W9-BRB-779

WEST OAHU COLLEGE

0 000023775

WITHDRAWN

Humanism and the Physician

DATE DUE

UNIVERSITY OF TENNESSEE PRESS
LIBRARY

'23
'38
)81

Pellegrino, Edmund D.
    Humanism and the Physician / Edmund
D. Pellegrino. Knoxville : University
of Tennessee Press, c1981.
xiii, 248 p. ; 24 cm.

Includes bibliographical references and
index.

1.Medicine-Philosophy2.Mendicine and the
humanities3.Humanism4.Medical Ethics
5.Medical Education-Philosophy I.Title

ISBN 0-87049-218-7

Humanism
and
the Physician

EDMUND D. PELLEGRINO

THE UNIVERSITY OF TENNESSEE PRESS

KNOXVILLE

Copyright © 1979 by The University of Tennessee Press/Knoxville.
All rights reserved.
Manufactured in the United States of America.
Second printing, 1981

Clothbound editions of University of Tennessee Press books
are printed on paper designed for an effective life
of at least 300 years, and binding materials
are chosen for strength and durability.

Library of Congress Cataloging in Publication Data
Pellegrino, Edmund D
  Humanism and the physician.

  Bibliography: p.
  Includes index.
    1. Medicine—Philosophy. 2. Medicine and the
  humanities. 3. Humanism. 4. Medical ethics.
  5. Medical education—Philosophy. I. Title.
  [DNLM: 1. Humanism. 2. Medicine. 3. Ethics,
  Medical. W61.3 P386h]
  R723.P38   610'.1   78-23174
  ISBN 0-87049-218-7
  ISBN 0-87049-311-6 (paperback)

For my parents,
my wife Clementine,
and "the seven"

Medicine and the Idea of Humanism

Next to autobiography, a collection of previously printed essays is the least discreet of literary exercises. It presumes that the author's old wine ought to be re-sampled—and without the advantages of new bottles. Sadly, it may reveal, instead, only a deteriorating palate no longer able to distinguish fine bottles from the spoiled. Still, once the initial indiscretion is committed, there may be some redemption in an explanatory preface, the least courtesy we can offer the intrepid reader gracious enough to open the book. Tasting old wines is a chancy business, and a little guidance through the musty cellar may not be out of order.

These essays were written for, and delivered to, a variety of audiences for purposes mostly pedagogical. Time for their composition was painfully extracted from a life in which patient care, teaching, scientific research, administration, and public service were, and are, inextricably and sometimes hopelessly intermingled. The essays therefore lack the more palpable sobriety and reflection of true scholarly work, but they have gained, perhaps, by being written under the pressure of urgent questions of immediate and daily concern to academicians and practitioners in the sixties and seventies. The essays have been shaped, too, by the uncompromising demands of medical audiences for relevance to what occurs at the bedside and in the classroom or office. So the esoteric appearance of their subjects notwithstanding, the aim of these essays has been eminently practical.

The circumstances of their writing militated necessarily against the anterospective development of a unifying theme. But happily in the task of selecting those essays to be included in this book the expectation of utter haphazardness did not materialize. Retrospectively, at least, a unifying theme does emerge. That theme is the mutual relevance and immediacy of the ideas of humanism and medicine in the twentieth century.

Medicine oscillates today, as never before, between the antipodes of the sciences and the humanities, never resting long in one or the other. It must look at embodied man as an object of science, yet never forget him as a thinking and feeling subject of the humanities. Medicine thus must always balance fact and value. If it is pulled too closely by one pole or the other, it becomes inauthentic and even dangerous.

The humanities too are beset by their own peculiar dangers. They can range too far from the admittedly untidy, noisome, and intimidating exigencies of daily life. They lapse easily into remote specialism, or value-free idealizations of a pseudoscientific kind. These defections weaken them as teachers of us all. Science, society, and medicine then lose the source of the critique of values and purpose they so urgently need.

These essays therefore grant no easy acquiescence to either the humanities or medicine in their claims to be "humanistic"; they offer rather a critical scrutiny of a too eager adoption of this sobriquet. They try to clarify the many faces of humanism as they become manifest in the intersections of medicine and the humanities. This is the leitmotif which recurs in one form or another in every essay.

The collection opens with an attempt to locate the source of our contemporary idea of humanism. It places that concern in the ambivalence and anxiety of modern man in the face of his growing technological prowess. When so much is possible, how can we tell what should be done from what can be done? Do the humanities, the traditional conduits of humanism, still have something to offer in making these value choices?

Medicine epitomizes these dilemmas because it is at heart a moral enterprise. Its moral center is the moment of clinical truth when fact and value, possibility and purpose must be weighed in the interest of a particular human being in the vulnerable state of illness. What are the medical uses of the humanities? In truth, what can the humanities gain from closer intercourse with modern medicine which encompasses so much of what we know phenomenologically about them?

These questions and themes are examined in three major sectors of the intersection of medicine and the humanities and at several points of engagement in each sector: first, as intellectual disciplines in the university; then, as substrata for some of the significant moral and ethical decisions our culture must now make; and finally, as interacting forces in the education of physicians and other health workers.

The essays in Part I concentrate on the relationships of medicine and the humanities and particularly, medicine and philosophy. The unique position of medicine at the confluence of the sciences and the humanities fits it ideally as the bridge over the gulf of the "two cultures"—in the university as in the world of practical decisions. Medicine has humanistic uses; indeed, it may be taken in some sense as one of the humanities. The humanities have medical uses and are essential if medicine is not to lapse into technicism; their juncture is important for the fullest maturation of our contemporary culture.

Another point of mutual engagement is in the idea of man. Here the history of that idea illustrates how the dominant values of a culture have influenced theories of medicine, and how medicine in turn, with its close study of man's psychophysical constitution, deeply influenced our ideas of what and who we are in every age. If there is any possibility of a "new" humanism compatible with contemporary existence then, it will emerge from a conscious interaction between medicine, the humanities, and the social sciences around the idea of man. Philosophical anthropology and even the metaphysics of man can now be reinvestigated without necessarily succumbing to the twin seductions of gross romanticism or materialism, as in the past.

This entails a reengagement of philosophy with medicine, of Minerva with Aesculapeus. Historically they have never been able to ignore each other totally, though their relationship has often been stormy. Until recently philosophy has, for the most part, been the dominant partner, with deleterious effect upon medicine. These two ancient disciplines are now ready for a more mature, bilaterally more secure and fruitful relationship. Medicine has today achieved unprecedented stature by its infusion with experimental science; philosophy is getting over its excessive infatuation with analytic and positivistic modes of thought, though cleansed by them of its nineteenth-century idealistic excesses.

The essays in Part II explore another critically important point of engagement, that between medicine and ethics, the branch of philosophy which deals systematically with the rightness and wrongness of all human conduct. For most of the history of medicine its most practical expression of the idea of humanism has been in the Hippocratic ethic. Although one of the most inspiring moral guides in the Western world, the oath and the other ethical books of the

Hippocratic collection have certain deficiencies for today. In a democratic, increasingly educated society in which the physicians' powers are enhanced beyond the imagination of the ancients, we need a far less paternalistic relationship.

We now face moral issues unknown to the ancients or even to our forebears of recent centuries. How do we assure a morally defensible climate for medical decision-making? How assure that the values of the patient are protected; that consent is based in disclosure of needed information; that the physician and patient both be free moral agents, not just the physician?

There are questions, too, that simply could not be anticipated in any traditional code: the questions of social ethics, for example. What are the physicians' responsibilities to society? How does a physician balance these against his obligations to his patients when these forces are in conflict? What are the ethical principles which should guide physicians and other health workers when they are acting as a team? Is there a right to health care? What are the ethical obligations of hospitals and other institutions as institutions since something akin to the physician-patient relationship now exists frequently between a patient and a hospital? Is there a humanistic framework within which human experimentation can be morally conducted?

No medical matter has received more public interest and concern than the new issues in medical ethics: abortion, euthanasia, behavior control, and the allocation of scarce resources. To deal adequately with these issues requires a critical reconstruction of the philosophical bases of professional ethics—one which is humanistically inspired.

Such a reconstruction might well begin with the fact of illness and the way it compromises the humanity of the person who is ill. The special vulnerability of illness creates a relationship of inequality which imposes special obligations on the physician. Out of this vulnerability and the physician's act of "pro-fession" the possibility emerges of a genuinely humanistic reformulation of professional obligations.

The essays in Part III move to the next logical point of engagement —the idea of humanism with medical education. If the image of the physician and his ethics are to be reconstructed or reshaped, then the education of physicians must be impregnated with the humanistic ideal. A humanistic medical education encompasses two components, an affective and a cognitive, which must be united if we are to have competent, considerate, and conversant physicians.

The humanities have a unique place in this effort. They sensitize to values, they inculcate the liberal arts as attitudes of mind, and they prepare the physician for a life of satisfaction as well as competence. How the humanities should be taught in medical schools —when, by whom, and through what content—are questions of current exploration. The move among so many medical schools to teach the humanities, and to examine values, promises to be the most important innovation in medical education in the next quarter century.

The obligation to educate humanely leads to those even more fundamental questions about the special social purpose and consequent moral obligations of medical schools. What obligations are owed to society, students, and patients by virtue of the special nature of medical schools? Thus far, while teaching something of medical ethics, medical schools have been innocent of any critical examination of the nature or extent of their own moral obligations as institutions.

Humanism and the humanities are essential to the fullest maturation of the physician not only as a professional, but as an educated human. They are indispensable to the fullest expansion of the medical intellect, allowing for a life of competency and responsibility and of satisfaction and delectation. No education can assure that every physician will savor the arts and the humanities for their intrinsic worth. Those who do can hope to approach the ideal of the Compleat Physician. In him the profession is graced by a complete human in whom science and art, profession and life, morality and competence are inseparably united. This is the ideal toward which each of the engagements between the idea of humanism and medicine ultimately must tend.

While that ideal will always be attainable only for the few, there is a more crucial measure of medical humanism which every true physician must strive to achieve. The epilogue summates that measure by elucidating what it means to *be* a physician, to *be* a patient and to make a "pro-fession," in the realization of both these realities. The collection ends, then, on a practical note, relating the ideal of humanism to the physician's daily encounter with the vulnerable sick and thus with the moral center of his whole enterprise. Medical humanism on this level is no longer a mere adornment; it becomes a moral imperative and the standard by which the authenticity of individual and profession may be measured.

ACKNOWLEDGMENTS

How can I give credit to all who have influenced this work? The idea of medical humanism has grown perceptively in the public and professional consciousness for almost two decades. During that time I have had numerous conversations, heard countless speeches, and read hundreds of papers on the subject. Each offered some insight I either found congenial, or wanted to oppose. A chance phrase here, a patient's response there, a critic's telling barb—these too initiated some train of thought. I must shamefacedly admit I can no longer trace the provenance of all the ideas or even some of the phrases I have used. So, I acknowledge my deep indebtedness to all—patients, friends, colleagues, family, and the authors I have read. I have tried to transmute their explicit or subliminal influences into my own idea of the humanist physician.

Some special thanks are owed to those friends who took me seriously enough to criticize in detail. For their candor and mordant wit, I thank Nicholas Pisacano of the University of Kentucky, Richard Zaner of Southern Methodist University, David Thomasma of the University of Tennessee, and Ronald McNeur and Thomas McElhinney of the Institute on Human Values in Medicine in Philadelphia. Andrew Lasslo of Tennessee deserves my special gratitude for his combination of faith in the work and his kindly "needling" to get it done.

The really hard work was done by a succession of remarkably efficient technical assistants: Sr. Marcella Tucker, O.P., Karen Wright, and Carol Winch-McVety. They typed, corrected, and improved with unexcelled tolerance for my unintelligible notes, curious phraseology, and proclivity for procrastination. Marilyn Gredinger, my administrative assistant, kept everything else in order so as to enable me to steal a few moments for writing during many busy days.

Finally, and most of all, I must thank my wife, Clementine, and my family for suffering the uncertain clackings of my typewriter at the most dubious hours.

CONTENTS

xiii

Humanism and the Physician

Medical Uses of the Humanities

Rarely are the humanities in medicine assessed for what they really are—neither educational flourishes nor panaceas but indispensable studies whose everyday use is as important for the quality of clinical decisions as the basic sciences are now presumed to be. This may seem a pretentious stretch of rhetoric. When the demands for technical competence are so insistent, are we justified in further eroding the physician's time and his education with such vanities?

If at the outset we dispense with the illusion that we can make every physician a Renaissance man, there are three clear uses of the humanities in medicine: (a) they are essential to understanding the ethical and value issues which underlie so many clinical decisions today; (b) they are indispensable to the critical self-examination the profession so urgently needs; and (c) they confer those attitudes which distinguish the educated from the merely trained man.

We cannot expect the individual physician to encompass all three uses. But neither can we excuse him from apprehending those uses which are most pertinent to his own life and practice. For the profession as a whole, however, the mandate to grasp the humanities at all levels in unequivocal.

The terms *value* and *purpose* are beginning to appear for the first time as respectable subjects for clinical inquiry. With the effective means modern science provides, the physician must determine whether or not he should use the techniques he possesses, for whom, for what purpose, and according to what value system. The prolongation of life, abortion, genetic counseling, dangerous operative and diagnostic procedures—all involve an intersection of the values of the patient, society, and the physician. How does the clinician dissect these three, respecting each and balancing them to avoid the tyranny of his own values on the one hand and the aban-

This essay appeared in similar form under the title "The Medical Uses of the Humanities" in the commencement issue of *University Medical*, The University of Texas Medical Branch, Galveston, Vol. 5, No. 6, pp. 4–6.

donment of his values to those of the patient and society on the other?

The complexity of today's clinical decision, compounded by the capabilities of modern medicine, dictates a moral formal knowledge of how to think about ethical issues. Where values are in conflict, intuitive decisions based solely upon one's own ideologies are socially and ethically unacceptable. Current public demands for accountability and participation accentuate the need for a fuller understanding of ethical problems than we now possess.

The humanities have always dealt with the root questions of human values—in ethics, philosophy, history, law, and theology. Although science is in no sense "value-free," it is an insufficient instrument for dealing with the spectrum of age-old questions about human value and purpose. Moreover, the sciences are too susceptible to seductions of the "technological imperative" to be safe guides through such intricacies. The humanities, at their best, teach us to deal with the unmeasurable phenomena of human existence with confidence and sensitivity.

The humanities will not of themselves teach values. This is a common misconception of their too-ardent protagonists. But they can teach us how to reflect critically on our decisions and their impact on the personal integrity of those we serve. Those things which science must expurgate from consideration—the personal, the ambiguous—are the very things which the humanities recognize as universal qualities of human experience, the very things especially heightened in confrontation with death or disease.

It was Plato who said that "the unexamined life is not worth living." I would add that the unexamined profession is not worth practicing. Never in its long history has medicine as a profession been more in need of critical examination. What is medicine? What are its responsibilities? What is the physician? What will he become in the future? How do we think medically? What is medicine's relationship to general culture? What ideological assumptions underlie our logic and our behavior? Everywhere society is asking us to scrutinize our self-image and to make it more consonant with our contemporary challenges.

Social, political, and economic events outside medicine are forcing a reexamination of the content, methods, and goals of our profession. We are in one of those recurrent periods of history where all of society's assumptions and our assumed prerogatives—medicine is among them—require scrutiny.

Medicine cannot examine itself critically with its present intellectual tools. The key questions are philosophical and they require some familiarity with use of the critical intellect, not to assure certitude but to guarantee that we ask the right questions and that we rigorously and honestly examine possible answers to their fullest depth.

The humanities have traditionally served this purpose in every mature culture. Lately, the humanities have become overspecialized and have defected somewhat in this reexamination. Their inquiry into medicine and the other professions should help the humanities revitalize their own functions in society as teachers and questioners of all of us.

It is unrealistic to expect every physician and student to engage in this fundamental inquiry into the purposes of medicine. But each must be constantly aware that the idea of medicine and of the physician is today in a process of change more drastic than any yet encountered.

The final medical use for the humanities is enabling the physician to function as an educated man as well as a proficient craftsman. Each physician must first be technically competent and practice with compassion. A few will, in addition, enrich both life and practice with the grace of the liberal arts.

The truly educated man is one who can deal sensitively with those works which are uniquely the works for man—capacity to use words, to reason and judge, to appreciate beauty, to criticize, and to create one's own works when possible. The arts which set man free—that is, free him from enslavement by the opinions of others—are the liberal arts, those which enable us to develop opinions of our own. There is no more effective antidote to the ennui that so easily afflicts the successful practitioner than cultivating one of the humanities throughout life.

The physician educated in the liberal sense is a better physician. He sees his patient in his human frame, so to speak. His practice radiates that special felicity of feeling and expression we expect of a learned professional. Moreover, the physician himself derives a degree of intellectual satisfaction which in turn elevates his daily work.

The Cartesian conviction that rational thought is confined only to the measurable and the observable has served medicine well. But it must now be modulated with the conviction of the humanities, that rational thought is possible equally among the unmeasurable ambiguities which are so uniquely and so frustratingly part of human existence.

The humanities in medicine are neither fripperies nor panaceas, but indispensable studies if medicine is to be as humane as it has been scientific. The three uses of the humanities require cultivation if our profession is to be a responsive instrument of human purpose. It is no overstatement to say that, for both medicine and society, the dialogue with the humanities will become as significant as the dialogue with the experimental science has already proven to be.

Part I
Medicine and the Humanities

Medical Humanism
and Technologic Anxiety

M edical humanism is one of those intriguing word combinations with the power to engender passionate responses. For one thing, the word *humanism* is seductive and vague enough to attract a variegated host of followers, each with a personal version of its meaning. What is more, everyone wishes to qualify as a "medical humanist"; the only antihumanists turn out to be the holders of contrary opinions about what constitutes medical humanism. Self-confessed antihumanists are rarely encountered.

Only a deeply felt human challenge or threat can underlie so powerfully beguiling a rubric. What is there about contemporary medicine that has generated so much talk about "humanism"—a term not very much in currency a few decades ago. Temerarious as the attempt must be, anyone writing under this tenuous rubric is compelled to expose the roots of the challenges and threats it subsumes.

Medical humanism has achieved the status of a salvation theme, which can absolve the perceived "sins" of modern medicine. The list of those sins is long, varied, and often contradictory: overspecialization; technicism; overprofessionalization; insensitivity to personal and sociocultural values; too narrow a construal of the doctor's role; too much "curing" rather than "caring"; not enough emphasis on prevention, patient participation, and patient education; too much science; not enough liberal arts; not enough behavioral science; too much economic incentive; a "trade school" mentality; insensitivity to the poor and socially disadvantaged; overmedicalization of everyday life; inhumane treatment of medical students; overwork by house staff; deficiencies in verbal and nonverbal

This chapter appeared in somewhat different form under the title "Technologic Anxiety and Humanism" in *Patterns for Progress, from the Sciences to Medicine*, proceedings of a symposium held in Kalamazoo, Michigan, October 17–19, 1976. Ed. John A. Hogg and Jacob C. Stucki. Miami, Symposia Specialists, 1977, pp. 61–66.

communication. No list can be complete. Every conceivable failing is admissible in the critique of so human-centered an endeavor as medicine.

The remedies depend upon which of these sins, singly or in combination, a critic finds most upsetting or disappointing. Hundreds of forms of "medical humanism" can thus be elaborated. Each defines a path which purports to lead physicians, patients, and all of us back from the brink of dehumanization to the haven of humanism.

Like all salvation themes the debate about which remedy should predominate in medical education and practice is only too often confusing and passionate. These perils notwithstanding, engagement with the issues is curtailed only at even greater risk. Medical humanism is really a plea to look more closely at what medicine *should be*, and increasingly *seems not to be*. It encapsulates a pervasive ambivalence felt even by the most ardent devotees of modern medicine: Can we balance the promises of medical technology against the threats it poses to persons and societies by virtue of its powers to fulfill those promises?

In subsequent chapters of this volume, a variety of meanings and senses of medical humanism will be examined. The reader, I hope, will have a better feel of the range of issues and the author's construal of them. To offer suggestions for any final resolution of the complexities would be illusory and naïve. Some of the social and cultural significance of the prevalent ambivalence and some of the actions designed to ameliorate it perhaps may emerge.

The challenge and the threat medicine poses to man are really overwhelming. It is only a short time since men fashioned the first extensions of their human capacities by making tools. Now while our species is barely in its adolescence, those tools have taken on a life of their own. Those who guide their use and the values these people hold can shape the whole of man's future life.

Medical humanism expresses in a very concrete way the anxiety which comes from the admiration and fear man has of the tools he himself has fashioned. Men have always sensed that the more tools they forged and the more machines they built, the more they were forced to know, to love, and to serve these devices. As long as the appearance of new technology was slow and its effectiveness uncertain, there was time to choose between each new convenience and to avert the danger of becoming enslaved by it.

In these times, however, our ability to make such choices has been overwhelmed by the endless capacity of our techniques and the awesome rate at which they are produced. We suffer acutely the twin fears of reverting to a barbarous existence either by using them too much or using them not enough. We oscillate between two lethal options—alternately yielding to a Luddite passion to destroy the machines that menace our humanity or capitulating mindlessly to the theme of salvation through technology.

In the last sentence of his *Technics and Civilization*, Lewis Mumford said that modern science had taught us one lesson: "that nothing is impossible" (1). This came less than a century after God had been declared dead, and as Alyosha said in *The Brothers Karamazov*: "Then everything is possible." Traditional moral and technical restraints have been removed, and the full weight of what Kierkegaard meant by the "despair of possibility" has descended on all of us.

Consider the enormous weight of that anxiety and the depth to which it challenges our metaphysical presuppositions, whether we call them by that name or not. When all things are possible, then we must decide which ones we shall have. What we choose, however, unerringly reveals what we value and that, in turn, peels back the layers of protection covering what we think we are and what we think humans are for.

Not only must we then recapture our humanity, but we must confront first the question of what we think that humanity is and ought to be. We are compelled to reverse the frenetic flight of modern man away from himself. It is no longer possible to escape the tragic choices an infinitude of possibilities opens to us. The most ordinary man must examine his life and discover exactly what he really treasures.

These challenges might have seemed indirect and distant when we first contemplated the cosmic disaster of atomic explosions. But they become concrete, personal, immediate, and urgent when we face the choices biomedical science places before us daily. We now choose between preventing, shortening, or lengthening life of humans; modifying their behavior; replacing their vital organs; and changing the genetic endowment of future generations.

The choices must be made in a minefield of tricky ambivalencies. The patient who regained all or part of a normal life with bypass surgery, kidney transplantation, or cancer chemotherapy cannot easily condemn medical technology, no matter what it adds to the

11

hugeness of our national medical-care bill. Yet even the beneficiaries, when the benefit is more remote or runs counter to some more deeply felt value, will seek to control the threats of unrestrained technological imperatives.

There comes a time when the cancer patient, the recipient of a transplant, or the patient with recurrent angina may seek to protect himself against further technological manipulation that may produce only marginal results. The woman who accepts amniocentesis and prophylactic abortion may stop at eugenic sterilization; the parents of a child with leukemia who benefits from chemotherapy may in the past have opposed experimentation with children; the physician who has discovered ways to prolong life may make a "living will" for himself. The combinations of value choices individuals may make in the presence of such ambivalencies are almost endless.

The same complexity obtains when we make choices on a broader social scale. Here, we are free of the immediacy of personal decisions about ourselves or members of our families. We can step back and talk of euthanasia, abortion, the right to die, the quality of life, "pulling the plug," and the like as semi-abstract entities. The absence of a common set of values and the feeling that there is a certain categorical imperative in technology further complicate the matter. Still, the ultimate decision is the choice between accepting another gift of technology and yielding further aliquots of our freedom and humanity in return for its benefits.

Anxiety about the possibilities in personal and social decisions is exacerbated and enhanced by the ethos of modern science. People are beginning to understand, inchoately but with increasing accuracy, the values in that ethos: (a) a dedication to rationality as the only means for ultimately eliminating disease; (b) a commitment to the universality of the scientific criteria of truth, criteria which transcend sociocultural and historical values; and (c) a conviction that knowledge must be sought even if it does not benefit us immediately because the enterprise of science reaches beyond time, place, and person (2).

The scientist who embraces this ethos is seen as a man apart, a member of a brotherhood responding to values outside the ordinary run of human affairs. Like captives of a benign foreign power, the general public recognizes its dependence upon technology for the kind of life to which it has become accustomed; what it cannot divine precisely is when those gifts might be withdrawn or when the hegemony of science might change into a paternalistic or even oppressive dictatorship.

Recognition of these complicated value conflicts has generated a mounting interest in reshaping science, technology, and medicine toward more humane ends. How can we become participants in the decisions that affect us? Should we slow our Promethean advance toward goals still only obscurely seen? The watchword of this movement is "humanism." We hear pleas to "humanize" technology, medicine, bureaucracy, indeed all our instruments of collective purpose.

That the precise content of that concept is ill-defined adds to the unsettled state of our thinking. "Humanism" has become a slogan, evoking a multitude of images of what we find good or lacking in the modern spirit. It comes in many varieties: theistic and atheistic, democratic and socialistic, Christian and Judaic, classical and modern, scientific and literary, psychologic, economic, political. Each version summates some set of metaphysical presuppositions on which its proponents take their stand. The term has thus become a shibboleth, apprehended for its own purposes by every human activity and discipline from aesthetics to zymurgy.

There is, however, a common set of assumptions that each version of humanism interprets in its own fashion. This is what Abraham Edel calls the "humanist strain"—the centrality of human dignity, justice, respect for man as individual and person in any activity we would term humanist (3). Humanism is less, therefore, a specific doctrine than a focus on the primacy of human values as the determinant of whatever relationships we establish with each other.

Hyphenated humanism, like hyphenated Americanism, is an intensified term with special coloration. Calls for "medical humanism" are now increasingly heard from many quarters. They summate the intense desire all of us share as patients, that the science and technology of medicine, as well as our encounters with physicians, be conditioned by respect for our own values. As we are ushered through the techniques, mystiques, and bureaucracies that constitute modern medicine, we want to avoid the humiliation and degradation of our humanity so often a part of the process.

Medical humanism and humanism in the general sense, if they are to serve as an antidote to the potential tyranny of technicism, must confront the value presuppositions upon which our decisions are based. The enterprise is, therefore, in significant degree a philosophical and ethical one. What is required is no less than a return of critical philosophy to the market place, the home, the hospital, the laboratory, and even the legislative chamber. Philosophy, as Cicero urged in his Tusculan disputations, must be "summoned from the heavens." He praised Socrates because: "He transferred it [philosophy] to the actual cities inhabited by mankind, and moved it right into people's homes; and he compelled it to ask questions about how one ought to live and behave, and what is good and what is bad."

Of the many versions of medical humanism, the most fundamental is that which grapples with these central issues of what man is, why man exists, and what is meant by humane purposes for technology. This in no way denigrates the equally important need we have for a more humanitarian, responsive, sympathetic, and compassionate experience of human illness. Feeling and thinking are not the opposite of each other, as so many polemicists like to believe.

Whether starting with the obligations imposed on medicine by the conditions of human affliction or with the philosophical questions about the nature of man, the medical humanist ends up worrying about the same values—the preservation, enhancement, fulfillment, and enrichment of human life. To be humane, all technology must make it more possible for us to be free, fulfilled, and self-determining, as well as more comfortable, efficient, or productive.

Although the formulas are uncertain, the means debatable, and the ends conflicting, few social and cultural aspirations are more important than those subsumed under "medical humanism." We may begin with the medical experience, but patently the same questions and concerns color every other feature of the fabric of human existence. Medical humanism is a convenient starting point from which to launch into the larger issues of how to root technology and values in our "center."

Lewis Mumford in the *Pentagon of Power* has epitomized the general dilemma very well: "If we are to save technology itself from the aberrations of its present leaders and putative gods, we must in both our thinking and our action come back to the human center; for it is there that all significant transformations begin and terminate" (4).

The efforts to define and actualize a more humane medicine are part of the larger effort to return to that "human center." The way to the human center must come from a deeper engagement with the disciplines of humanistic psychology, as well as with the humanities more classically construed. Different kinds of people and disciplines subscribe to these approaches, but both are indispensable because man is indivisibly a feeling and a thinking being.

It would be tragic if the humanistic psychologies or the humanities engaged in ideological warfare to capture the soul of medical humanism. Medical humanism, for all its pretensions, would then itself become another force for "dehumanization."

The Most Humane of the Sciences; the Most Scientific of the Humanities

There are no subjects in which, as a rule, practice is not more valuable than precept.

Quintilianus, *Institutio Oratoria* (1)

Reasons of exquisite urgency impel the examination of an ancient and much labored subject: the humane education of the physician.

The physician of today works in the wake of a metaphysical rebellion, which on the one hand exalts man and on the other overshadows him in technology and mass organization. Things and services designed for the presumed benefit of man too often end up dehumanizing him. Man's most daring creations promise to annihilate him as a person unless he can decide who he is and what his existence is for and where it should lead.

The physician has had to become part of the technological apparatus of society in order to attain mastery over many of man's bodily ills. Yet, as never before, he is also compelled to remain the practitioner of the most humane of all the sciences. Is it possible to be at once a practitioner of the new biology and an advocate for the person against the dehumanizing thrust of a mass civilization? Can the doctor simultaneously attend Man the molecular aggregate and Man the person; Man the unit of a complex society and Man the ineffable?

Society can tolerate no answer except that the impossible must be achieved: medicine must become master of its technologic base and, at the same time, use that technology within a humanist

---

This chapter is based on the Sanger Lecture entitled "The Most Humane Science: Some Notes on Liberal Education in Medicine and the University" which was delivered at the Medical College of Virginia of Virginia Commonwealth University, Richmond, on April 10, 1970.

framework. No other solution is equal to the tensions medicine itself creates in human values—tensions far more critical to human welfare than the cure of individual illnesses.

Few would deny that medicine today needs a more vigorous and more penetrating intercalation with humane studies than ever before. But this intercalation is too simplistically equated with larger or more sustained doses of liberal studies assembled according to a traditional formula more romantically than critically conceived. These, once taken, are expected to guard the nascent physician against the narrowness, insensitivity, and hubris his education is thought to inculcate.

This view is too firmly rooted in a romantic, nineteenth-century ideal of the educated man. It depends too heavily on a naïve hope of resurrecting the Renaissance man as prototype of the physician. It propagates the myth that there is something sacred in the four-year liberal arts education for inculcating human values, hence making it a necessary prelude to specialized studies of any kind and of medicine in particular. Most fundamental of all, this conception misreads the history of the humanities and liberal studies and their meaning in contemporary life.

The prevailing conception that everyone can be, or needs to be, liberally educated before undertaking professional studies must be countered with a goal that is less pretentious, more realistic, and more consonant with both the inclinations of today's students and the need for more competently trained manpower.

The aim should be to provide liberal education a variety of ways, but probably most often by reversing the traditional order of liberal and professional studies. Medicine is the most humane of sciences, the most empiric of arts, and the most scientific of humanities. Its subject matter is an ideal ground within which to develop the attitudes associated with the humanistic and liberally educated. Pursued simultaneously with medicine or even later, the humanities can more effectively humanize practice and cultivate the mind of the practitioner.

To advance this thesis, I must examine several questions: What *precisely* is the nature of the deficiency in the physician's education that has aroused such concern? How have the humanities failed in their own purposes? What alternatives are being tried as remedies? What is a viable formula for today? What are its implications for medicine and the university?

It is a common assertion nowadays that the physician is too often an uneducated man, technically proficient but insensitive to values, ideas, and esthetics. These deficiencies are presumed to lead to neglect of the person of the patient, to disregard of the needs of the total community, and even to economic rapacity. They are to be eliminated, it is said, by a "humanistic" education prior to entering medicine and by deeper study of the humanities.

The charges are not new. In one form or another they have been popular with the literati from Molière to George Bernard Shaw and Mark Twain. They are more stridently proclaimed by the medically disenfranchised and by patients in every class of society. Medical students sensitive to any trace of hypocrisy in their teachers have added their voices and have called for changes in medical education designed to avoid replication of the same pattern in their own lives (2).

The medical educator interested in instant education can achieve it with his university colleagues by reciting the same litany. He will often be rewarded by being called a humanist himself, thus being separated from that rude band of technicians, his colleagues.

There is considerable justification both for the criticism and for the demand that in today's world the physician must be more responsive to what society and his patients expect of him. Clearly, medicine's responsibilities have grown along with its capabilities. The physician must look at himself with uncommon candor. He does not need defense, but a clearer delineation of the reasons for the criticisms and more effective antidotes than are now available.

The questionable feature in current criticisms of the physician's humanistic education lies in the line of reasoning generally followed. Two aspects of the physician's life, that of the educated man and that of the compassionate person, are confused; lacks in either are assumed to stem from insufficient exposure to the humanities or to liberal education. Such studies are presumed automatically to confer on the physician a sense of human values and thus make him a humanitarian and a man educated in the use of the liberal arts—a humanist physician. This is too much to expect of any formal educational method, liberal arts or other. The misconception arises from a perennial vagueness in the definitions of such terms as *humanism, humanitarian, humanities,* and *liberal studies.* They are too often lumped together as a mithridatic prescription to insure a human approach by professionals to their work. Some dis-

tinctions in defining these terms are essential for development of
my thesis.

Few words are as entrancing in concept or as varied in interpretation as *humanism*. It has been subjected to a wide range of definitions. Some see it as a literary concept based in a knowledge of
classical languages and literature; others equate it with a mode
of education. Still others see it as a democratic or socialist theory of
politics, or as a form of man-centered religion, or as an instrument
for the suppression of the working class, or as the antidote to voca-
tionalism (Babbitt and More). Most commonly today it is applied
to any study or endeavor which is man-centered or places primacy
on man and human values. In this latter sense, it is indistinguishable from humanitarianism.

Thus, it is clear that an education which emphasizes studies of
the works of man may be conducted from divergent points of
view, based in differing sets of values and priorities. When critics
demand a more humanistic education for physicians, they may be
talking about any of these humanisms—though most will mean
that they want physicians who are more interested in patients as
people, an attribute which does not necessarily result from any of
the *humanisms* formally defined.

Equal confusion pertains to definitions of the conglomerate of
studies called the *humanities* or *liberal studies*. Professor Albert
Levi has recently reanalyzed the difficulties in defining the humanities today. He illustrates well the problem of separating them from
the social sciences and the natural sciences, also concerned with
human values. He concludes that the humanities are best limited to
three arts: communication, continuity and criticism—i.e., language and literature, history, and philosophy. These are in turn
equated with liberal studies and then sharply distinguished from
the sciences (3).

Although Levi's definition is acceptable, it is apparent that the
studies thus defined may or may not teach values. They might
make the physician a learned or an educated man, but not necessarily a humane or compassionate one. As Levi himself points out:

> The "conviction," the "faith," the "presupposition," that
> the humanities teach values is not enough. They must be
> taught with this constant aim in mind and with an exper-
> imental willingness at every point to explore the actual
> relationships between the content of the liberal arts and

the humanitarian values and the humanistic attitude
which are their reasons for existence, their card of accreditation in the spectrum of teaching and research. (4)

This point has special pertinence for liberal studies in a medical
education.

Clearly society today needs physicians who, in addition to being
technically competent, are compassionate and educated—physicians
who can understand how their work intersects with the culture of
which it is a part, physicians who can work empathetically with
other humans in distress. All of these attributes rarely will be found
in one man. One mode of education, even if based in humanistic
studies, cannot guarantee all. This conclusion is essential to any restructuring of medical education to meet the full flavor of the criticism now leveled at it.

Other professionals are as susceptible to deficiencies in their liberal education and in their abilities to react empathetically to their
clients. But such lapses have a moral tone in medicine. The physician is most intimately in touch with suffering man, with the mis-
ery and the joys of the human condition. Behind the vehemence of
the criticisms is society's hope that medicine, more than other endeavors, can heal the rift between science and technology on the
one hand and art and wisdom on the other. Since Descartes, man
has been told he is a machine. Yet, all his strivings since have been
toward becoming more of a person.

The imperative, then, becomes this: medicine must become more
humane, more infused with the spirit of liberal studies, and more
willing to address itself to the metaphysical dichotomy between the
arts and the sciences. This is an undertaking fraught with presumptions, but no other science or art has the potential for attempting
such a task successfully. Indeed, the need for drastic revision of the
mode of the physician's liberal education derives intellectual impetus from the need for this synthesis. Without it, medicine can
justifiably be reduced to what its severest critics say it has already
become—just another technology.

THE EROSION OF THE HUMANITIES

Before the humanities are fixed into the framework of medical
education, their state in the contemporary university needs to be

ascertained. Liberal studies have been transformed by the potent influence of science and technology, the needs of education in a democratic society, and changing motivations of the student body.

Today's university is no longer essentially a training ground for an elite corps of leaders, as it was in the nineteenth century. In an egalitarian society, it has become mainly an instrument for mass education and the most effective means for socioeconomic advancement. Society expects our universities to prepare large numbers of young people for socially useful roles. It supports higher education with this expectation, not primarily to increase the number of "educated" men or scholars.

Students too have changed their perception of the university experience. They see it mainly either as a means of providing the tools for some profession, including specialized scholarship in this definition, or as a means of "finding" themselves as persons. Very few enter universities nowadays to train their intellects in the sophisticated mode advocated by Cardinal Newman. Refinement of the intellect and the cultivation of tastes and aesthetic values as lifelong endowments for work and leisure are not conscious goals. Rather, these goals are consciously rejected by increasing numbers of students, who see in them the remnants of an outmoded social and economic caste system.

As universities and students have changed character, so have humanistic and liberal studies. Europe inherited from the Italian Renaissance and the Enlightenment a special ideal of the educated man. He was steeped in the Greek and Latin tongues and classics, at home in the Scriptures, knowledgeable in the history of his country, and skilled in the artful use of its language. These endowments were not considered inconsistent with competence in some profession; and indeed they enhanced professional pursuits. We in America have been most influenced by this ideal as exemplified in nineteenth-century Oxford and Cambridge and epitomized in Newman's *Idea of a University*. This ideal has suffered substantial attenuation in the past century under the impact of science and technology, the needs for mass education, and the trend toward specialization through graduate studies. Even at its height, the traditional ideal was really effective in only a few exemplary men of letters, science, and government. Today it has been deprived of meaning for the majority of students who attend universities for more pragmatic and more immediate goals. It can only be a limited formula for education in a democratic society needful of large numbers of professionals, technicians, businessmen, and bureaucrats.

The humanities themselves have been compelled to assume the stance of specialties and to adopt the research attitudes and the objectivity of the sciences. In today's universities the departments in the humanities are primarily the training ground for scholars, and, as Northrop Frye so aptly points out, scholarship is distinctly not the same thing as education (5). The professional practitioners of the humanities now direct their major energies to the replication of research specialists in their graduate students. They have lost their capability for communication with the general undergraduate and with their colleagues in other faculties. Indeed, from being the teachers of all, they too have become specialized teachers just like all the rest.

The humanities today seem well along the road of abandoning wisdom for information. In so doing, they have become the antithesis of liberal studies, which were originally intended to free the mind and the spirit. The professional humanists still insist that their disciplines have value for all educated men, and lament early specialization in other fields. Students still hope that by some magical formula the humanities will somehow become relevant. Professional schools continue to speak piously of educating the man first and the professional second.

Medical educators, hoping to preserve medicine as a "learned" profession, are especially susceptible to these illusions. They assert that all medical students should first receive a liberal education, and the professionals believe that today's collegiate experience can provide such an education. Two annoying factors militate against the reality of these assertions. The first is the attenuation of the humanities as liberal studies. The second is the notorious imperviousness of premedical students to genuine liberal studies when those studies are obstacles that must be hurdled to enter medical school.

The clear reality is that few of the purposes of a traditional liberal education are provided in today's undergraduate experience. The fact is that most students enter professional schools without the "broad" base they are assumed to have acquired. Medical education can no longer be postponed until this dubious base has been acquired by all students.

None of this is to say that the attitudes traditionally called "liberal" are in any way less essential to an educated man and to the profession of medicine. Without them, medicine cannot be a humane science or avoid the confusion of purposes to which its unprecedented knowledge makes it so susceptible. Manifestly, we must seek some better way to free the minds of some physicians at least, so that they can see the relationship of their work to the whole fabric of culture and society. Where can one look for an approach consistent with the state of contemporary science, society, politics, and student interests? Under what conditions can the humanities be revitalized?

SOME INSUFFICIENT ALTERNATIVES

In the past two decades medical educators and students have striven to fill the vacuum left by the defection of the humanists by modifying the medical curriculum several ways: adding behavioral sciences, religion, real-life experiences, and involvement. It is worth examining each briefly before turning in more detail to another possible approach.

The social and behavioral sciences—sociology, anthropology, economics, and psychology—do contribute much to understanding the person, the family, and the institutions that figure so intimately in the genesis of health and illness. They are fundamental studies for the psychiatrist, specialists in community medicine, and for all physicians who hope in some measure to understand the "whole" patient. These studies serve to sensitize students to the importance of personal and social values in diagnosis, therapeutics, and prevention. Undeniably, the social sciences introduce new and valuable data into medical education as well as into the techniques of sociomedical research.

For several reasons, the social sciences do not, however, fully compensate for the deficiency left by the defection of the humanities.

First of all, the social sciences, striving like the humanities for the objectivity of the physical sciences, have become specialized studies. The "establishment" of social scientists relies heavily on descriptive or statistical language and eschews values and philosophical insights. At the same time, the younger generation of radical sociologists rejects any hope of understanding society. Instead, they perceive their roles as activists who must destroy existing social structures and remake them according to some private and viscerally apprehended formula. Such antirationalism is fashionable with the young, who, lacking experience with the genuine article, accept these views as the basis for a "new humanism," which is, in fact, nonhumanist at its roots.

Last, medical educators expect too much of the social sciences. These studies increase our understanding of certain critical factors in the care of the patient. They do not guarantee that physicians exposed to them will act in a socially responsible or compassionate manner. They must be reinforced by the behavior of clinical teachers who actually use these data in their daily practice and teaching, and most importantly, in the care of their own patients.

Another alternative to the humanities is theology. Some medical schools have filled part of the gap in humanistic education by introducing the theologian and the minister into the clinical setting. These are admirable beginnings and hold promise for the future, providing theologians can make the transition from a doctrinaire to an evolutionary stance in treating human values. Theologians today are increasingly interested in a more existential examination of human problems and seem willing to deal with the transcendent in more contemporary terms. As they become less dogmatic and less sectarian, religion and theology might well offer a more substantial base for liberal studies in the professions than many other disciplines.

Theology is, however, only rarely represented in universities and medical school faculties. Its practitioners, as in the humanities and social sciences, are also susceptible to the pull toward specialization and scholarship. Like the social sciences, religion and theology can indeed sensitize many students to some very significant questions in medicine. But these studies also suffer from the special handicap of centuries of misunderstanding and misuse. Although the process of the intellectual rehabilitation of theology and religion has begun, we are a long way from reestablishing their authenticity for most of today's secular-minded students.

In the last three or four years medical students have initiated a third and quite imaginative method for remedying some of the insensitivity to humane values in contemporary medicine, education and practice. They have plunged into early and direct clinical experiences and roles of advocacy for medically disenfranchised patients and communities. These efforts have effectively revolutionized certain aspects of the medical curriculum. In the process, even faculties and deans have become more responsive to the importance of "involvement" in the major social medical issues of our day.

This approach, like the others, supplies only part of what is missing. It provides direct experience with human distress and thus enables the student to confront questions of values early in his professional education. The emotional impact is significant, and motivation of the student to help others is reinforced. But the cogitated assimilation of these direct experiences with human distress must still be sought if the student is to emerge as a truly educated person in the liberal tradition.

These three approaches—via the behavioral sciences, religion, and direct clinical experiences—are partial solutions to the educational deficiencies created by the present state of the humanities. These efforts will surely be expanded further, but to be fully effective they must be complemented by a drastically altered view of the place of liberal studies in general and professional education. What form might this assume?

HUMANITIES IN MEDICINE: A NEW SEQUENCE

Every culture has expected its physicians to function at several levels. The first is concerned with professional and technical competence—the detection and treatment of disease by the most effective means; the second deals with the management of the personal dimensions of illness—the promotion of health and the adjustment of the patient to those things medicine cannot cure; the last is providing society a critique of the quality of life from the special viewpoint the physician brings to questions of population, environmental pollution, drugs, and sociopathy, for example (6).

Educating each physician to perform adequately at all these levels would compromise competence to the point of absurdity. We live in a complex society, moving toward equal opportunity for education and service and away from restriction of these rights to the privileged. A socially responsible and more realistic goal for medical education is to provide a sufficient number of physicians able to function at one level only, not just a small number who can meet all expectations of individuals and society. The totality of personal and technical services needed by every patient can best be provided by a judicious combining of the efforts of physicians and other health professionals. What we must seek is the appropriate organizational pattern in which the limitations of each can be complemented by the strengths of each.

Many physicians will function at more than one level, and in a properly designed structure this can be encouraged. What must not be encouraged is the dangerous pretension that some form of education can generate a host of Renaissance men, capable at all levels. Even in the Renaissance, the true polymath was a rarity.

Education must, therefore, recognize the unique capabilities of each student and match these with the most congruent level of professional function. Some will do best at the technical and craftsman tasks, some at the personal and social, others at the investigative and speculative, and still others at the public expressions of medicine. There is a special compulsion today to advance the student as expeditiously as possible to the socially useful goal which best fits his particular capabilities.

To attain this end, current insistence on a traditional "liberal" education for all students before they enter specific medical studies must be abandoned, permitting these liberal studies to be pursued in a variety of ways—before entering medicine, during medical education, after medical education, or not at all. The reality is that some physicians will assimilate the liberal attitudes completely, some partially, and some not at all. Yet, all will be useful to society.

The traditional sequence of liberal studies prior to medical studies will still profit many. But many more will not want it or perceive their need for it. Forcing every student to "take" the humanities as a tonic or as an initiation rite or as a fulfillment of retrospective dissatisfactions with education is no longer reasonable. To do so is to encourage a superficial exposure to humane studies and to engender a self-defeating, lifelong distaste for them.

The same admonition was voiced by so astute and so humanist a clinician as Peter Mere Latham in the nineteenth century: "The different professions have one way of glorifying themselves, which is common to all. It is by setting forth a vast array of preparatory studies, and pretending they are indispensable in order to fit a man for the simple exercise of the practical duties that belong to them" (7).

While some students will continue in the usual sequence, a different pattern seems more consistent for many others, perhaps the bulk of students. For them, higher education can begin with the craftsmanship of medicine, and the route to liberal education and cultural awareness can be through their professional and technical studies. These students should be allowed even to choose a field of major study within medicine and acquire special skills as soon as feasible. Such goal-oriented students are notoriously immune to humane studies until they are relieved of anxiety about getting into medical school and until they acquire some competence in their chosen craft. There is little to be gained from blunting their motivation with the illusion they somehow will be "better off" if they postpone technical studies.

Capturing student motivation by early immersion in medical studies should have a high yield in enthusiasm and application, qualities often only mechanically exhibited in the first years of a traditional medical education. This enthusiasm can also be channeled into the acquisition of a humanistic outlook, provided it is an intrinsic part of medical education. A wide variety of humane studies—sociology, ethics, history of ideas, social psychology, anthropology, philosophy—can be taught around the cases with which the student becomes involved as a physician-in-training.

There can be no real question about relevance here. The starting point for thinking is always a real human being facing a real human problem in values, hopes, and aspirations. Ample opportunities in the everyday matter of patient care exemplify most of the perennial questions of human concern. Can there be more pertinent grist for the mill of the committed humanist than these: the cancer patient facing death, pain, and loneliness; the sick and lonely aged; the disaffected; the depressed; the alcohol- and the drug-addicted; the "better off" with their less dramatic but significant neuroses? All the existential problems of being human in a terrifying mechanistic world are exemplified in the medical student's daily work. Health and disease are entry points to the whole range of personal and social concerns of mankind.

Problems that transcend individuals are abundant too: the ethics of experimentation, the justice of distribution of health resources, the human uses of technology, the social and cultural roots of dissent. All problems of human life—alienation, affection, social and cultural relationships, and even salvation—come to a focus in the existential laboratories of human problems we call hospitals. Every humanistic question takes on poignancy when embedded in the concrete situation: to discuss the value of life when deciding

27

whether or not to abort, to relieve pain, to desist from overtreatment in hopeless situations; or to discuss the ethics of confidentiality and consent when actually facing the decision in a proposed investigation; or to discuss the question of dehumanization when patients become lost in the institutionalized underbrush of the system.

The full range of perennial questions can thus be experienced and cogitated in their contemporary form by both faculty and students. Starting with the concrete case also can instill those qualities of mind classically associated with a liberal education—the capacity to search for truth, to understand the values of others and thus evaluate one's own, to frame a personal response to the problems of existence, and to communicate clearly, if not eloquently.

Even esthetic experiences can grow out of these encounters with the concrete phenomena of human life. The seminal works of art and literature are, after all, more sensitive insights into the same world, transmuted by the special responsiveness of the artist and the poet. The most general, philosophic, and abstract considerations usually flow from the concrete and the particular. The abstract need not precede experiences, as has been insisted in academic institutions for so long.

Teaching of the humanities and of humanist values in this way demands humanist teachers with special characteristics. They must first be bona fide members of social science or humanities faculties, not merely cultivated or talented physicians with an interest in these subjects. They particularly should maintain identification with their own disciplines for two reasons: to avoid the isolation which besets the humanist in a medical setting where there is usually an insufficient "critical mass" of colleagues and to maintain authenticity in their teaching. Attaining these two essentials usually requires joint appointment to both university and medical school departments.

These teachers must also have a real commitment to communicating the sense of their disciplines to students in medicine and the other health professions. They can do this in several degrees of depth: (a) introductory seminars for all students in the health professions, taught in interdisciplinary sessions; (b) elective seminars and courses in greater depth for those medical and other students stimulated by the introductory material; and (c) research and advanced study for students of the health professions who wish to pursue scholarly work in medical social sciences and humanities or to teach in these fields. Such students can drop out of the standard curricula for extended periods, or even pursue a combined Ph.D.-M.D. option as they now do in the basic health sciences.

The social scientists and humanists should be situated for a significant part of their time in the physical milieu of the health sciences center, living, so to speak, in the laboratory of their concerns. This will foster those daily fortuitous contacts with students, faculty, and patients so rich in unanticipated opportunities for dialogue, cooperative teaching, and research. Medical students and faculty will thus be exposed in an immediate way to how humanists view their daily problems; humanists in turn will gain access to the concrete human experiences that can make their cogitations truly relevant. Some humanists in such contact with those they teach may be stimulated to resume their forgotten, nonspecialist roles as teachers of the entire intellectual community.

An additional advantage of this arrangement for social scientists and humanists is freer access to every facet of activity in the health sciences centers as subject and source for research. The philosopher studying death phenomenologically, the political scientist interested in institutional policy and decision making, and the anthropologist observing the cultural transactions in patient care—these are examples of scholars whose work is enriched by open, direct contact with daily life in hospitals and clinics. Indeed, it is doubtful that such studies can have full validity or that the health sciences centers can be fully utilized as university resources without the physical presence of some of these scholars.

There are hopeful signs that some professional social scientists and humanists already see the unnatural constrictions imposed on their disciplines by the university and are bold enough to assume teaching within the context of health sciences centers. They are motivated by the need to ground their own work in the reality of human experiences and also by a genuine desire to influence and improve the education of health professionals who are to become practitioners of the applied social sciences and humanities.

Some modifications of customary teaching modes will be demanded of those social scientists and humanists who teach in the milieu of professional education. They will need especially to adapt to the individual clinical case as the usual launching point of discussion. Interdisciplinary presentations, occasioned by the multiple problems that patients so often present, will be common. Careful planning is essential to avoid the interjection of some artificial point important in itself but not arising naturally out of the clinical situation. Such teaching will take place in unfamiliar surroundings —on hospital floors or in clinics, often with the patient present and even participating to some extent.

These teachers will no doubt be dismayed at how much has been forgotten or unperceived by their students prior to "liberal" education. But they should be equally gratified with the depth of response and the flash of recognition when some idea suddenly opens the mind of a future physician to dimensions of life and thought to which he was previously unresponsive.

Reading in the classical and seminal works of history, literature, and philosophy is relatively easy to encourage when related to daily experiences in medicine and its contiguous fields. A substantial reinforcement of liberal education can be achieved quite painlessly and enthusiastically in the postgraduate years, even in the continuing education of the practicing physician. Indeed, to perceive the social and cultural intersections of one's daily work is one of the few effective antidotes to the intellectual ennui that afflicts too many successful practitioners in their middle years.

Clarity of expression, if not felicity of style, can also be taught this way. Correction and criticism of papers and assignments prepared to meet course requirements becomes a more valuable exercise in composition or rhetoric than the usual theme-writing of freshman English courses.

The interweaving of liberal studies and humanities with professional studies affords a viable opportunity for shared education experiences among students of medicine, dentistry, nursing, pharmacy, and the other health professions. The sharp differences in preparation among these groups that exist with regard to the laboratory sciences is usually not found with regard to the social sciences or humanities. All these students can profitably engage in discussion of the values, human purposes, and problems that arise in clinical situations. As a consequence, some of the barriers to future communication between health professionals may be less firmly erected. Opportunity exists, too, for sharing these sessions with university students outside the health sciences, an interface yet to be investigated.

This approach should help to soften the growing conviction, within and without the universities, that the humanities are isolated from life and work and are meant only for the leisure use of an elite class. Ideally, if a case-oriented liberal education could be provided in medical school and reinforced through the physician's life by continuing education in the humanities, it would contribute optimally to his growth as an educated man. The taste for liberal and humane studies matures late; it is focused and enhanced by life's experiences at a time when it can no longer be cultivated in the present schema. Liberal studies which seemed trivial or irrelevant in youth may provide that margin of rationality and delectation to lift us out of the mundanity of our workday functions in later years.

This pathway to a liberal education sharply reverses the traditional sequence of studies. Its utility is, of course, yet to be proved. It can, however, scarcely be less effective than the traditional method. Taking this new pathway might at least dispel some of the illusions fabricated to protect both medicine and the humanities from facing their current shortcomings in producing educated men.

With any method of liberal education, one must be prepared to find students for whom the realm of ideas, values, and esthetics will always be foreign. With the method proposed here, if students must reject these realms, they will do so only after having a still better opportunity to experience the potential significance for man and society.

THE MOST HUMANE OF SCIENCES: THE MOST SCIENTIFIC OF HUMANITIES

It has always been difficult to place medicine precisely among human intellectual endeavors. Medicine is unique in being so thoroughly steeped in the practical on the one hand and so dependent upon the humane and the scientific on the other. Plato recognized medicine as an essential ingredient of the Greek culture. Varro included medicine among the humanities. In his search for infallible demonstrations, Descartes attempted to mathematize medicine and thus to ground it. Modern-day reductionists would identify it as simply a sophisticated form of chemistry and physics.

One suggestion very congenial to the present thesis is set forth by Scott Buchanan in a seminal and neglected book, *The Doctrine of Signatures.* Buchanan very perceptively saw the clinical arts of diagnosis, prognosis, and therapeusis as applications of the liberal arts: "the clinical arts are applications of the liberal arts to medicine just as observation, experimentation, and verification in the laboratory are applications of the liberal arts to physics. In fact, any body of scientific doctrine has a fringe of tentative exploration and operation which consists in the application of the liberal arts" (8).

He concluded that medicine is "the medium and perhaps the focus in which the problems of wisdom and science meet" (9). He went further and saw it as the root of a new humanism, a unifying influence for philosophy and the laboratory sciences. Buchanan's thesis is unquestionably fraught with pretension, but it offers an invigorating challenge to medicine, science, and the humanities. To the contemporary humanist, medicine offers the most concrete grounding for his discipline; for the educated physician, it can become the vehicle for intensive application of the liberal arts. Interpreted broadly as "man's study of man," medicine might well be used to teach the sciences to the nonscience major and the liberal arts to the science major.

As the most humane of sciences, medicine is an excellent focus for problems of sociology, economics, political science, law, and every other discipline which concerns itself with human beings. The ethical, philosophical, and theological questions posed by modern medical progress are of the utmost consequence to all educated men. In examining abortion, population control, behavioral modification, drug use and abuse, psychopathy, neuroses, and the myriad concerns of modern medicine, there is unparalleled opportunity to treat some of the most important issues in the social sciences and the humanities. The great advantage of starting with the medical situation lies in its concreteness, immediacy, and urgency. All students have directly or indirectly experienced the challenges of disease, disability, disaffection, and death. Questions of human values and the choice of alternatives are posed in a most direct way. The relationship of thought to action is nowhere more clearly exemplified.

Underlying its intensive concerns with human values, medicine nevertheless continues to be scientific in its method. It must proceed by the careful collection of data, the critical evaluation of evidence, and reliance on experimental and empirical solutions. Medicine is nothing less than a "humane science," potentially capable of illustrating for the profession or the general student the meeting ground of traditional wisdom and science.

But medicine is equally one of the humanities because its concerns are for all dimensions of the life of man which in any way impinge on his well-being. Medicine is not one of the humanities *sui generis*; yet more than any other science it stands at the confluence of all the humanities. Its peculiar arts of clinical evaluation and decision exemplify all the major attributes of mind we seek from the liberal arts: the search for truth and the means of identifying it, the establishing of a system of values, the orderly presentation of observed data and their artful arrangement in making a specific diagnosis and in defending the case for that diagnosis. In short, the medieval trivium of grammar, rhetoric, and logic can be reified in every informed medical action.

Medicine thus can be extremely useful, in itself, in imparting the attitudes of the liberal arts and the content of the humanities to the medical student in the course of his professional education. Its value as a cultural subject and as a vehicle for the humanities and social sciences for the college undergraduate should be explored further. With certain modifications in content and depth of detail, the most human and humane questions could be introduced through an undergraduate study of medicine in both its personal and social dimensions.

All the sciences and many of the humanities were first seeded in the soil of medicine in the medieval universities. Medicine is expanding its social and human concerns as it becomes the agency of applied biology and sociology. Its potential to alter human life and nature have occasioned a deeper interaction with philosophy and theology as well. It could well become the meeting ground for all disciplines dealing with man.

But medicine may have an even greater cultural potential yet to be realized. Is it not a practical mechanism for bridging the widening gulf between the sciences and the humanities? The need for such a bridge is epitomized in the vigorous discussion which followed C.P. Snow's Rede Lecture on "The Two Cultures" (10). Never have people been so sensitive to the need to understand themselves simultaneously as subject and object, as person and machine. The marks of Descartes' hemisection of human nature are magnified in every irruption of technology into human affairs.

The reconciliation will not come, as naïvely suggested by some, from teaching the humanists the beauties of science or the scientists the rationality of the humanities. To hope to "humanize" the sciences and infuse the humanities with the scientific spirit is to ignore an essential contrariety between two fundamentally divergent views of reality. This contrariety is irreconcilable, and indeed it is necessary to the full expression of man's intellectual capacities. Levi has said it rather well:

> The natural sciences, for all that they are undeniably a human enterprise, are a tribute to man's ability to expurgate all mythical, teleological, and anthropomorphic elements from his thinking. They illustrate his interest in factuality. They show him at the utmost limit of his objectivity. The humanities, for all that they employ a logic and require a structure of their own, are a demonstration that drama, purposiveness, and self-concern are inescapable and indispensable elements of the human situation and the expressiveness which it requires. They illustrate man's dramatic instinct. They show in its most elegant form the propensity for teleological interpretation in man.
>
> This, as I have said, is a real dualism—a clear split down the center of the intellectual life, and it is difficult to see how, with such diametrically opposed cognitive needs, it could be otherwise. (11)

This fundamental split must be recognized, and its divergencies used to balance any excess trend in either direction if man is to be best served. Medicine has great, and almost unique, cultural force precisely because it is a discipline in need of both views. It does not "belong" strictly either to the sciences or to the humanities.

But it must use the languages and cognitive methods of both in the pursuit of its object: the health of man. Medicine is a humane science since it must examine man as person and object simultaneously. On the one hand, to understand Man the object, it uses the objective, factual, experimental language and method of the sciences, necessarily "expurgating" itself of myth; on the other hand, to understand Man the person, it must examine man in all his subjective, imaginative, purposive, self-conscious, and mythopoeic activity.

Taken thus, as a unification of the ramifications of man's existence as person and object, medicine has a unique opportunity to occupy the two worlds of the intellect and provide the ontologic bridge between them. This end will be achieved if medicine works into its fabric the practice of the humanities as well as it has the practice of the sciences.

SOME IMPLICATIONS FOR THE UNIVERSITY

Sir Eric Ashby recently probed the dilemma of today's academics confronting the uses of technology in the university. He notes the conflict between those who see the university as a precious haven of the free intellect and those who feel its obligations to solve pressing social problems. He proposes a new technologic humanism as the way to heal this rift; interestingly he uses medicine as a paradigm (12).

Ashby suggests that the cultural education of the physician and others who must perform technical tasks be acquired through their vocational and special training, not separately from it. He suggests that the pertinent studies are psychology, ethics, political science, and the like, rather than the classical studies, literature, and history traditionally taught. In propounding this thesis, Ashby is reinforcing in modern terms the notion expounded by Plato that medicine is a techné—a body of knowledge aimed at the benefit of man and incomplete until put into practice (13).

Clearly, the intercalation of medical with liberal studies and the humanities in the manner outlined here would provide an excellent example for the other university faculties of one potent way to heal the humanist-scientist dichotomy. I think medicine can thus stimulate the university to a fresher and closer examination of its fundamental purposes in society.

But the dilemma is deeper than this. The university today must regain its academic and intellectual authenticity. Its current difficulties are academic much more than political or social. Students and society now expect an education more congruent with our complex world. Most reforms have thus far been at the periphery of the life of the university and have been engineered to safeguard traditional academic concerns. Clearly, there is no general agreement on the intellectual language all educated men should share. A drastic revision of prevailing concepts of general education is urgently needed—one which confronts squarely the issues of goals, standards, and alternate routes for undergraduate education and which infuses them with new realities.

Universities, like medical schools, have rigidified formulas for general education, unmindful of the diverse expectations of today's student bodies. Some come to college because they know what they want to do; they are goal-oriented from the outset and want to enter a profession as soon as possible. Others, and these seem the largest number, expect college to be primarily an experience in personal searching—finding what talents they have, achieving some identity and some purpose for the future. A subset of this group wants to use college intermittently, interspersed with work or other pursuits and spread out over more than the usual four years. Greatly in the minority are the students who come to train the intellect in Cardinal Newman's sense, as a tool, useful in itself, and capable of being applied to any data in work or leisure.

Sadly, only for the last group are the traditional modes of liberal education applicable. The others need a wholly different academic approach, a different set of academic standards, and even different faculties with a lifestyle more consistent with that of the students they teach. To maintain, as many still do, that a single mode of liberal education is essential or even beneficial is to subscribe to an outmoded conception of the uses of the university. More than that, it is a defection of academic responsibility which threatens the intellectual freedom the university rightfully cherishes. The general public and the legislatures will not long accept "reform" efforts that do not permit revision of the inner life of the university—its role as the liberalizing force in all intellectual affairs.

A tripartite system of undergraduate university education, at least, seems in order: (a) early entry into professional and technical training for those who wish it, with liberal education integrated into their special studies; (b) work-study programs, community and social experiences, interspersed with formal course work for those who are seeking self-knowledge; and (c) for the few who wish it, a truly rigorous liberal and classical education. Three different faculties, as well as different standards of performance, are needed for these alternatives.

This is not the place to expand this notion of a tripartite university education. I wish simply to indicate that the troublous state of university education today demands alternatives less protective of customary modes and standards.

As the confluence point of the sciences and the humanities, medicine has a special responsibility to explore this new territory of alternatives. In thus revising its own educational forms, it can encourage the general university faculties to more candidly appraise their responsibilities. As the existential arm of the university most acutely in contact with pressing personal and community needs, medicine can lead the university toward a more effective role in contemporary society.

Medicine can thus bring the humanities into closer relationship with the world of practical affairs and help them regain their position as guardians of human values and advocates for man—an eventuality as essential to the humanities as it is to the future of mankind.

CHAPTER THREE

Medicine, History, and the Idea of Man

The philosophers are the most powerful makers of history.

(1)

Medicine is an exquisitely sensitive indicator of the dominant cultural characteristics of any era, for man's behavior while facing the threats and realities of illness is necessarily rooted in the conception he has constructed of himself and his universe. The system of medicine in each culture bears an indissoluble and reciprocal relationship to the world view of its adherents. The medical behavior of individuals and groups is incomprehensible if separated from general cultural history. Henry Sigerist has superbly demonstrated the fact that medical history should properly be considered one aspect of the history of culture (2).

The roots of disquietude in contemporary man are bifurcated; the disquietude springs not only from the insufficiency of naturalist and positivist ideals inherited from the nineteenth century, but also from the inadequacy of current medical thought to include man's social and personal dimensions within its recently acquired scientific framework. The mainstreams of culture and medicine must so mix that a new definition of the unity of man's nature will eventuate —a definition which will be satisfactory to both humanist and scientist.

Cultural history, in the view expressed by José Ortega y Gasset, is "the system of vital ideas which each age possesses; better yet, it is the system of ideas by which each age lives" (3). In this view, cultural history is the record of man's effort to understand his own nature and that of the world and his fellows, together with the order of relationships that should exist between them.

Important as the other manifestations of a culture may be, it is the prevailing philosophic conception of man that influences medi-

---

This essay is based on an article of the same title which appeared in *The Annals*, Vol. 346, March 1963, pp. 9-20.

cine most profoundly. Man's understanding of his own nature and of his relationship to his fellow man and to the world has determined the practice of medicine in each era. The ideas of disease have undergone evolution as successive cultures have influenced each other. And although each system of medicine evolves from an earlier culture, man sometimes reverts to and resuscitates older notions in times of personal or world distress or when scientific medicine fails to meet the expectations set for it by society.

A historic view of the interrelations of medicine and the prevailing concepts of man is requisite for an understanding of the rational premises for medical activity in the past and for a perception of the present state of medicine, history, and man.

PRIMITIVE MEDICINE

Primitive man, as Radin points out (4), engages in speculation about himself and his world. His world view is a complicated admixture of mystical and pragmatic elements still to be unraveled by scholars. He is far more immersed in the world of nature than civilized man and sees himself subject to forces beyond his control or understanding. Religion is intermingled in every action in an attempt, by ritualistic observance, to bring life into conformity with the mysterious world of spirits who infuse matter and events and determine man's fate. The primitive is pessimistic about life and experiences a sense of guilt not unlike modern man. His approach to religion is practical, even skeptical. The idea of an autonomous, natural order under man's control does not occur to him.

This world view is reflected in a medical system with certain identifiable characteristics. Disease, like other disasters, is construed as the result of a transgression against nature or against the world of an enemy. Disease is viewed sometimes as the intrusion of a foreign object or of an evil spirit into the victim's body and sometimes as the capturing or the loss of the soul from the body.

Granting these axioms, the medical practices of primitive man form a rational, effective, and practical system. To attain a cure, the intruded object must be removed by suction over the painful part or by bleeding; the evil spirit must be driven out by noise or violence; the soul must be recaptured and the spell broken by appropriate ritual, sacrifice, or incantation. Prevention is possible and mandatory—one can watch for and avoid taboo signs, wear talismans, and placate the omnipresent spirits by appropriate offerings.

Primitive medicine has had an enduring success. Until the recent era of specific therapy, it offered as much probability of cure as its more sophisticated competitors. No small part of its success lies in its admixture of empirically discovered techniques which are still valid—setting fractures, dressing wounds, using poultices, massage, and an extensive pharmacopoeia. Most important perhaps is the sharing between the primitive doctor and his patient of a common view about the disease, its causes, and treatment. Important, too, is the time devoted to the patient by doctor and community in the performance of the elaborate rituals necessary for cure. The elements of primitive medicine are viable today and form the basis of the medical beliefs of many antiscientific and nonscientific medical cults of the modern world.

EGYPTIAN AND BABYLONIAN MEDICINE

The Egyptian system of medical ideas was marked by a certain refinement of the concepts of primitive medicine. Although it had not yet the speculative elements that characterized Greek medicine, it did develop nonmagical principles based on observation. The accurate and astute observations of the Egyptian physicians recorded in the Smith Papyrus indicate an impressive empirical knowledge of the nature and treatment of surgical disorders. In the realm of internal diseases, as the Ebers and London Papyri indicate, the Egyptians made an attempt at causal explanation of the phenomena of life and disease. Unaided by experiment and lacking the Greek critical attitude, they produced a fanciful theory of disease, but one based at least on experiences.

The Egyptians lived in, and supported, a hieratic society which directed much of their energies to the elaborate preparations necessary for proper entry into the next world. From their observations of putrefaction in the embalming parlor, the Egyptians derived their most persistent and influential explanations for most illnesses (5). Disease was conceived to be caused by the absorption from the intestine of noxious substances resulting from the putrefaction of food. These toxins were thought to cause blood coagulation and pus formation. This in turn resulted in fever, rapid heart rate, and other signs of disease. Equally influential was the idea that blood vessels are canals whereby air, liquids, sputum, blood, and urine were distributed to all parts of the body. Disease arose if these canals did not function properly or were blocked.

The reasonable way to treat diseases caused in this way was with cathartics, enemas, purges, blood letting, or opening the abscess wherein putrefaction was localized. What system of medicine, in what age since then, has not indulged in these familiar maneuvers to relieve the body of noxious and mysterious toxins supposedly arising in the gastrointestinal apparatus? Intestinal intoxication as a cause of the widest variety of disease is one of the hardiest notions in contemporary medical cultism, as the modern devotees of colonic irrigation will attest.

Babylonian medicine and its theories of disease were essentially religious in orientation. The major cause of disease was spirit intrusion, and therapy proceeded along the lines of primitive medicine. It abounded in magical notions like hepatoscopy, dream interpretation, and astrology. The whole Mediterranean area was influenced by these ideas through the Hebrews and Persians in their contacts with the Greeks and Romans (6).

CHINESE MEDICINE

Chinese medicine is an excellent example of the influence of a world view on the content of medical ideas and medical practice. The Confucian philosophy held that in health Yang, the masculine element, and Yin, the feminine, are in balance and in dynamic equilibrium. Disease is due to a disharmony or lack of ebb and flow between Yang and Yin. Man, like the whole cosmos, is made of five elements: wood, fire, earth, metal, and water; these correspond to the five viscera, senses, colors, and tastes. Such an assured view of the constitution of man strongly discouraged the study of anatomy. Chinese medicine was characterized by the vaguest notions of human anatomy. Its therapy was directed at providing the missing Yang element by the administration of some animal organ presumed to have a high content of that material (7, 8).

Primitive and ancient medicine share this common ground: each derives from a religious, mythical, or magical intuition of man's nature. Empirical elements are found in each, and each approaches disease in a manner consistent with its idea of what man is. Each system is practical; speculation is applied to the philosophical system underlying medical practice but not to the data of medicine itself. With such initial postulates, scientific medicine could not be a possibility.

THE GREEK IDEA

In the Greek era, philosophy and medicine were intimately interrelated; from their fruitful relationship came a medical system which went far beyond earlier empiricism and provided the requisite base for the evolution of scientific medicine. The Greeks not only accumulated observations, as had their predecessors, but added the vital elements of critical appraisal of experience and an interest in universal laws. They were intrigued with the causal relationships between observations and developed the first rules of logic and epistemology. They made scientific medicine possible by giving it a rigorous, intellectual framework.

The dominant conception of man held by the pre-Socratic Greek philosophers was that he was part of nature. Health and disease were determined by whether or not a man was in harmony with the cosmos. One of the first attempts to develop a real philosophy of disease was made by Alcmaeon of Croton (9,10). He proposed that health was a state of *isonomia*—that is, in health there was a cooperative relationship of the separate elements in man's nature. Disease was conceived of as a disequilibrium of the harmonious balance between the various potencies of man's animal nature. This same idea is reflected in the *eukrasia*, "the good mixture," mentioned in the Hippocratic writings. Here, health resides in an equilibrium between the four humors: yellow and black bile, phlegm, and blood. These views somewhat resemble the Chinese idea of the harmony of Yang and Yin.

Plato and Aristotle in their conception of man went considerably beyond the cosmologic views of the earlier Greek philosophers. They introduced the first major modification of the primitive view that man is an intrinsic part of nature. They posited, instead, that he was different in essence from inanimate objects, plants, and animals. They realized the distinctiveness of man as being manifest in the operations of his mind. The idea of the human soul was adduced to account for the thinking and feeling operations of man; forever after, the philosopher of man has had to deal with this added dimension.

Plato was much concerned with medicine. He insisted that in health, harmony of the soul, *sophrosyne*, was just as important as harmony with the material universe. Health is possible only if there is a right order between the different components of the soul itself: its impulses, emotions, and knowledge. Aristotle, in his *Nichomachean Ethics*, takes an ethical view and regards health as synonymous with virtue.

The close relationships between Greek philosophy and medicine eventuated in a body of medical principles and practice subsumed under the heading of the *Hippocratic Corpus*. This collection of medical writings showed influences from the leading medical schools of ancient Greece, Cos, and Cnidus, and it also contained ideas derived from the philosophy of Pythagoras.

There is a considerable unity of doctrine in these writings despite their varying sources. They emphasize the need for a proper sense of proportion and a right relationship between the individual and the universe. The effects of the emotions on health and disease were understood. Much attention is given to the social significance of medical activity and especially to the social responsibilities of the physician as a public servant. As Jaeger points out, "The physician was classified as a *demiourgos*—a public worker" (11). There was insistence on the importance of the relationship between physician and patient at all points in the recovery and treatment process. In contrast with the enormous pharmacopoeias of Egyptian and Chinese and Babylonian medicine, there was a certain distrust of medication and more reliance on diet, exercise, and rest. The physician was considered ancillary to the healing forces of nature and instrumental in reestablishing the right relationship between the sick man and the world around him.

This sophisticated pattern of Greek medicine, modified in Rome and Alexandria, was transmitted to the Western world in the writings of Galen. He essayed a synthesis of the Hippocratic teachings with elements of Christianity and the philosophy of Aristotle. This Hippocratic-Galenic system preserved in the monasteries of Spain, France, and Italy provided the raw material for the teaching of medicine when it emerged as a university discipline in the early

Middle Ages. Very much the handiwork of the Greek idea of man and philosophy, it still serves as a valued foundation for the clinician of today.

THE ROMAN IDEA

In clear contrast to the speculative nature of Greek medicine is that of the Roman world. Greek in origin and inspiration, it nevertheless acquired the practical orientation of the Roman mind, which as Virgil (12) so accurately sensed, was more attuned to administration, practical politics, and the propagation of the *Pax Romana*. The dominant Roman philosophical systems were the Stoic philosophies of Seneca, Epictetus, and Marcus Aurelius. These thinkers were mainly concerned with ethical conduct and the noble acceptance of the miseries of human existence. Their focus was on a world of action, not of contemplation.

Many of the Roman ideas of disease were corruptions of the Greek. It was during this period, for example, that the methodist school originated, which claimed all diseases were caused by patency or obstructions of the pores in the skin. All treatment was directed at restoring the state of the pores to normal. This is another idea which has been popular many times in the history of medicine and has vitality today.

Conditioned by its practical world view, Roman medicine was chiefly oriented to public health and social medicine. Its accomplishments included laws for the regulation of medical practice and the punishment of medical negligence, swamp drainage, the provision of a pure water supply, the establishment of sewage systems, the public baths, the supervision of street cleaning, markets, and foods—even the establishment of the first hospitals to care for the sick soldiers of the Roman army.

THE IDEA OF MAN AS PERSON

The most profound development of the idea of man came from the amplification of the Judaeo-Christian tradition in medieval Christian philosophy. Neither the primitive cosmologic view nor the Greek naturalistic conception could encompass such Christian doctrines as the Incarnation, Redemption, Resurrection, or the idea of the ultimate responsibility of the person before God.

Much of the thought of St. Augustine, St. Thomas Aquinas, and the other medieval philosopher-theologians was directed to harmonizing the potent philosophizing of the Greeks with these requirements of the Christian world view.

A crucial problem in this synthesis has always been the nature of man. Medieval Christian philosophy reasserted the ideas of Plato and Aristotle that man was a unique being and had a soul. But this soul had to be spiritual and immortal, not chained to materiality like Aristotle's entelechy. The doctrine of Aquinas on the unity of man amplified and complemented the earlier views of Boethius and provided a metaphysical basis for the destiny of man. St. Thomas insisted upon the unity of man, which was derived from the permeation of body and soul with each other to form one substance—the metaphysical sense—the person (13). It is the person who thinks and feels, not the body alone or the soul alone.

The most important implication of this metaphysical unity lies in the notion of person as the suppositum for all the higher functions of man. His conduct, responsibility, intellectual activity are expressions of his person. The dignity and ultimate value of the human is deeply rooted in this metaphysic, the final independence of the person from the determinism of nature imposed upon him in the Greek naturalistic view.

"No philosophy ever insisted more than did the scholastic philosophy upon this independence and upon the dignity and value of human life—by virtue of this doctrine of personality," according to Maurice DeWulf (14). The medieval personalist and the Greek naturalist views of human nature are profoundly different. They define two fundamental aspects of the idea of man, of which all others are variants.

The effects of medieval philosophy and its otherworldly orientation on medicine were paradoxical. Observation and the collection of verifiable data were largely neglected; medical ideas were mainly those of the Hippocratic-Galenic corpus, and medical writing consisted of translations and commentaries. There was an over-infatuation with logic. On the other hand, the contributions of medieval philosophers in providing a framework for scientific inquiry have been undervalued. Medieval metaphysics had an abiding faith in the power of human reason to apprehend the orderly structure of the universe. Careful attention was given to the rules of inductive and deductive logic. Cultivation of the tools of reason provided the Western world with a further extension of the intellectual structure of Greek philosophy and greatly enhanced development of the method of science.

The assertion of the doctrine and worth of the person and the exhortations to practice charity contributed to the origin of hospitals for the poor and the neglected. These flourished all over Europe and many are still extant. Although its daily practices were still empiric and magical, medieval medicine did maintain and refurbish the traditions of Greek medicine and establish the teaching of medicine as a university discipline. It enlarged upon the social and public health bequeathal of Roman medicine. The providential view of human history held by medieval man enabled him to endure the mysteries of disease at the personal level when prevailing medical practices were inadequate to the task of cure.

EXPERIMENT AND QUANTIFICATION

Modern man was born sometime in the Renaissance at that indefinite but crucial point when his thought turned from a primary interest in philosophy and theology to the investigation of himself and his world with the tools of experimentation and mathematics. The adequacy of reason and authority had been realized in the thirteenth century by Roger Bacon and Robert Grosseteste, who called for a return to the observation of nature as the only means of discovering its processes. Two physicians of the thirteenth century, Arnold of Villanova and Raymond Lull, had already called for a reestablishment of medicine on the solid foundations of observations, examination, and reason, as exemplified in Hippocrates. But these views were prefigurements, born before their time and lost in the excessively speculative tendency of the Middle Ages.

Restoration required that remarkable concordance, in the Renaissance, of notions from almost every branch of culture to return man's thought once more to the world of immediate phenomena. The transduction of ideas from one discipline to another was unprecedented. The philologists injected a critical spirit into writing, thinking, and the evaluation of ancient texts; the anatomists reinstated dissection and precise information on the structure of animals; the philosophers like Francis Bacon extolled the virtues of the inductive method; the artists studied and depicted common objects and refocused people's attentions on the attractions of this world. Harvey exquisitely demonstrated what could be learned by experiment, and Galileo affirmed that true science was impossible without quantification of data.

These interactions between medicine, philosophy, art, and science fructified in that attitude of mind we still call "modern." For the development of scientific medicine, the ideas of the importance of observable phenomena and the indispensability of verifiable data for any theory of disease were crucial. We are currently in the midst of the continuing efflorescence of these ideas.

DESCARTES AND KANT

While the outlines of scientific medicine were being drawn, the postmedieval philosophers were profoundly altering the traditional ideas of man, especially the medieval concept of person—the unity of body and soul underlying all our actions.

Perhaps the greatest transformation of the idea of man, the source of a still vital challenge to medicine, came from the French philosopher, René Descartes. His famous *Méthode* has influenced almost all branches of contemporary philosophy, science, and medicine. Descartes attempted to resolve disagreements among postmedieval philosophers by applying the methods of mathematics to philosophy. "We should busy ourselves," he said, "with no object about which we cannot attain a certitude equal to that of demonstrations of arithmetic and geometry" (15). Descartes completely demolished the Christian idea of the unity of man as person. Instead of regarding man as a complete being, he proposed that the human soul is pure spirit and the body pure matter.

As a consequence, Descartes' philosophy gave a powerful impetus to the mechanistic view of man and of life; for as Gilson remarks, "It was not long before John Locke soon did away with the disembodied Cartesian mind and left us only with its mechanical body" (16). La Mettrie, whom many regard as the father of modern materialism, carried Descartes' philosophy to its logical conclusion and called man simply a machine that thinks. Contemporary mechanistic views, and their variations, owe their origins to the phi-

47

losophies of Descartes and La Mettrie. Cartesianism had important implications for medicine even at the outset. Descartes himself tried to work out a whole theory of medicine based on infallible demonstrations, but shortly before his death he had to admit his complete failure. In his view, disease was nothing more than an accident in the human machine and could be set right by approaching the sick man as if he were an ailing watch.

Direct descendants of the Cartesian philosophy were the iatrochemical and iatromechanical schools of medical thought. These schools tried to reduce medicine to chemistry, physics, and mathematics. Their attempt was a bold one which could only be realized in the twentieth century with any realistic hope of success. In their own times, the efforts of Sylvius, Borelli, Bellini, and others were severely limited by the rudimentary state of experimental chemistry and physics. Their ambitious scheme did, however, serve to introduce quantitative methods into human physiology and medicine, thus to prepare the way for the sophisticated clinical investigators of today.

One very influential philosophic response to the mathematicism of Descartes was espoused by Immanuel Kant, the father of transcendental idealism. In his *Critique of Pure Reason* (1781), he postulated that "though our knowledge begins with experience, it does not follow that it arises out of our experience" (17). Kant then emphasized the importance of man's mind in ordering sense impressions into *a priori*, intelligible unities. Instead of a knowledge of things in themselves, we have only knowledge of the sense impressions made by them in our minds.

When this view is extrapolated, as it was by some of Kant's less critical followers, it leads to a subjectivist interpretation of the external world as a creation of the human mind. Indeed, as Kant himself avowed in his *Critique of Practical Reason*, the will can become a law to itself in moral experiences.

The Kantian philosophy, through Schelling and Fichte, produced theories of medicine with less interest in the external and mechanistic phenomena of disease and more interest in aberrations of the mind (18). At its worst, the philosophy led to a series of transcendental, subjective, imaginative systems that neglected observation of phenomena. At its best, as Galdston points out, the Kantian philosophy reintroduced the notion of disease as a total disturbance and encouraged the foundations of psychology and psychiatry.

Some progress was made in the formation of the personalist conception of man from the fragments left by the Cartesian method.

SCIENTIFIC MEDICINE

During the nineteenth and early twentieth centuries, the maturation of mathematics and the physical sciences seemed at last to give more substance to the immature hope of the seventeenth century that man and the universe could be explained in mechanistic terms. Classical physics seemed to demonstrate that the cosmos was a neatly functioning machine; evolution questioned man's privileged status in the biological order and imposed upon him the determinism of natural selection. Mendel showed that we are, to a large extent, what our genes make us, and Freud exposed how much man is a victim of his own unconscious strivings.

The closed, explicable, mechanical universe seemed established with man firmly trapped within it. Human progress and happiness were to be assured if the scientific method could be applied to political and social phenomena, as Comte suggested. The idea of man once more became essentially naturalistic, like that of the pre-Socratic philosophers, although the interpretation was far more sophisticated and the data supporting the view seemed much more secure.

Medicine thrived on these advances in the physical and biological sciences. Its greatest progress has occurred in the past hundred years as a consequence of the application of their techniques to the problems of the bedside.

In reality, however, we are in another of those periods of confusion experienced in the post-Hippocratic, postmedieval, and romantic periods. The scientific method has itself exposed the frailty of the idea of the closed universe and the mechanistic interpretation of man within that framework. The physicists to whom many now look for absolutes assure us that they can only approximate the structure of the physical world and that no single theory can explain all natural phenomena. Individual events at the atomic and subatomic levels are probabilistic in character, but are not predictable as such. "Even physics volatilizes our material world" (19).

The absolutes of medieval philosophy and theology were shaken by the rationalist and idealist philosophers. The absolutes of a me-

49

chanical universe and of material welfare were then substituted in their place. With these now threatened by the continuing explorations of science itself, man is in another of those exciting but anxious periods in which he must resynthesize an understandable picture of himself, out of which he can draw inspiration for his individual and group actions.

MEDICINE AND THE CONTEMPORARY IDEA OF MAN

The physician is in a peculiarly sensitive position to detect the bewilderment in the contemporary idea of man. The confusion, despair, and anxiety in our cultural life are personalized in his patient facing the realities of sickness and death. Faced with the individual person in all his mystery, the physician enjoys the benefits of the scientific revolution in the specific things he can do to heal the body. Simultaneously, he experiences the consequences of that gradual corrosion of the identity of the person which has been in process since the sixteenth and seventeenth centuries.

The struggle for personal identity has become a prime source of anxiety in our times. In the seventeenth century, man derived his identity from the fact that he was a thinking being, though Pascal's reference to the frailties of the *"thinking reed"* was more consistent with reality. The romanticists and the idealist philosophers tried to give identity to the person through his feelings and emotions. The optimistic nineteenth-century hope of an ever-progressive evolution and Hegel's dialectic view of history as the process of becoming revealed the instability and the evanescence of both thinking and feeling as marks of identity.

What is the status of our culture today with respect to those ideas which are most important to the development of an optimal medical system? What has been the effect of the current indecision about a hierarchy of values important to man? Can the polarization of the sciences and humanities be prevented? We know that C.P. Snow's simplistic dichotomy of the two cultures is somewhat naïve. Yet it does point to a disturbing reality which is increasingly apparent to the educated public, as well as to the scholar.

A large portion of contemporary culture is a construct of experimental science. Although there seems to be no real limit to what can be achieved when science is applied to dealing with the world of phenomena, there is an immediate lacuna when it is applied to ultimate explanations, the determination of value, and the meaning of reality. Herein lie the "imperfections of science" (20).

Poised as it is between the need to apply the physical sciences and the need to understand and heal the person, contemporary medicine is stymied by the breach which simultaneously heals and fragments. The practice of medicine is more acutely affected than any other human endeavor. To fulfill its potentials, it requires an idea of man that will more satisfactorily meet the requirements of both the scientific mode of thought and the needs of the person.

A new and closer relationship between medicine and philosophy in the formal sense may be imminent, perhaps approaching that happy confluence of these two disciplines which contributed to the greatness of Hippocratic medicine. Such a relationship draws its justification from several contemporary concerns of medicine and society. We are trying to understand illness holistically, to integrate knowledge from all conceivable sources, and to adjust diagnosis and treatment to the multiple needs of the sick person. Most of the new knowledge available to the physician is of things rather than of persons. We are all witness to the paradox of a medicine capable, on the one hand, of doing more for the alleviation of human ills than ever before conceivable and subject, on the other hand, to increasing disaffection on the part of patients and society.

The root deficiency lies in failing to deal constructively with the needs of patients on the personal, social, and community levels. The mechanical man of Descartes, the feeling man of Kant, and the bewildered, hopeless man of Sartre are insufficient concepts for dealing with all the dimensions of personal reality. The future physician should understand the philosophic origins of man's present state, collect data on its effects on health and illness, and widen his own perspectives so that he can provide raw material for the philosopher of man.

Demanding though these requirements may be, they will assuredly be a major concern of future medicine. Because of the dissolution of absolutes outside man, the physician is called upon increasingly to perform hieratic functions. He is being forced continually to penetrate to the true person and to make contact with the intimate regions of personal goals and ultimate beliefs. He may afford for many the only possibility for a truly personal human experience. The privilege and the power of this intimate contact will impose grave responsibilities in the regions of human values, both social and private—responsibilities not contained in a purely scientific medicine.

What applies to the individual is equally pertinent to the ills of the social organism. The social effects of present and future scientific medicine on altering all aspects of human life are just being felt. Many already turn to medicine for guidance in problems as varied as overpopulation, selective breeding, aging, recreation, and even the right use of leisure time. These, too, are rooted in the patient's idea of himself and his world and solving them necessitates a greater sociocultural orientation for physicians than is now commonplace.

Yet in all of these problems the physician must attend to an immediate knowledge of individuals and their particular problems. He has, indeed, a unique role in preserving the person and his identity from the oblivion peculiar to the units in the gigantic social structures of our times.

CHALLENGES

Reconciliation between the science of medicine and the practice of medicine—and between the importance of the person who is practitioner and the person who is subject of scientific application —will require a fundamental reorientation in medical education and practice. More attention must be focused on the growth of the physician as a person. His own ideas about the nature of man can seriously aid or impede his contact with the person behind the symptom complex he encounters in the examining room.

There are substantial evidences that medicine and philosophy are approaching a new interpenetration. The existential bias of so many of the influential philosophers of man—like Maritain, Tillich, Buber, Camus, and Marcel—leads to the human and personal situation as a starting point for their thinking. They share a common concern with the experiential aspects of man, his individual uniqueness, and his societal relations. They are all immersed in the here-and-now problems of modern man, and all share a distrust of the easy solutions of positivism and naturalism.

It is possible that in our culture we may elaborate a conception of man which can fit the requirements of many more of his dimensions than hitherto has been possible. Without seeking refuge in idealized notions of the past, we may yet rehabilitate the concept of the person out of the confluent meditations of medicine, science, and philosophy.

If current metaphysical disquietude is to be ameliorated, the age-old dialogue between medicine and the mainstreams of culture must be intensified. Out of this dialogue, a more profound medicine could emerge, more capable of satisfying the tasks society sets before it and closer to realizing its still rich potentialities for human good.

R.G. Collingwood states: "Man who desires to know everything, desires to know himself" (21).

Medicine, Philosophy, and Man's Infirmity

Pascal said, "By space the universe embraces and swallows me up like an atom, by thought I embrace the universe" (1). In the tenth book of the *Confessions*, St. Augustine raised, for the first time, questions about man from what might be called the modern viewpoint. In the midst of what would now be called an existential analysis of the mystery of human existence, he writes, "And I directed my thoughts to myself and said, 'Who are thou?' and I answered, 'a man'" (2). In another place, he inquires, "What then am I, O God? Of what nature am I?" (3). And further on, "I have become a puzzle to myself, and this is my infirmity" (4).

Contemporary man, at the apex of his Promethean attempt to capture the physical world, is more than ever beset with this infirmity. Caught in the dilemma of the finite and infinite dimensions of his being, not only does he have doubts about the answers, but also doubts about the hope for finding the answers, then finally doubts about the meaning of the questions.

Every man must philosophize. Either he deals constructively with the ultimate questions or he denies their meaningfulness. In either case, a philosophical decision is involved. The configuration of his personal philosophical choices conditions the dimensions of each man's behavior. Indeed, the intellectual and psychologic adjustment of all men in an era depends upon the concept of man predominant in that era, in the light of its own knowledge and its own problems.

The central problem of modern philosophy, then, is open confrontation with this infirmity of man—his puzzlement about his way of being and his existence. For the first time in history, he faces this problem alone, stripped of supports from demonology, traditional philosophy, mythology, or theology.

Today, man's image of himself is fragmented to the profoundest

This chapter appeared under the same title in *Conditio Humana, Festschrift for Professor Erwin Straus*. Springer Verlag, October 1966, pp. 272–84.

degree in history. As Martin Buber has put it, "The difficulty of this concern with his own being soon overpowers [man] and exhausts him, and in silent resignation he withdraws—either to consider all things in heaven and earth save man, or to divide him into compartments which can be treated singly in a less problematic, less powerful, and less binding way" (5). As a consequence, there are philosophical anthropologies based in a dozen disciplines, each declaring itself the absolute as it exalts some facet of man's existence —the social, psychologic, biologic, economic, political. These anthropologies are monochromatic, necessarily incomplete, and, except to a few devotees, unsatisfactory.

If some order could be established among them, there lies in the very diversity of contemporary interpretations the possibility of a fuller comprehension than ever before. The multidimensional character of man allows application of a variety of analytic methods, each directed to its appropriate object. Can these conceptions in some new way synthesize without compromising their special individual contributions?

This question is particularly pertinent to medicine and philosophy. Each in a sense subsumes the many other attempts to sound the depth of man's being. As it reveals the facts of modern biology, medicine increasingly needs a clearer conception of what man *is*. Philosophy in its turn, seeking a fuller explication of the many levels of man's existence, is compelled to take into account the reductionistic analyses of biology and medicine. Are the concepts of man emerging from these two disciplines that approach their subject differently amenable to each other?

If the concepts are not, then there appears little hope of a rapprochement between the humanist and scientific conceptions of man's existence. But if, as I believe, these views are open to each other increasingly, then there is the potential for a redefinition of man which can enrich the efforts of physician and philosopher alike. Indeed, the exciting hope from what appears to be an emergent dialogue is the possibility of healing one of the great intellectual schisms of our time.

The mutual reinforcements of phenomenology, existentialism, and psychiatry have already advanced productive results. Little or no interchange, however, has taken place between contemporary philosophy and the more traditional interests of the physician in

disease, disability, and death. Here more concern and more intensive cultivation seem needed.

The unique point of contact with philosophy is the metaphysics
of man—what is man? what is he for?—Augustine's questions
again. As medicine deals with the potentialities of modern biology
—like the modification of evolution and behavior and the promotion of health—it cannot avoid questions about ends and values of
happiness and purpose. While attempting to gain fuller insight into
man's being and existence, medicine has an expanded and a unique
responsibility. Its present concern with all the physical and psychosocial determinants of health and disease is favorable for synthesizing data from diverse sources. Indeed, all sciences that study man
sooner or later feed their knowledge into medicine. The interface
between medicine and philosophy is worthy of special cultivation.
These disciplines deal more pertinently than others with man as
man, with his uniqueness and with his predicament. Answers to
many of the questions now put to medicine are linked with the
dominant themes of contemporary philosophy. Philosophers in
their turn, look frequently to medicine for the details of man's constitution and his experience confronting death and disease.

The most influential idea of man during most of the intellectual
history of the Western world is contained in the formula propounded by Aristotle in the *De Anima*. He identifies the soul as
"the specifying principle of a body potentially alive" (6). All living
things have souls which form a substantial unity with the body so
that "it is unnecessary to inquire whether the soul and body are
one, any more than whether the wax and an impression made in it
are one" (7). Applied to man, this formula defines him as the substantial union of two disparate elements, body and soul, each essential to a complete human nature and interdependent. Aristotle
recognized the contrariety of these two elements and the importance of harmony between them to health. He recognized too that
different aspects of this unity could be studied by different disciplines like natural science, medicine, and philosophy. Physiology
and philosophy both may study man, but each is distinct; human
psychology should not be confused with either (8).

Aristotle's idea, upon which he firmly insisted, of the unity of
mind and body contradicted the prevailing Platonic notion that
man was essentially a soul using a body, eager to shed this tempo-
rary prison for the life of pure thought. It also contradicts the Car-

tesian assertion that soul is the first certainty and the opposite idea, that mind is a mere curious epiphenomenon of brain. Aristotle's concept of the substantial unity of man would render absurd all recurrent monisms—materialistic or idealistic—as well as any dualism combining distinctly different substances.

This strict belief in unity of soul and body created some very subtle problems for St. Thomas Aquinas, who was committed to augmenting the Aristotelian conception with the insights of Christian revelation. Aristotle was noncommittal about the immortality of the soul and, in the *Ethics*, even denied the possibility of man achieving his true end. While realizing the merits of the Aristotelian synthesis, Aquinas had to satisfy the requirements of Christian belief—a soul which could survive the body, and a body so much a part of the soul and human nature as to be resurrected with it. Aquinas' solution was a complicated one: he proposed that man was not two substances united but a complex substance in which one of the principles, the soul, substantializes the other, the body. This subtle distinction was not acceptable to all Christian philosophers, e.g., Scotus and Cajetan, but it did both reaffirm the unity of man postulated by Aristotle and take into account the Christian requirement for immortality (9).

Even more significant in establishing the unity and meaning of man was the development of the concept of *person* by Aquinas and the other medieval philosophers. They accepted the definition of Boethius, put forth seven centuries earlier, that the person was "an individual substance of a rational nature." St. Thomas, in the *Summa Contra Gentiles*, identified the person as that which was "most perfect" in nature. The person became the substratum of all man's activities, itself unchangable and destined for immortality. This doctrine of person as a rational substance underlies much of Christian ethics and provides a rationale for ideas about personal liberty (10).

Although he may have denied some detail of the Aristotelian-Thomist synthesis, Western man accepted it as substantially correct for a long time. The existential anxieties of medieval and later European men centered less on the absence of a philosophy of man than on the consequences of defying this philosophy. The Renaissance humanist, while often profane and hedonistic, still maintained a belief in the substantial unity and destiny of man. In the modern era, the Aristotelian-Thomist synthesis has undergone progressive dissolution and transformation. This dissolution is one of the most significant events in the formation of the modern mind, and the explanation of some of its present crises. Man's chronic "infirmity" worsens in direct proportion to the increasing variety and severity of his doubts about the meaning of his own existence.

Doubts about the validity of the medieval synthesis began in the later days of scholasticism and have grown progressively greater under the impact of a growing skepticism about metaphysical knowledge and the rise of experimental science. Men like Ockham, Nicholas of Autrecourt, Nicholas of Cusa, and Montaigne reacted to the convoluted disputations of late scholasticism by questioning the validity of first philosophy in arriving at certain knowledge.

Undoubtedly the blow with most lasting effect was dealt by Descartes. Cognizant of Montaigne's skepticism, he sought a more doubt-resistant base upon which to rebuild Western philosophy. He hoped to achieve in philosophy the same certitude he had experienced in mathematics. He thought he found it, as expressed in his famous *Cogito*, when he reduced to doubt all things except the existence of the thinker. The thinking subject, therefore, is the first reality and the foundation of thought: (a) "This 'me,' that is to say, the soul by which I am what I am, is entirely distinct from the body, and is even more easy to know than is the latter; and even if body were not, the soul would not cease to be what it is" (11). (b) "For it might possibly be the case if I ceased entirely to think, that I should likewise cease altogether to exist . . . to speak accurately, I am not more than a thing which thinks, that is to say a mind or a soul" (12).

That both the concept of substantial union of soul and body and the medieval concept of person were destroyed by Descartes' radical schism affected every subsequent system of thought. A radical dualism was established, in which a man became either a machine or a disembodied thinker. La Mettrie, Berkeley, Locke, and Hume fell upon the pieces and gradually dismantled the Cartesian system (13). The ideas of the substantial unity of man was torn apart, and it has not yet been reconstituted in terms comprehensible to scientist and philosopher.

The history of Western philosophy since Descartes is a catalog of attempts to deal with the fragments left by his assault on the philosophical unity of man. A wide variety has been proposed—mechanism, logical and scientific positivism, the Hegelian absolute, the economic determinism of Marx, the evolutionary determinism of Darwin, the psychologic determinism of Freud, and many others less creditably founded. Each provides a valuable insight into some feature of man's activities, but none is capable of exhausting the full potential of man's being.

The last explanation for man's existence outside himself was finally destroyed when Nietzsche announced what many thinkers had felt but feared to say—that God was dead. Man, who had by then lost confidence in philosophy, saw theology demolished as well. Soon, even the certainties of the Newtonian universe and the nineteenth-century faith in human progress were to be compromised. Man entered the twentieth century with himself as the center of the universe, with nothing outside himself to account for his existence and with little likelihood of reuniting the finite and infinite dimensions of his existence.

In this atmosphere of philosophic instability, and in reaction to it, the existentialist philosophies emerged. Although differing in doctrinal content, the philosophies of Kierkegaard, Sartre, Camus, Jaspers, Marcel, and Heidegger still share certain common features relevant to our present inquiry. Each focuses on man as its central theme —Kierkegaard on man's relation to God, Marcel on the transcendental implications of human relationships, Heidegger on man's apprehension of being, Camus on the absurdity of his existence, and Sartre on his absolute freedom. Each is concerned with the individual in the concrete situation of his life as a starting point. Existence is seen as experienced rather than objectively given. Man is not as much an object of thought as an experiencing, involved subject.

The existential bias is that the study of human life begins with the experience of living in the human, not by analogy with the reactions of other objects or species. This is not too different from the commentary of Aquinas or Aristotle's *De Sensu et Sensato* that the way to study the soul is by an introspective awareness—*"quasi in quadam abstractione"* (14). Here and in certain aspects of the existential view exists a possibility for amplifying and restructuring traditional philosophy in terms more understandable to the men of our times.

Like much of post-medieval thinking, the existential philosophies are antispeculative in their bias, and they vary widely in their attitude about the transcendental. Sartre and Camus are frankly atheistic and explore the consequences of this atheism for a man who is alone, free, and the arbiter of all values. Marcel and Jaspers on the other hand rediscover God in a subjective analysis of human existence. In each case, conclusions are drawn from a subjective, metalogical analysis of the concrete details of life as seen by the subject, not from a metaphysical analysis of the traditional sort.

An invaluable analytical tool for the existential philosophers is the phenomenological method of Husserl. Like Descartes, Husserl sought an answer to the recurrent challenge of skepticism and looked for a doubt-resistant base for all thought. He proposed an explication of experience that would be beyond question by disengaging the mind from all belief in the real world and directing it instead to analysis of the phenomena of things as they are present to the intending self, the transcendent Ego (15).

Husserl's method provides the existentialists with the minute, descriptive analyses of concrete experiences so essential to their consideration of existence as experienced, and not objectively given. This methodology is useful too for all thinkers, in recalling the uniqueness of the human person, in which the intending subject and its perceptions are closely related in a being that inhabits a material body and can at the same time reflect on that body's experiences.

The existentialist philosophies have of themselves proven insufficient to satisfy the continual need of man to understand his existence in all its dimensions. Indeed, they have contributed to the contemporary ontologic crisis by laying bare the roots of man's dilemma and the despair which follows when he questions the reasons for his existence and can find no reasons. Yet, by clearly delineating the alternatives, the existentialists have sharpened awareness of the needs for a new synthesis and of the possibilities for its development.

In their exploitation of the concrete details of individual human experience, the existentialists open themselves and all of contemporary philosophy to closer articulations with the behavioral sciences, as well as with the science of human biology with its increasing interest in man's higher functions as an individual and social being. Likewise, the existentialists, by their emphasis on the experiencing person and his responsible condition open the possibility of a dialogue with traditional philosophy that emphasizes the notion of the person, so badly corroded by post-Cartesian materialism and idealism. Thus, the existential bias can find responsive elements in certain trends in the science of human biology and the perennial philosophies, a finding not possible for nineteenth-century philosophy.

In what directions may we look for a new synthesis and for the next developments in the philosophy of man? What are the prospects for post-existential man? What can medicine, which has always recognized a need to understand man's multiple experiential dimensions, contribute?

Biology, like philosophy, was impelled along certain lines by the Cartesian attack on the medieval unity of man. During most of its recent history, biology has studied man's body as a machine. The methods of chemistry and physics have been turned on smaller and smaller units of life, and thereby unprecedented knowledge has been gained about the constitution, structure, and energetics of human life. The successes of this reductionistic approach have, until recently, discouraged experimental study of man's more complex and highly organized activities.

Yet, this same success, in reductionistic biology, has accentuated the need for explaining the physiological, psychological, cultural, and social responses that are not observable when man is studied at the molecular level. The nature of brain mechanisms, memory, cultural development, and responses to stress, as well as such things as circadian rhythms, emotions, and factors conditioning the quality of individual and societal life—these are some of the dimensions of human biology which should receive explication. The science of biology will undoubtedly continue to exploit the reductionistic approach, but it must inevitably expand its interests in man's total or unique behavior, even including his cultural and humanistic activities (16).

This expansion of method to encompass more of man will merge with medicine, which now seeks a total understanding of man, healthy or diseased. The mutual interests and methods of contemporary philosophy, biology, and medicine will converge. A new synthesis more suitable to contemporary minds will emerge—undoubtedly to be replaced in future ages by still more suitable syntheses.

The dialogue between medicine and philosophy, which always has been in process intermittently, has recently borne fruit in psychiatry. Knowledge of the neuroses and of some of the psychoses has been enriched, as has psychotherapy, by an analysis from within, so to speak, using such existential and phenomenological approaches as are in the works of Binswanger, Straus, Frankl, and Von Gebstettal. There is excellent promise of an even more comprehensive understanding of man as a psychologic, material, and

61

spiritual being—with acknowledgement of his relation to a transcendental order—in the work of Frankl, Baruk, Von Weizsäcker, Niedermeyer, Lopez Ibor, and I. Caruso. The latter has proposed an ambitious, personalist depth psychology based upon a synthesis of elements of the Judeo-Christian tradition, Aristotelian-Thomist philosophy, and his own clinical experiences (17).

But as yet there has been little exploration of the possibilities of extending dialogue to include the broader applications of medicine and human biology. In individual clinical medicine and in social medicine many problems of mutual concern could be illuminated better by an interchange between philosopher and physician. Currently, a "reimmersion of philosophy in the data of the empirical sciences which deal with human experience in any manner" (18) is taking place. This reimmersion will move philosophy closer to many concerns and findings of everyday medicine.

In some respects medicine appears to be retreating from the encounter by overconcentration on technical, experimental, and molecular dimensions.

Yet, when the physician subscribes to the Hippocratic idea of caring for all the dimensions of his patient, he implicitly commits himself to delving into the depths of the ill person. To a greater extent than he may acknowledge, the doctor deals with existential phenomena, with the world as seen from the viewpoint of his patient. Today, with the metaphysical substratum of the person very much in question, the doctor encounters a variety of discordant images of man, or commonly, the consequences of the denial of an ontology of man.

Each patient's world view colors his illness, his response to that illness, and its meaning for him. The patient's philosophy is a part of his posture as a person.

The prevailing ontologic deficit affects the patient's behavior as much as his unconscious drives. The failure of the existentialist philosophies, except perhaps in the case of Marcel and Jaspers, to solve or successfully to avoid the problem of ontology, has produced a crisis, heightened by the apocalyptic potentials of modern biology and physics. Many decisions about how best to direct what science can do are contingent upon definitions of the good and of man which transcend the existential analysis. Sciences can provide means, but only a philosophy can define ends. A stable system of values is needed equal to the challenges, for good or evil, latent in the technical information man is accumulating.

The physician cannot himself make up the ontologic deficits. But he must understand some of its genesis in ideologic history and of its affect on the development of his patient. For, the loss of belief in an objective order of values outside man often compels the patient under the stress of illness to reveal his inner needs. The physician is often asked to fill the hieratic role, to ponder ethical and even religious problems with his patient. He is one of the few kinds of persons left in a democratic society who holds individual, direct power over the well-being of others. Even for the educated, he wields powers which verge on the magical. In a highly organized society, he is perhaps the last refuge to which the patient, as an individual and as a person, may repair. Although he should not substitute for the minister or the theologian, he may have to provide "medical assistance in the direction of conscience" (*Seelsorgehilfe*) as Niedermeyer has suggested (19). He clearly has, in any case, a responsibility to gain some insight into the history of ideas so that he can understand his patient's world view. Most important, he needs to contemplate these questions himself because philosophic maturation is a part of emotional maturation, without which he can be of little help to others.

The philosophic notions of the object he studies cannot be ignored by any scientist, no matter how objective he tries to be. Like the measuring instrument in physics, the observer's notions alter the object by the very act of measurement. The physician's understanding of the nature of man and of the person determines the facts he chooses to study, the questions he considers meaningful, and the hypotheses he generates.

Whether he recognizes it or not, then, the physician must be aware of whatever his idea of man is from which his actions derive, and he needs some understanding of the intellectual history of that idea and its implications. Because medicine involves a personal relationship, the most critical contact with philosophy will be on the subject of the nature of man and of the person. The major concern of contemporary philosophy is man's existence; here a dialogue fruitful to the physician can begin.

The functions of physician and philosopher are not to be confused. The doctor proceeds by hypothesis, observation, experiment, and the empiric. He uses a concept of man to frame his questions, but he does not derive the concept from his methodology. The philosopher, with his special view, clarifies and augments the concept, relates it to the general history of ideas, and raises fundamental questions about ends and values.

The relationship of the two disciplines should not involve subordination of one, but a true synthesis. Philosophy needs to explore the actual ontologic state of man. Its task today can be achieved in a much fuller way by a close collaboration with the many branches of clinical medicine that examine the facts of existence with verifiable methods. Medicine can better decide what factors to seek out in answering some of its most profound questions by a dialogue with philosophy, which can acquaint it with the emergent conceptions of man.

Disease is itself a disorganization of a patient's whole world. Its meaning to a man is related to how he views himself and the world. What a man believes of himself forms his personality and even the kind of disease he may have. The nature of disease, the ontologic definition of medicine, the comprehensive understanding of the psychosomatic unity, and its disorganization in disease are all matters about which the clinician can be illuminated by contact with the philosophers of man.

Most of the questions about the life of man, brought up by recognition of the phenomenal potentialities of biological science, can only be answered by some reference to a system of values that confronts squarely the problem of what humans are and what they are for. How many organs can we transplant and still assure that the identity of the person is retained? How should heredity be controlled, if at all? In what direction should the human race be modified by genetic manipulation? Behavior, memory, and intelligence can be modified by chemical means, but to what ends? Who will decide and who will set the values if the transcendental order is abrogated? Should technology be directed to societal ends emphasizing utility and function, or to individual happiness instead? These are questions which will be put to medicine; its methods alone are inadequate to answer them. These are all ethical questions, and ethical questions are meaningless without a clear definition of man from which thinking can start.

One benefit of the present closeness of medical schools and universities is ease of interchange between medicine and philosophy. The university hospital is potentially a laboratory for closer scrutiny of man in all his experiential dimensions. The openness of phenomenologists to all human phenomena and the contemporary tendency to philosophies rooted in existence should encourage contacts with medical school colleagues. It is to be hoped that medical faculties will include a few members interested in providing data pertinent to questions raised by the philosophers. Such dialogue would be greatly advanced if formal philosophy were more often a part of the liberal education of the premedical student. The importance of raising philosophic questions in medicine should prompt further exploration of the place of philosophy in the medical school curriculum.

We are a long way still from answering the anthropologic question posed by St. Augustine: "What am I that I have become a problem to myself?" Augustine raised the question in wonder, not so much at man as part of the world but rather at that in man which cannot be understood as part of the world. Man, as Pascal understood so clearly, is too much a fusion of the finite and infinite to be understood fully by any system. As long as man has a mind, he will never cease to sound the depths of this mystery.

Today, an expanded understanding of man consistent with our own problems and knowledge appears possible. The metaphysical unity disrupted by Descartes can never be reconstituted in its old form. Our ontologic anxiety will persist and deepen, however, if the spiritual, psychologic, and material levels of man's existence are not reconstituted in contemporary language. The time is propitious for another interchange between the ancient disciplines of medicine and philosophy, an interchange which could be as fertile as that of ancient Greece. In this there would be hope for reunion of the experiential and the ontologic views of man. The healing of the cultural rift between the human and scientific experiences of man and the maturation of both disciplines depends significantly on the success or failure of dialogue. An excellent beginning for such dialogue was suggested centuries ago by Aristotle:

> But it behooves the Physical Philosopher to obtain also a clear view of the first principles of health and disease, inasmuch as neither health nor disease can exist in lifeless things. Indeed, we may say of most physical inquirers, and of those physicians who study their art philosophically, that while the former complete their works with a disquisition on medicine, the latter usually base their medical theories on principles derived from physics. (20)

CHAPTER FIVE

Medicine and Philosophy

Phaedrus: *Hippocrates the Asclepiad says that the nature even of the body can only be understood as a whole.*

Socrates: *Yes friend, and he is right—still we ought not to be content with the name of Hippocrates, but to examine and see whether his argument agrees with his conception of nature.*

Plato, Phaedrus (1)

Medicine and philosophy oscillate about each other like the strands of a complex double helix of the intellect. They are intermittently drawn together by their immersion in man's existence and driven apart by their often opposing preoccupations with that existence. Special tensions arise from their conflicting claims to universality—medicine divinizing the body and the particular, and philosophy the intellect and the abstract.

The state of the relationship is, however, always of profound cultural significance. When medicine and philosophy converge they can greatly advance man's search for a unified image of himself and the world; when they diverge, that image becomes fragmented, puzzling, and even absurd. Today, the intersections of medicine and philosophy are fraught with uncommon possibility and urgency. The problematic state of that intersection is one of the most significant challenges our culture faces.

The ambiguities and the tensions inherent in the relationships of medicine and philosophy have been expressed in ancient and modern terms. Plato, with his usual prescience, exposes these ambiguities. In the *Protagoras*, the *Gorgias*, and elsewhere, he stresses the

---

This chapter is a modified version of an essay entitled "Philosophy of Medicine: Problematic and Potential" which was published in *The Journal of Medicine and Philosophy*, 1:1 (1976), pp. 5–31.

close congruity of medicine and philosophy as practical disciplines aimed at the promotion of the good life. For both Plato and Aristotle, medicine and philosophy share a concern with the normative —the first prescribing the right conduct of the body, the latter the right conduct of the soul as well as of the social and the political life (2, 3).

In the *Symposium*, however, the emphasis is on the antithetical claims of medicine and philosophy. Eryximachus, the physician, is a symbol of technicism in his promulgation of the cultivation of the body as the true end of human life—"And this is what the physician has to do, and in this the art of medicine consists: for medicine may be regarded as the knowledge of the loves and desires of the body, and how to satisfy them or not" (4,5). But later on, Diotima speaks for Socrates, of a higher form of Eros: "But what if man had eyes to see the true beauty—the divine beauty, I mean, pure and clear and unalloyed, not clogged with the pollutions of mortality and all the colors and vanities of human life?" (6). Or, as Socrates says to Simmias in the *Phaedo*," the body is always breaking in upon us, causing turmoil and confusion in our inquiries" (7).

These dichotomies are expressed in more modern terms as an opposition of method, the antithesis between contemplation and understanding, and fact and observation. Claude Bernard stated what is still a dominant medical view: "philosophy does not teach anything, and is unable to teach anything itself, since philosophy makes neither experiment nor observation" (8). Scott Buchanan, calling for a philosophy of medicine, says that medicine "stands at the head of the natural sciences, and does not know which way to go. It has a record maximum of knowledge and a minimum of understanding. It has art, and wonders if it has science. It is suffering from an intellectual imbalance of virtues" (9).

Medicine and philosophy have inherent tendencies to a special kind of hubris which has complicated their relationship for centuries. Medicine is pulled toward technicism, especially today when its technologic apparatus is so impressive. Philosophy leans toward detachment, as the emphasis in the recent past on speculative metaphysics or linguistic analysis illustrates. Paradoxically, a deeper perception of the advantages of these tendencies has now revealed the need in both disciplines for a conscious balancing of these tendencies. Medicine is recognizing the need for understanding and critical reflection; philosophy has recently addressed itself to some of the more practical issues in legal, political, and social philosophy.

Contemporary medicine and philosophy, therefore, are at the moment in their intellectual histories when each needs the other to redress the tendency to internal imbalance.

I will inquire into one problematic aspect of the ground between philosophy and medicine—the philosophy of medicine. Is a discipline under this rubric possible? Can there be a formal discipline which has as its object the philosophical issues specific to medicine and medical phenomena? If so, can it be distinguished from other branches of philosophy? What particular problems does it subsume? What value does it have for philosophy itself, for medicine, and for society? In what specific ways can philosophy engage medicine, and how can it avoid spurious and contrived relationships?

My aim will be simply to map out these questions as they appear to a nonphilosopher who believes that medicine must become increasingly an "examined" discipline—one critically justified as science and practice. My stance is that of the academic clinician, educator, and administrator, aware of the presuppositions upon which medicine is built and their exquisite significance for individuals and society. My hope is to engage bona fide philosophers in examination of the conceptual bases of medicine, leaving to them the more rigorous, more distinctly philosophical treatment the issues demand and this essay must necessarily lack.

MUTUAL BENEFITS AND ATTITUDINAL OBSTACLES

In every culture, medicine rests on a structure of concepts which determine its character—that is to say, its method and practice as well as its ethos, ethics, and ideology. These are the ideas used to justify the expectations and the behavior of physicians, patients, and society. They are the source too for an idea or image of man which inevitably flows from medicine to the whole of culture. Never have the conceptual bases of medicine had a wider impact on mankind than today. Never has it been more urgent to examine them critically, dialectically, and speculatively—i.e., philosophically.

Philosophy, then, has a special cultural and social responsibility to help redress the "imbalance" of intellectual virtues in medicine to which Buchanan alluded. It possesses the intellectual tools—its own traditional and contemporary techné—to make the whole matter of medicine an examined activity. It can bring the understanding and clarification necessary to forestall the easy seductions of technicism. Few issues are more fundamental to human well-being than the humane use of medical knowledge. But the validity of the ends and means of medicine and of the models of man that emerge from them is a "transmedical" matter not susceptible to the methods of medicine itself.

Philosophy's engagement with questions raised by medicine is not without significant benefit to its own enterprise. Anglo-American philosophy, more so than European philosophy, has too assiduously eschewed a concern with the central issues of human existence. As it re-engages those issues, philosophy will need a fuller input from what medicine has learned about man's encounters with his body, his world, and his psyche. Medicine abounds in concrete, verifiable, and measurable data about human life and offers these as ground for cogitation and inquiry. Out of this ground, philosophers can find new stimuli to their traditional concerns for apprehending human being, thought, knowledge, and value. It is very much as Wartofsky said: "I believe philosophy has to get beyond philosophy to remain philosophical" (10). For the dialogue to be mutually beneficial, each party will have to overcome its temptations to universality.

Philosophers must learn to see the immediate and grave issues in medicine as philosophically legitimate, not unworthy of respect because they originated in such a practical domain. To be of service to medicine and to itself, philosophy must learn to turn to medicine even for understanding some issues of its own concern. A less precious, though no less rigorous, image of philosophy must emerge.

For its part, medicine must overcome its antiphilosophical bias and its own claims to preciosity and sacerdotal privilege. These barriers to a critical examination of the conceptual structures of medicine are now being breached by reevaluations of the social purposes of medicine. The most effective way medicine can generate a new, more realistic image of itself is through the kind of scrutiny philosophy can bring. This scrutiny need not abandon the scientific fundaments of medicine. In fact, a realistic appraisal of what medicine is, and must be, should reinforce the validity of that effort.

The dialogue between Eryximachus and Diotima is entering a new phase, one in which medicine and philosophy may have to compromise about their competing claims to universality, in the interests of the mankind each presumably serves.

MEDICINE AND PHILOSOPHY: THE HISTORICAL ANTECEDENTS (11)

Medicine as a discipline began under the domination of religion and myth. In the Western world it freed itself from this influence by becoming a part of pre-Socratic, Ionian natural philosophy. From this it imbibed an interest in the explanation of the natural world through reason, as well as a fascination with the ideas of cause and effect and change. In this period, physicians and philosophers—as well as medicine, science and philosophy—were largely indistinguishable.

Medicine became an independent profession in the fifth century B.C. with the development of the Hippocratic School. As Edelstein points out, medicine took on two distinct features: it emphasized the importance of basing its art in the observation of the individual patient and within an ethical framework (12).

Medicine and philosophy became independent and strong disciplines. Because of this, Hippocratic medicine and Attic philosophy enjoyed the most fruitful of relationships, not equaled since. Each contributed conceptually to the other, and their congruence eventuated in *paideia*, the ideal of Greek culture, as Werner Jaeger so well documents (13). It was in the spirit of this felicitous conjunction that Hippocrates likened the physician who was a philosopher to a demigod (14). Aristotle posited that philosophy properly ended in medicine (15), and Galen insisted that the best physician was a philosopher (16).

But even in that most salubrious of relationships, there were discordant notes. The treatise *On Ancient Medicine* in one sense fortifies the analogies between medicine and philosophy, as exemplified in the *Protagoras*. But in another sense that same treatise warns explicitly against speculations undisciplined by direct observation of patients (17). Hippocratic medicine even developed some attributes of a philosophy of its own. Thus, even at the happiest conjunction of medicine and philosophy, the tensions which Plato symbolizes in the *Symposium* were clearly discernible.

The usual historical pattern has been for medicine to be intermittently influenced by whatever philosophical school had currency in a given era. It took the methodological potency of modern science to fortify medicine against overspeculation and philosophical domination.

In the Hellenic and Greek worlds, whole medical systems were fashioned out of bits and pieces of the philosophies of Aristotle, Plato, Pythagoras, or Zeno—as the multiple and successive schools of Dogmatism, Methodism, or Eclecticism attest. In the Middle Ages, scholasticism and Christian theology suffused medical thought and practice. Later, Descartes' mechanistic biology became, and remains today, a powerful influence, from the iatromechanists, iatrochemists, and iatrophysicists of the seventeenth and eighteenth centuries to the biological reductionists of our time.

More recent is the influence of German idealist philosophy on the medical systematists of the eighteenth and nineteenth centuries such as Hoffman, Stahl, John Brown, and William Cullen. Risse and Galdston have documented how such notions as nervous ether, animism, or vitalism could be derived from readings—or misreadings —of Hegel, Kant, Schelling, or Fichte (18, 19, 20). Systems of diagnosis and treatment unrestrained by empiric or scientific observations proliferated in the romantic era and for a time inhibited the growth of scientific medicine.

In reaction to these transfers into medicine of poorly comprehended philosophical models, modern medicine has become distrustful of philosophical intrusions. Its historical susceptibility to the domination of philosophical systems came from the lack, for so many centuries, of a scientifically verifiable base of knowledge. Thought unopposed by fact was too powerful to be gainsaid. But in the last century, the triumph of Bernard's experimentalism and the infusion of the chemical and biological sciences into clinical medicine have reduced this susceptibility to a large degree. The philosophical temptation for medicine no longer is unrestrained system-building, but excessive faith in positivistic modes of thought and explanation. Medicine is now strong enough and independent enough to engage philosophy without fear of domination.

Philosophy has successfully completed its century-long reaction to speculative overemphasis of idealist and romantic philosophical systems. Logical positivism and the analytic and linguistic emphasis of Anglo-American philosophy have served this purpose well. Many philosophers, among them the philosophers of science, have already recognized the need for grappling with some of the more traditional metaphysical concerns, as McMullin shows (21).

Both medicine and philosophy have renewed interest in the recurrent and fundamental issues of purpose, value, and the meaning and mode of human existence. Medicine manifestly cannot grasp

71

the full reality of its subject—man—or learn to use its knowledge morally without relaxing its positivist bias, just as philosophy has already done. Philosophy cannot adequately deal with the new questions about man without continuing its own recent turn to the phenomena and the realities revealed by human biology and the medical encounter.

The serious normative issues in medical ethics, for example, demand more than can be extracted from "meta-ethics." If these issues are not treated in a genuinely philosophical way, they will be resolved in the crises of the clinical situation, and by individual practitioners applying their own philosophical or pragmatic leanings. These issues are too important for society to be decided without serious critical reflection and the participation of thinkers outside, as well as inside, medicine. Philosophers are taking an interest in questions about the value and purpose of human life and about the uses of professions as instruments of personal and social purpose.

European philosophy, with its phenomenological and existential emphases, has turned to some of the non-scientific dimensions of human existence and to some of the issues medicine is examining. One thinks notably of the work of Marcel, Merleau-Ponty, Lain-Entralgo, Foucault, and E. Straus. These thinkers observe a conscious fastidiousness about ontological questions and eschew the ancient idea of a "first" philosophy which confronts the unanswerable, but perennially relevant, questions. European philosophy, however, on the whole has been responsive to the fact that questions of another kind must now be addressed and that those questions must bear once again on this human condition, its meaning, and the central questions of what man "is." Marcel, Camus, and Sartre, as they grappled with the complexities and absurdities of the human existence, at least faced the questions, even if their answers are not acceptable.

At this late date, in the English-speaking world there is no recognition of a formal discipline under the rubric of the philosophy of medicine. We do acknowledge the philosophies of law, education, science, religion, and history. But even Edwards' comprehensive *Encyclopedia of Philosophy* has no article under this heading; indeed, its only reference to medicine is an article on Hippocrates (22).

In continental Europe, the philosophy of medicine has had a more definable status. Since the beginning of the nineteenth century, a substantial number of studies under this category have been made in Germany, France, Poland, Italy, and Russia, as Szumow-ski's valuable review attests (23). A wide variety of topics has been covered, such as the logic and epistemology of medicine, the concepts of health and disease, medical ethics, causality in medicine, the mind-body problem, mechanism, and vitalism. In the 1920s several chairs of philosophy were established in Polish universities.

The significance of the European efforts is not to be denied. They are notable exceptions to the predominantly antipathetic attitude of the majority of physicians toward philosophical exercises. These efforts represent, however, a rather all-encompassing notion which suffers from diffuseness and includes much that would not be strictly defined as the philosophy of medicine.

Doubtlessly, many thinkers in both fields will continue to see an impassable gulf. The stereotypes of philosophy contemplating the world of untestable ideas and of medicine confining itself to practical and technical concerns are too comfortable to be speedily abandoned. The artificiality of these extreme positions is becoming plain in light of the kinds of issues medicine now raises and of the kinds of questions philosophy itself must confront. As their interests reach beyond the peripheral intersections we now observe, a true dialogue must emerge—one which will force each to break its traditions and biases of the recent past.

The need for a genuine dialectic is increasingly obvious. The philosopher cannot really clarify the ontological status of man without relying on the most accurate statements he can obtain about man's existence. Many of these can be found in the kind of data medicine alone can provide. The physician, on the other hand, needs an ontological conception of man that can give order and intelligibility to his objective search—and this is the business of philosophy. The ontological encounter between science and philosophy, which De Waelhens feels is so important for our understanding of each, can have its paradigm in the encounter of medicine and philosophy (24).

The possibilities inherent in such an encounter are exemplified by the increasing number of philosophers in recent years who have examined questions highly pertinent to medicine or the medical context. We can cite only a few to make the point: the deep interest in the philosophy of the body evidenced in the work of Marcel (25), Merleau-Ponty (26), and Spicker (27); the philosophical foundations of psychiatry, psychology, and perception in works by Straus (28),

Natanson and Ey (29), and Grene (30); Engelhardt's concern with concepts of health and disease and the philosophical bases of medical ethics (31, 32); Buytendijck's fusion of physiology and anthropology (33); Lain-Entralgo's analyses of the patient-physician encounter (34, 35, 36); Wartofsky's inquiry into human ontology and medical practice (37) and Zaner's series of papers underscoring the character of the human self, interpersonal bonds (as exemplified in medical contexts), and the concept of "enabling" in medical education (38, 39, 40).

These explorations speak eloquently to the genuinely philosophical nature of many medical issues. They underscore the need for an orderly, detailed inquiry into the matter of medicine, from its prelogical assumptions to its method and modes of thought and their applications to persons and society. Serious philosophers are now examining this totality with a variety of philosophical tools. The increasing frequency and depth of these engagements raise the possibility of the philosophy of medicine as a formal discipline, distinct from other branches of philosophy. The subject is still in an inchoate state. It is toward its maturation that Engelhardt and Spicker have established their series on philosophy and medicine (41), that *The Journal of Medicine and Philosophy* was initiated, and that the American Philosophical Association formed its Committee on Philosophy and Medicine. (*The Journal of Medicine and Philosophy* is published under the auspices of the Society for Health and Human Values by the University of Chicago Press. The journal was first published in March 1976. The Committee on Philosophy and Medicine is under the chairmanship of Professor John Ladd, Brown University.)

The historical wariness of the two disciplines is being overcome, and the ground between them is again being actively tilled. We are entering a new era of dialogue, perhaps as promising as that between Greek medicine and philosophy. Considering the historical antecedents, the relationship will be a delicate one nonetheless.

THE PHILOSOPHY OF MEDICINE:
DISCIPLINE OR PHILOSOPHICAL MÉLANGE

Do the medical forays of philosophers in Europe and the current interest in the U.S. prefigure the emergence of a definable discipline

—the philosophy of medicine? Opinions range from flat denial to full acceptance. Jerome Shaffer categorically denies the possibility; Toulmin regards it as problematic; and Szumowski accepts the notion, going so far as to define it. We will first examine these opinions, then lay out the requirements the philosophy of medicine must satisfy if it is to be a distinguishable discipline.

Shaffer's denial of the possibility is unequivocal (42). He doubts there are any problems common to medicine and philosophy. Those alleged to be are either misclassified or not philosophical problems at all. He would reduce all philosophical efforts in the medical context to philosophy of science, philosophy of mind, or moral philosophy. Shaffer freely acknowledges the significance of the issues for philosophy, but sees nothing to distinguish medicine from a mere summation of biology and psychology.

Toulmin partially agrees with Shaffer by finding no real distinction between medicine and physiology (43). Physiology itself is a derivative of physics and chemistry. Physiology, however, deals with "the special field of life" where the laws of physiology are not independent of chemistry and physics, but still are not fully equated with them. Thus the somatic elements in medical science are subsumed under the philosophy of science or of biology. Toulmin, however, allows for the possibility of a philosophy of medicine based on the psychosocial dimensions of medical practice and the realm of values and choice that remain outside the concepts of medicine as science.

Szumowski, who traced the history of medical philosophy in Europe, is the least critical, and proposes a very broad definition:

> The philosophy of medicine is a science which considers medicine as a whole; it studies its position in humanity, society, the state, and the medical school; it embraces at a glance the totality of the history of medicine; it sets forth the most general problems of philosophy and biology; it analyzes the methodological forms of medical thought, mentioning and explaining the logical errors committed in medicine; it borrows from psychology and metaphysics the knowledge and ideas of moment to the whole of medicine; it touches on medical praxiology; it discusses the principal values in medicine; it formulates the principles of ethics and medical deontology; finally, it discusses aesthetics in medicine. (my translation; 44)

75

None of these views is really adequate. Shaffer ignores too much; Szumowski embraces too much. Toulmin occupies a halfway house; on further analysis, he must leave that position and either go with Shaffer or accept philosophy of medicine as a discipline, though not necessarily in the diffuseness of Szumowski's definition. Toulmin is right that the first step is distinguishing medicine from science. Then we must show the specific philosophic issues within medicine susceptible to comprehension by no other discipline than philosophy.

In recent times, philosophy has examined many special disciplines for their meaning and essence, their modes of explanation, the metaphysical assumptions upon which they are based, and the possibility of some unifying theory of the realities they encompass. Thus the logical, epistemological, and metaphysical examinations of what historians, lawyers, or scientists do, and the meaning of what they study, comprise the philosophies of history, law, or science. One can ask the same questions about philosophy itself—the philosophy *of* philosophy. Indeed this has been a preoccupation of some major thinkers like Ortega, Heidegger, Husserl, and Merleau-Ponty (45, 46, 47, 48).

Special difficulties do arise when we consider adding the philosophy of medicine to this list. Medicine does derive much of its method, logic, and theory from the physical and biological sciences, and so it is to a certain extent a branch of those sciences. Medicine is also a praxis in the Aristotelian sense—knowledge applied for human ends and purposes—and can be classed among the technologies. But medicine also tries to modify the behavior of individuals and societies and thus has roots in the behavioral sciences. Finally, medicine operates through a personal, and therefore an ethical, relationship intended to "help" the person to "better" health; it is a value-laden activity, with roots in ethics and the humanities.

At first glance, it would seem that Shaffer's position is correct—medicine is totally derivative. Because it has no distinctive subject matter, its philosophy is nothing but the sum of the philosophies of the biological, mind, and moral sciences. But is this so? Let us first see if we can distinguish medicine from science, then from the social sciences and the humanities. Only then can we properly speak of a philosophy of medicine.

Medicine is, in part, a truly scientific endeavor. It shares with chemistry and physics the aim of understanding physical processes. Medicine as science studies man by observation, mensuration, hypothesis-formulation, and experiment under controlled conditions. In studying *man as object*, it follows the canons of good science—proper experimental design, validity of observation and method, correct logic, and verifiable conclusions. This surely is the content of the basic sciences of medicine, even though they pursue these ends in the most complicated of biological systems. Granting that the "special field of life," as Toulmin suggests, imparts special features to the laws of chemistry and physics, the basic sciences of medicine could indeed be subsumed under the philosophy of biology (49).

But, the basic sciences are not sufficient by themselves to constitute medicine either as clinical science or medical practice. As clinical science, medicine must study the human entity, in which purpose, values, consciousness, reflection, and self-determination complicate interpreting the laws of chemistry and physics even more than do the special micro-environments of living things in general. Medicine, even as science, must encompass the special complexities of *man as subject* interacting with *man as object* of science. Physiology, unlike the clinical science of medicine, studies physical processes while ignoring the lived reality of the experimental subject —his or her self-perceived history, uniqueness, and individuality. Thus even when it functions as clinical science, medicine must correlate the explanatory modes of the physical sciences with those of the social and behavioral.

But, neither the basic sciences nor the clinical sciences can be properly considered as medicine until they are used in a particular clinical context, on a particular individual, and for a particular purpose, to attain health. The purpose of medicine qua medicine, then, transcends that of medical science per se, which primarily is to know. Medical science, basic or clinical, becomes medicine only when it is used to promote health and healing—that is, only when it intervenes in an individual life to alter the human condition. Medicine thus construed has a telos which distinguishes it from its component sciences, whose telos is to understand physical processes in as general a way as possible, and certainly is not to particularize that knowledge in an individual human life. For medicine qua medicine cannot deal with general scientific laws alone, but must apply them in a time, a place, and a person.

77

Medicine is, in short, a practical application of theory about human reality. It is a moral activity, since it operates through a relationship of persons, the physician and the patient, who co-participate in defining the goal and achieving that goal—cure of illness or promotion of health. The patient is not a passive object to which a technique is applied; the patient seeks help about what he "ought" to do and modifies his behavior in conformity with the physician's advice. This dimension of the "ought" impinges directly on the person and his values. It involves two persons interacting, each in his own sociohistorical moment. The intersection of their values, together with those of medicine, science, and of society, creates a nexus of choices and priorities. The unraveling of that nexus for this patient, here and now, constitutes medicine. The resulting synthesis includes more than the sum of the component sciences—physical, social and moral—that contributed to the unraveling.

This synthesis, moreover, is constrained by the fiduciary responsibility imposed on the physician by the very nature of the contract between him and the patient. He is *presumed* to help and not to harm, and to advocate the "good" of the patient at all times. The patient presents himself in a wounded state of humanity. He has lost some of his freedom because he must come to the physician; he must give consent when he is in pain and discomfort, and he does so in the midst of an information gap which can never be fully closed. Medical science, therefore, becomes medicine only when it is modulated and constrained in unique ways by the humanity of physician and patient. Its telos takes it out of the realm of *téoria* and puts it into the realm of *praxis*.

It is the totality of this unique combination that constitutes the clinical moment and the clinical encounter, without which authentic medicine does not exist. No simplistic neo-Cartesian reduction of medicine to sciences of mind, arithmetically added to sciences of the body and tied together with a ribbon of moral science, adequately explains this synthesis. Nor is this merely biology. Neither plants nor animals—though they become ill just as humans do—can enter into a relationship with the healer in which the patient participates as subject and object simultaneously. Plants and animals can be simply the objects of applied scientific knowledge; in that sense, botanical and veterinary medicine are simply applied biology.

Medicine might be considered in one sense a technology because its purpose is the application of knowledge to meet specific human needs. But, technology cannot be the same as medicine: technology's use is determined by the clinical encounter, as I have just explained, not by technology itself. Technology, like the sciences, becomes part of a larger synthesis when used within medicine. The question of "usefulness for what" goes beyond both medicine and technology into the realm of philosophy, as Jonas points out (50).

We have thus far said nothing of medicine as art. Here too, medicine has an autonomy very much like that of music, for example. Music depends upon physics, acoustics, and mathematics. But it operates with an autonomy which results in an entity called "music," which is not completely definable in terms of its derivatives.

The same kinds of distinctions can be made between medicine and the social sciences or the humanities upon which it depends. Medicine differs from psychology because it works on and through the body to affect health, while psychology works only through the senses to affect the psyche—as does religion to affect the spirit. Medicine differs from the humanities, which also deal with values and human existence. But, they do not do so with the direct purpose of affecting health or curing illness through manipulation of the body. The philosophy of medicine, therefore, is not congruent with the philosophy of the humanities, any more than it is with the philosophy of sciences.

Finally, we must add the social dimensions of medicine as medicine —the applications of medical knowledge on an aggregate of humans rather than on an individual. This social encounter parallels the clinical encounter with an individual patient; scientific knowledge can also be used to improve the health of the community. Here medicine is concerned with values, choices, and priorities relating to the good of society. Such issues as the distribution of health services, the purposes for which medicine is used, for whom, who decides, and upon what principles, constitute the elements of a social philosophy of medicine.

Medicine, then, is an activity whose essence appears to lie in the clinical event, which requires that scientific and other knowledge be particularized: in the lived reality of a particular human, for the purpose of attaining health or curing illness, through the direct manipulation of the body, and in a value-laden decision matrix. It is in this sense that medical theory is a theory of practical reality, and not just the theory of the sciences which contribute to it.

Up to this point, I have tried to distinguish among three parts of the total meaning of the term *medicine*: (a) the basic sciences component, a seeking to understand physical processes in a living being, healthy or ill; (b) the clinical sciences component, a seeking to understand physical processes in a perceiving subject in whom mind and body are united; and (c) medicine per se, or medical praxis, a particularizing of the clinical and basic sciences in the clinical moment or encounter, amidst all the complexities previously discussed. In medicine qua medicine, the sciences are not only means of understanding, but means of intervening in the lives of persons or societies.

Thus I would agree with Shaffer, that the basic science portions of medicine are derivative and that their philosophy is the philosophy of biology or the sciences. Clinical sciences, however, attempt a larger understanding which includes the entities of mind and psyche. The contemporary Cartesian would consider even clinical science completely derived from physical sciences and psychology, and its philosophy to be some combination of the philosophies of biology and psychology. I prefer to regard clinical science as a type of synthesis which encompasses more than biology and psychology, so that its philosophy must be a philosophy of clinical science. Finally, medicine as medicine—i.e., medical practice as I have explained it in the clinical encounter—cannot be totally congruent with either basic or clinical sciences; hence, the philosophy of medicine cannot be congruent with the philosophy of biology, plus the philosophy of mind, plus that of moral science.

I might summarize my line of reasoning in Aristotelian terms in this way: the *final* cause of all disciplines, scientific and otherwise, is understanding. The *final* cause of the physical and biological sciences is understanding of physical processes; the *final* cause of the humanities is the understanding of man in the human context—and of the social sciences, man in the social context. The distinguishing *final* cause of medicine is the understanding of physiological processes in a human being who is a part of the human context and who exists in a social milieu—particularly as his being is modified in health and disease. The *efficient* cause of all the disciplines is "to know," and, in this, medicine is not unique. The *material* cause of medicine is the body of the individual or the body politic. The *formal* cause of medicine—its unique feature, which is not shared with other disciplines—is the clinical encounter, operationally delineated above.

Medicine clearly is a domain of activity as distinctive and distinguishable as science, art, and praxis. It comprises a set of legitimate philosophical issues and questions which derive from the unique nature of the clinical encounter. This is the singular, ordering concept that distinguishes medicine from the sciences and which is the ground for the logic, the epistemology, and the metaphysics of medical practice. It cannot be reduced to the philosophies of science, mind, and morals, as Shaffer proposes; nor is it so all-embracing, as Szumowski's definition would have it. By failing to emphasize the clinical moment, Szumowski's definition includes everything about medicine—not only its philosophy but its sociology, economics, politics, education, and esthetics. In his definition, both the terms *philosophy* and *medicine* are too loosely used.

PHILOSOPHY AND THE MODES OF ENGAGEMENT WITH MEDICINE

The philosophy of medicine must emphasize genuinely philosophical questions and define them with care. These are the questions not answerable by medicine itself or by any of the other scientific or humanistic disciplines which enter into it. It is important, therefore, to elaborate somewhat upon the sense in which the term *philosophy* is used here. The term has been particularly misused by medical writers, as Temkin's observations about even so revered a figure as William Osler make clear (51). Osler's *Way of Life* is an example of many works of opinion and belief written by eminent physicians about medicine, works which are commendable but which have been too gratuitously termed "philosophy" (52).

The nonphilosopher cannot presume to enter into the question, "what is philosophy," which has engaged almost every major modern philosopher. Nor would I exalt one mode of philosophizing above the others as most suitable for the specific issues raised in medicine. The number and variety of problems are sufficient to challenge the whole range of philosophical methods. Some problems are best approached phenomenologically, others analytically, and others speculatively. This is not to sanction an undiscriminating collage of philosophical notions or some mysterious process of intellectual *épluchage*. In the nascent state of the inquiry, however, a pluralistic methodology has certain advantages. The precise nature of the questions may be more clearly revealed by divergent modes of inquiry, particularly if they eventuate in similar formulations.

There is little room for an autocratic notion of philosophy, sitting in judgment over the other special disciplines. This tendency is too easily manifest in dealing with medicine, whose immersion in the practical may range from the sublime to the sordid. There is already something of a backlash among medical people, a consequence of misunderstanding the intent of some philosophers who have ventured into the troublous arena of bioethics (53).

What is needed is a systematic set of ways of articulating, clarifying, defining, and addressing the philosophical issues in medicine. The philosopher can contribute by critical discussion of the physician's thought and action and by dialectical dissection of the presumptions behind them. The aim is the same as in philosophizing about any human activity: to grasp something of its reality, of the value of the things which comprise it, and of the nature of man as revealed in the medical act, the clinical encounter. What is essential is the act of philosophizing on the whole domain of the clinical moment, not the particular mode of that philosophizing.

There are three distinct ways by which philosophy as philosophy can engage medicine. I have devoted most attention to one of them, the philosophy *of* medicine, because it is the most problematic and also is the most in need of delineation. There are two others, philosophy *in* medicine, and philosophy *and* medicine. They can be distinguished by the ways in which medicine and philosophy address each other and the types of issues with which they deal.

These distinctions are a modification of the distinction my colleague Robert Straus has made between sociology *in* and *of* medicine (54). He did not make a third distinction, sociology *and* medicine, which I add in the case of philosophy.

Philosophy *and* medicine comprises the mutual considerations by medicine and philosophy of problems common to both, or problems in medicine that are not limited to the special rubric of the philosophy of medicine as I have outlined it above. Here the effort is collaborative. Medicine and philosophy retain their identities. Each draws on the resources of the other, is enriched, and elaborates some new medical or philosophical concept of its own. Some of the recurrent problems of philosophy—the mind-body debate;

the meanings of perception, consciousness, language; the special or nonspecial character of chemical and physical laws in living things —are susceptible to this type of collaborative attack. The findings of neuropathology, neurosurgery, and the physiology and pharmacology of the nervous system are essential, for example, to any serious deliberation on the philosophy of mind or psyche. Out of the interaction of medicine *and* philosophy may come part of a synthesis of the constellation of interpretations which now constitute the idea or image of man. A true philosophical anthropology must start with the full range of observations medicine makes of individual men in health, in illness, and in facing death. It cannot end there, of course.

Philosophy *in* medicine refers to application of traditional tools of philosophy—critical reflection, dialectical reasoning, uncovering of value and purpose, or asking first-order questions—to some problem defined as medical. The problems can range from the logic of medical thought to the epistemology of medical science as science, the problem of causality, the limitations of observation and experiment, and, of course, the whole range of vexing issues in the active field of biomedical ethics. These are problems that medicine shares with other sciences, professions, and technologies. The philosopher serves an invaluable function *in* medicine, that is, in the medical setting as educator and trained thinker showing how philosophy can illuminate and examine critically physicians' everyday activities.

This is a common form of interaction in the United States, especially on medical campuses and in hospitals that have formal programs in medical ethics. Philosophers in these settings are making significant contributions without necessarily addressing questions about theories of medicine as medicine. Most problems of the basic clinical sciences as sciences fall under this rubric.

When philosophy turns to the meaning of medicine as clinical practice and examines its conceptual foundations, its ideologies, its ethos, and the philosophical bases for medical ethics, then it becomes the philosophy *of* medicine. The questions examined by philosophy *in* medicine are then carried to the unique realm of the clinical encounter with a human being experiencing health, illness, neurosis, or psychosis in a setting which involves intervention into his existence. The questions then transcend those of the philosophy of science per se and grapple with the meaning of medicine—its nature, concepts, purposes, and value to society—what can be called the philosophical problem of medicine. The philosophy of medicine seeks explanations for what medicine *is* and *ought* to be, in terms of the axiomatic assumptions upon which it is based. This is the realm of the transmedical meaning of medicine, the realm which neither medicine nor any other science can explore itself. "And yet, there is another side in every science which that science as such can never reach: the essential nature and orgin of its sphere, the essence and essential origin of the manner of knowing which it cultivates" (55).

These three types of engagement (*and, in, of* medicine) are rarely separable: philosophers can, and do, engage in all three. I have dissected them to show the importance of the philosophy *of* medicine, i.e., the philosophical issues innate to the theory of medicine as a practical human activity. Ultimately, the more proximate issues dealt with by philosophy *and* medicine or philosophy *in* medicine must be rejoined to the philosophy *of* medicine.

SOME URGENT PHILOSOPHICAL ISSUES IN MEDICINE

Whatever mode or level of philosophizing one chooses, there are a series of interesting and genuine philosophical problems arising in contemporary medicine.

First, there are the questions which medicine shares with the philosophy of science, such as the analysis and meaning of medical language and explanation, the criteria for verifying medical theories, the notion of causality, the logic of discovery and experimental design, and the limitations of statistical and stoichastic analyses. These questions are modulated in medicine because they must be examined in reflecting, conscious subjects in the clinical context. Some mode of explanation must be found to overcome the pretensions of reductionism and vitalism. How, if at all, is the scientific enterprise to be modified in medicine?

Another set of questions, not usually part of the philosophy of science, also demands philosophic inspection. These relate to the unique existence of humans as a unity of mind and body. The meanings of the phenomena of embodiment and corporeality, and their perception by the subject, have a deep impact on medical theory and practice. Both Cartesian dualism and monistic materialism are glaringly deficient in satisfactory explanations of these phenomena. Still, no alternative to these polarities is at hand. Resolution of the deficiency is fundamental to any theoretical development of medicine.

To what extent are the methods and modes of explanation of sociology, psychology, and philosophy valid in tackling the realities of man's existence as a thinking being? Can intelligence, for example, be reduced to engineering concepts and be totally simulated by computer? Or, as Dreyfus suggests (56), are the metaphysical assumptions upon which such an assertion rests in error? Medicine and philosophy should be able to reinforce each other in dealing with such issues. Philosophy is still far from drawing fully on the large base of neurophysiologic, neuropsychiatric, and neuroendocrinologic data medicine has collected; medicine has yet to appreciate the insights metaphysical or phenomenological analysis can contribute to the interpretation and intelligibility of these data. This conjunction should help to reconcile the scientific with the common-sense images of man.

This reconciliation is a most important step in the persistent search for a philosophical grasp of the idea of man. Philosophical anthropology is still a diffuse exercise of quite recent origins. The "image of man" is fractured and in need of restoration, as Buber, Scheler, and Cassirer have told us (57, 58, 59). There is a growing need to weave together the numerous separate strands of information about human existence. (Stent, an unusually philosophical biologist, has sketched the limitations of both the positivist and structuralist formulations of man [60].) Difficult as the effort may be, such a scientific-philosophic synthesis is fundamental and must come prior to the choices we must make about human life, death, health, and disease. There must be some idea of man to order our definition of what is good for the person and society, and for the optimal relationships between them. Individual and social bioethics both derive from this context of our idea of man.

Intimately related to the philosophical conception of man are the definitions of health and disease, of cure and of disability. The suppositions physicians hold about these conceptions shape medical theory and practice. Since health is the end and purpose of medical knowledge, the clearer definition we can give to that term, the more order and priority we can give to our uses of medical knowledge. The intersection of human, societal, and historical values characterizing the medical encounter can only be dealt with rationally if both physician and patient each understand the other's suppositions about the purposes and perfection of human existence.

The idea of man underlies a whole set of humanistic issues which arise out of the technological potencies of modern medicine. Matters formerly the concern of the speculative and imaginative intelligence are now technological realities. Medicine can prolong or terminate life, control conception and fertility, elevate our moods or blunt our pain and anxieties. To apply these measures is to challenge traditional meanings of the value and dignity of individual life, of the family, of suffering and dying, or of individual versus social good. The ancient metaphysical question of what is "the good" has resurfaced with an unprecedented urgency. We cannot use medicine for the attainment of health "or the good life" unless we clarify these conceptions in the light of our technological possibilities (61).

The philosophical foundations of contemporary biomedical and professional ethics also are derived from the ideas of man, the person, and the balance which should obtain between the life of man as an individual and as a member of society. Samuel Gorovitz has sketched out a very complete topography of the philosophical issues at the heart of medical ethics. He underscores the urgent need for a closer examination of the assumptions about the primarily philosophical questions which underlie medical decisions, and he calls for their examination by philosophers. In fact, Gorovitz puts the matter squarely in terms of social responsibility: "That science exists in the final analysis, for the pleasure and for the benefit of society, is a point to which philosophers generally accede readily. What is perhaps less often noted by them is that philosophy too, is a social enterprise supported in the final analysis by the public, to whose interest it accrues" (62).

But what value system should we use in addressing these humanistic questions? Do we follow the ideology of modern science, which has influenced so many medical men today? Bronowski and Holton have ennobled the community of science, and the pursuit of science is an ethic of unique proportions in itself. Bronowski praises the value system of science—the capacity to tolerate dissent, to foster freedom and independence of thought (63). Holton holds that the scientist has no choice but to pursue creativity and new knowledge, even if we have not the means at hand to cope with the challenges to human values created by the scientist's activity (64).

Hans Jonas, on the other hand, calls for an ethic of limits, prudence, and restraint, to balance the ethics of endless progress (65). The more a technique has the possibility for modifying human life, the less free the scientist should be to pursue it without some restraint. This is in direct contradiction to the freedom which the ethics of science holds as a fundamental requisite—"The demand of each discipline to choose its own problems and fit them to its own concepts and techniques and instruments, suggests that science is not eager to undertake to solve the problems of society, as society would define them" (66).

The ethos, as well as the ethics of science and medicine, demands critical examination. How do we reconcile the image medicine has developed of itself and the concept society holds of its functions? The ideology of science has taken firm hold in medicine. But, can medicine provide answers to the questions it creates using only the method of science? Medicine must be reintegrated with all the humanities, as I have argued elsewhere (67). Isolation of technique from purpose poses an antinomy whose perpetuation can only confuse, and possibly subvert, the humane use of medicine.

The process of modernization is associated with bureaucratization and technology, which have become values in themselves. They are prime shapers of the cognitive style of our culture and of modern medicine. They are part of what Foucault calls our *"episteme"*—the aggregate history of a human endeavor which enables it to occupy a specific space in a given culture (68). Has the episteme of medicine arising from its own bureaucratization already determined what society seeks from medicine and created a self-perpetuating cycle carrying man ever further from what is distinctly human? Will this distorted "view" contribute further to man's philosophical infirmity (69)?

These are some of the questions which may constitute the content of the formal philosophy of medicine. This topography, necessarily incomplete, illustrates that there are several truly philosophical questions which medicine can neither pose clearly nor discuss critically if it relies only on its own modes of inquiry. These questions may be more deeply explored by the methods of ancient and modern philosophy. The choice of questions and the emphasis placed on them will depend upon the philosopher's own conception of his subject and of the act of philosophizing.

WHAT THE PHILOSOPHY OF MEDICINE OUGHT NOT TO BE

Several dangers lie in any effort to use the critical and speculative intellect on the matter of medicine. Risse and Galdston, as noted above, have shown how medical theory, when not securely based in the data of experimental science, can become a vast speculative enterprise that inhibits the growth of medical science. These authors use the example of the German physicians of the eighteenth century who hoped for "ultimate" causes of life, health, and disease. The conflict between those physicians who sought truth in speculative constructs and those who sought it at the bedside was a vigorous one, felt even today. The deleterious effects of thus making medicine into philosophy have been all too evident in the history of medicine. The greatest disservice to modern medicine would be done by a resurgence of that error. Medicine should not become bad philosophy, nor should philosophy become bad medicine.

MacIntyre recently warned against the unrealistic expectation the public and physicians might have of philosophy (70). The philosopher, particularly the ethicist in medicine, cannot hope to provide ready answers or formulae for all the moral problems of modern medicine; nor can ethicists be society's only monitors of the actions of health professionals. Some medical people are too eager to delegate the making of moral guidelines to philosophers or ethicists, while others resist even the asking of ethical questions by those outside medicine.

Philosophers cannot, on the other hand, avoid their responsibility as "delegated intellects." They must not, however, compromise the integrity of their discipline or be lured by sudden prominence and attention to indulge in pontifications beyond the limits of the method they master. Philosophers are as susceptible as others to the temptation of all intellectuals to see their special mode of inquiry as the universal way to truth. One way to offset this tendency is to place philosophers of medicine in the company of other humanists. Historians, theologians, and specialists in literature are also entering the medical setting. Their interaction with philosophers may be salubrious for all.

Nor should the philosophy of medicine become *medical philosophy*—that is, the musings, ruminations, and meditations of physicians on the state of medicine, the professions, health, or other related matters. These mental processes serve a hortatory, interpretive, and inspirational purpose, important in education and practice. They might become a matter for the pondering of the philosophers of medicine, but they must not be confused with the philosophy of medicine.

The philosophy of medicine also should not become a quest or crusade for *the* philosophy—some unified theory for all of medicine which would explain all human biological phenomena. We should seek instead continual examination of the crucial philosophic questions which arise from the substance of medicine, not a final system of medicine to end all questioning. We conceive of *a* philosophy of medicine as some theoretical construct to be tested against experience on the one hand and dialectical reasoning on the other. *A* philosophy of medicine as a set of propositions *about* medicine is valid only in the way hypothesis is valid in experimental science.

The philosopher contemplating medicine must be careful to avoid the twin seductions of overly serene detachment on the one side and total submersion in medicine on the other. He should remember the unfortunate plight of some social scientists who have lost their identity in the medical setting and their credibility as social scientists, contributing little to the medical milieu. The philosopher will be helpful to medicine and advance his own discipline only if he remains a *bona fide* philosopher.

SOME EDUCATIONAL IMPLICATIONS

If there is any cogency in this explication of the necessity and nature of the philosophy of medicine, then its nurture becomes of concern to educators and practitioners as well as scholars. Wartofsky's analysis of the impact of human ontology in shaping the concept of disease, and thus of medical practice, illustrates clearly how important the seemingly academic considerations of the philosophy of medicine can be in the practical world (71).

The questions subsumed by the three forms of engagement of medicine with philosophy—philosophy *of* medicine, philosophy *in* medicine, philosophy *and* medicine—outlined here will have varying degrees of immediacy for physicians and other health workers. Practitioners need, most of all, to develop some capacity for critical examination of their own value systems and their concepts of man. Teachers of medicine will require a deeper understanding of theological and epistemological questions in medical science and clinical practice. Those who make public policy decisions will require a better grasp of the social ethics of medicine. The medical scholar will want to probe the more ontological and metaphysical issues.

It would be palpably unwise to attempt to make every physician a philosopher in Galen's or Plato's sense. It does seem reasonable to expose every student to critical discussion of the issues explored here, particularly those relating to medical and professional ethics. But every physician, because he is involved with values, concepts, and ideas of medicine, must have some philosophical *sense*. Medical schools are becoming more cognizant of the centrality of issues of human values in medical practice. Approximately thirty schools have developed programs to integrate ethics, philosophy, and the humanities into professional education (72). Similar efforts have been initiated to involve the practicing physician as well.

A minimal aim should be to sensitize all students in the health professions to the reality and meaning of their personal values, so they can understand more clearly the basis of their own daily decisions and recommendations. Some exposure to the rigor of philosophical inquiry may balance some of the antiphilosophic bias of medical education. For those students who wish to probe more deeply, opportunities for extended study, research, or a career in the problems at the interface of medicine and philosophy, may help to expand the number of physicians able to take responsibility as educated men in the consideration of how medicine shall be used to advance human purposes.

What is needed is the cultivation of the humanities and philosophy in the medical and health-care setting with something of the vigor we dedicate to the basic sciences. Indeed, for most practitioners, the utility and importance of humane studies equals that of the clinical and basic sciences. Charles Fried has shown how philosophical, legal, and economic values and principles overlap in practical decision-making—not only in human experimentation, but in personal health care and in the social ethics of medicine (73). Few physicians who wish to be more than technicians can ignore the philosophic bases of these practical, daily choices so integral to their authenticity as professionals.

SUMMARY

The congruence between medicine and philosophy which we find in the *Protagoras* and the *Treatise on Ancient Medicine*, as well as the tensions symbolized in the dialectic between Eryximachus and Diotima, will always be with us. Both the congruence and the divergence of these ancient disciplines are important to human well-being. By opposing one another, medicine and philosophy can each balance the other's pretension to universality. By converging, they illumine some of the most important questions of human existence.

This essay has examined ways medicine and philosophy can converge in our times as philosophy *and* medicine, philosophy *in* medicine, and philosophy *of* medicine. The present moment in our intellectual history is particularly propitious for nurturing the engagement of medicine and philosophy. The most fruitful form of that interaction may be in the philosophy *of* medicine, a definable discipline with a set of issues specific to it. If the obvious intellectual dangers can be avoided, those who practice medicine, those who think about it, and those who are served by it can gain deeper insight into the nature and the purpose of medicine, as well as the nature of the profession and of man himself.

Perhaps—positioned as it is at the intersection of the sciences, the humanities, and technology—medicine can become "a medium and the focus in which the problems of wisdom and science meet" (74).

Part II
Humanism and Medical Ethics

The Hippocratic Ethic Revisited

Custom without truth is but the seniority of error.
Saint Cyprian, *Epistles* LXXIV

MORE IS NEEDED

The good physician is by the nature of his vocation called to practice his art with high moral sensitivity. For two millennia this sensitivity has been provided by the oath and the other ethical writings of the Hippocratic Corpus. No code has been more influential in heightening the moral reflexes of ordinary men. Every subsequent medical code is essentially a footnote to the Hippocratic precepts, which even to this day remain the paradigm of how the good physician should behave.

The Hippocratic ethic is marked by a unique combination of humanistic concern and practical wisdom admirably suited to the physician's tasks in society. In a simpler world, that ethic long sufficed to guide the physician in his service to patient and community. Today, the intersecting of medicine with contemporary science, technology, social organization, and changed human values has revealed significant missing dimensions in the ancient ethic. The reverence we rightly accord the Hippocratic precepts must not obscure the need for a critical examination of their missing dimensions—those most pertinent for contemporary physicians and society.

In fact, some of the major proscriptions of the Hippocratic Oath already are being consciously compromised: confidentiality can be violated under certain conditions of law and public safety; abortion has been legalized; dangerous drugs are used everywhere; and in human experimentation a conscious but controlled invasion of the patient's rights is permitted.

Based on a chapter entitled "Toward an Expanded Medical Ethics: The Hippocratic Ethic Revisited" in *Hippocrates Revisited*, ed. Roger Bulger, pp. 133–47. Copyright 1973, The Williams & Wilkins Co. Reproduced by permission.

Some important dimensions of medical ethics are not included in the Hippocratic ethic; in some other ways, medical ethics are obscured by a too rigorous application.

An analysis of the questions regarding the ethics of participation, the questions raised by institutionalizing medical care, the need for an axiology of medical ethics, the changing ethics of competence, and the tensions between individual and social ethics reveal the urgent need for expanding medical ethical concerns far beyond those traditionally observed. A deeper ethic of social and corporate responsibility is needed to guide the profession to levels of moral sensitivity more congruent with its expanded duties in contemporary culture.

THE HIPPOCRATIC ETHIC

The normative principles constituting what may loosely be termed the Hippocratic ethic are contained in the oath and the deontological books *Law, Decorum, Precepts,* and *The Physician.* These treatises are of varied origin and combine behavioral imperatives derived from a variety of sources—the schools at Cos and Cnidus, intermingled with Pythagorean, Epicurean, and Stoic influences (1, 2).

The oath (3) speaks of the relationships of the student and his teacher, advises the physician never to harm the patient, enjoins confidentiality, and proscribes abortion, euthanasia, and the use of the knife. It forbids sexual commerce with the women in the household of the sick. The doctor is a member of a select brotherhood dedicated to the care of the sick, and his major reward is a good reputation.

Law discusses the qualities of mind and the diligence required of the prospective physician from early life (4). *The Physician* emphasizes the need for dignified comportment, a healthy body, a grave and kind mien, and a regular life (4, pp. 311–13). In *Decorum,* we are shown the unique practical wisdom rooted in experience which is essential to good medicine and absent in the quack; proper comportment in the sick room dictates a reserved, authoritative, composed air; much practical advice is given on the arts and techniques of clinical medicine (4, pp. 279–301). *Precepts* again warns against theorizing without fact, inveighs against quackery, urges consideration in setting fees, and encourages consultation in difficult cases (3, pp. 313–33).

Similar admonitions can be found scattered throughout the Hippocratic Corpus, but it is these few brief ethical treatises which have formed the character of the physician for so many centuries. From them, we can extract what can loosely be called the Hippocratic ethic: a mixture of high ideals, common sense, and practical wisdom. A few principles of genuine ethics are often repeated and intermingled with etiquette and homespun advice of all sorts. The good physician emerges as an authoritative and competent practitioner, devoted to his patient's well-being. He is the benevolent but sole arbiter who knows what is best for the patient and makes all decisions for him.

There is in the Hippocratic Corpus little explicit reference to medicine as a corporate entity with responsibility for its members and duties to the greater human community. The ethic of the profession as a whole is assured largely by the moral behavior of its individual members. There is no explicit delineation of the corporate responsibility of physicians for one another's ethical behavior. On the whole, the need for maintaining competence is indirectly stated. There are, in short, few explicit recommendations about what we today call "social ethics."

These characteristics of the Hippocratic ethic have been carried forward to our day. They were extended in the code of Thomas Percival, which formed the basis of the first code of ethics adopted by the American Medical Association in 1847 (5). The Hippocratic norms can no longer be regarded as unchanging absolutes, but as partial statements of ideals, in need of constant reevaluation, amplification, and evolution. The necessity for a stringent ethic of competence and a new ethic of shared responsibility, stemming from team and institutional medical care, are understandably not addressed.

It is useful to examine some of these missing ethical dimensions as examples of the kind of organic development long overdue in professional medical ethical codes.

THE ETHICS OF PARTICIPATION

The central and most admirable feature of the oath is the respect it inculcates for the patient. In the oath, the doctor is pledged always to help the patient and keep him from harm. Elsewhere, in *The Physician, Decorum,* and *Precepts,* the physician is further enjoined to be humble, careful in observation, calm and sober in thought and speech. These admonitions have the same validity today that they had centuries ago and are still much in need of cultivation.

But in one of these same works, *Decorum,* we find an excellent example of how drastically the relationship between physician and patient has changed since Hippocrates' time. The doctor is advised to "perform all things calmly and adroitly, concealing most things from the patient while you are attending him." A little further on, the physician is told to treat the patient with solicitude, "revealing nothing of the patient's present and future condition" (4, pp. 297–99). Although this advice is currently at variance with social and political trends and with the desires of most educated patients, it too often forms the *modus operandi* of physicians dreaming of a simpler world of authority and paternalistic benevolence.

Indeed, a major criticism of physicians today centers on this very question of disclosure of essential information. Many educated patients feel frustrated in their desire to participate in the decisions that affect them intimately, as medical decisions invariably do. The matter really turns on establishing new bases for the patient's trust. The knowledgeable patient can trust the physician only if he feels the latter is competent and uses that competence with integrity and for ends which have value for the patient. Today's educated patient wants to understand what the physician is doing, why he is doing it, what the alternatives may be, and what choices are open. In a democratic society, people expect the widest protection of their rights to self-determination. Hence, the contemporary patient has a right to know the decisions involved in managing his case.

When treatment is specific with few choices open, the prognosis good, and side-effects minimal, disclosing the essential information is an easy matter. Unfortunately, medicine frequently deals with indefinite diagnoses and nonspecific treatments of uncertain value. Several alternatives are usually open: prognosis may not be altered by treatment; side-effects are often considerable and discomfort significant. The patient certainly has the right to know these data before therapeutic interventions are initiated. The Nuremberg Code and others were designed to protect the subject in the course of human experimentation by insisting on the right of informed and free consent. The same right should be guaranteed in the course of ordinary medical treatment as well.

So fundamental is this right of self-determination in a democratic society that to limit it, even in ordinary medical transactions, is to propagate an injustice. This is not to ignore the usual objections to disclosure: the fear of inducing anxiety in the patient, the inability of the sick patient to participate in the decision, the technical nature of medical knowledge, and the possibility of litigation. These objections deserve serious consideration, but on close analysis do not justify concealment except in special circumstances. Obviously, the fear of indiscriminate disclosure cannot obfuscate the invasion of a right, even when concealment is in the interest of the patient.

Surely the physician is expected by the patient and society to use disclosure prudently. For the very ill, the very anxious, the poorly educated, the too young, or the very old, he will permit himself varying degrees of disclosure. The modes of doing so must be adapted to the patient's educational level, psychologic responses, and physiological state. It must be emphatically stated that the purpose of disclosing alternatives, costs, and benefits in medical diagnosis and treatment is not to relieve the physician of the onus of decision or to displace it on the patient. Rather, it permits the physician to function as the technical expert and adviser, inviting the patient's participation and understanding as aids in the acceptance of the decision and its consequences. This is the only basis for a mature, just, and understandable physician-patient relationship.

DEONTOLOGIC VERSUS AXIOLOGIC ETHICS

The most important human reason for patient participation in decisions that affect him is to allow consideration of his personal values. Here, the Hippocratic tradition is explicitly lacking because its spirit is almost wholly deontological; that is, obligations are stated as absolutes without reference to any theory of values. Underlying value systems are not stated or discussed. The need for examining the intersection of values inherent in every medical transaction is unrecognized. The values of the physician or of medicine are assumed to prevail as absolutes, and an operational attitude of *noblesse oblige* is encouraged.

A deontologic ethic was not inappropriate for Greek medicine, which did not have to face so many complex and antithetical courses of action. But a relevant ethic for our times must be more axiologic than deontologic, that is, based in a more conscious theory of values. The values upon which any action is based are of enormous personal and social consequence. An analysis of conflicting values underlies the choice of a noxious treatment for a chronic illness, the question of prolonging life in the case of incurable disease, or the setting of priorities for using limited medical resources. Instead of with absolute values, we deal more frequently with an intersection of several sets and subsets of values: those of the patient, the physician, sciences, and society. Which shall prevail when these values are in conflict? How does one decide?

Professor Kenneth J. Arrow argues that, in matters medical, the individual should be free to reject knowledge of what is harmful to health and to make this own choice as to whether he shall smoke, wear seat belts, drink excessively, or use heroin.

The limitation to the axiom lies in the social burden of cost in money, facilities, and personnel required to treat the victims of self-abuse. In some instances, society places a higher value on the individual's life and comfort than he himself places on them.

A further limitation lies in the information gap that separates physician from patient. Freedom of choice involves much more than transfer of knowledge.

But granting that the physician tries consciously to close the deficiency in knowledge between himself and the patient, is the patient ever totally free to act on that information? He is after all seeking help; he is anxious, perhaps in pain, or otherwise discomfited. He sees his life-style threatened, his own values put awry, and his person subjected to the indignity of petitioning another for help. The patient's capacity to deal with the information is modulated by multiple factors that make his transaction with the physician an unequal one. If the patient is a child or elderly or distraught, there are psychologic and physical barriers to the reception of information. Socioeconomic, ethnic, and cultural inequalities compound the difficulties. The mere transfer of available knowledge does not suffice for most cases; thus, the libertarian principle, even if it were valid *a priori*, would be difficult to apply to most of the decisions clinicians and patients must make.

Perhaps the most subtle influence that limits the freedom of the physician as well as the patient is the intersection of their value systems in each transaction. The disparity between these value systems may be as great as the disparity in information. What each thinks of the meaning of life, pain, disability; the value or nonvalue of suffering; the existence or nonexistence of God; and a hundred other like issues will all color *how* the information is delivered by the physician and received by the patient.

The patient's values must be respected whenever possible and whenever they do not create injustice for others. The patient is free to delegate the decision to his physicians, but he must do this consciously and freely. To the extent that he is educated, responsible, and thoughtful, modern man will increasingly want the opportunity to examine relative values in each transaction. When the patient is unconscious or otherwise unable to participate, the physician or the family acts as his surrogate, charged to preserve his values as closely as possible.

The Hippocratic principle of *primum non nocere* (6), therefore, must be expanded to encompass the patient's value system if it is to have genuine meaning. To impose the doctor's value system is an intrusion on the patient; it may be harmful, unethical, and result in an error in diagnosis and treatment. Further, the concept of health as a positive entity is as vague today as in Hippocrates' time. Its definition is highly personal. The physician's view of health may be quite at variance with that of the patient or even of society. The doctor understandably tends to place an ideological value on health and medicine. Society should expect this from him as an expert, but his view must not prevail unchallenged. Indeed, society must set its own priorities for health. The amelioration of social disorders like alcoholism, sociopathy, drug addiction, and violence can have greater value to a healthy human existence, for example, than merely prolonging life in patients with chronic disabling disorders. Indeed, the patient and society now demand to participate in making the choices.

Each patient has a slightly different definition of health. The physician is also a person with values that invariably color his professional acts. His views of sex, alcohol, suffering, poverty, race, and so forth can sharply differ from those of his patient. His advice on these matters, as well as his definition of cooperation, often has a strong ideologic or moralistic tinge. The physician must constantly guard against imposing his own values as the good to which all must subscribe if they desire to be treated by him.

101

Disclosure is therefore a necessary condition if we really respect each patient as a unique being whose values, as a part of his person, are no more to be violated than his body. The deontologic thrust of traditional medical ethics is too restrictive in a time when the reexamination of all values is universal. It even defeats the very purposes of the traditional ethic, which are to preserve the integrity of the patient as a person.

INDIVIDUAL VERSUS SOCIAL ETHICS

Another notably unexplored area in the Hippocratic ethic is the social responsibility of the physician. Its emphasis on the welfare of the individual patient is exemplary, and this is firmly explicated in the oath and elsewhere. Indeed, in *Precepts,* this respect for the individual patient is placed at the very heart of medicine: "Where there is love of one's fellow man, there is love of the Art" (3, p. 319).

The physician's sense of responsibility toward his patient is one of the most admirable features of medicine and must always remain the central ethical imperative in medical transactions. But, it must now be set in a context entirely alien to that in which ancient medicine was practiced. In earlier eras, the remote effects of medical acts were of little concern, and the rights of the individual patient could be the exclusive and absolute base of the physician's actions. Today, the growing interdependence of all humans and the effectiveness of medical techniques have drastically altered the simplistic arrangements of traditional ethics. The aggregate effects of individual medical acts have already changed the ecology of man. Every death prevented or life prolonged alters the number, kind, and distribution of human beings. The resultant competition for living space, food, and conveniences already imperils our hope for a life of satisfaction for all mankind.

Even more vexing questions in social ethics are posed when we attempt to allocate our resources among the many new possibilities for good inherent in medical progress and technology. Do we pool our limited resources and manpower to apply curative medicine to all now deprived of it or continue to multiply the variety of services for the privileged? Do we apply mass prophylaxis against streptococcal diseases or repair damaged heart valves with expensive surgery? Is it preferable to change cultural patterns in favor of a more reasonable diet for Americans or to develop better surgical techniques for unplugging fat-occluded coronary arteries? Clearly we cannot have all these things simultaneously.

This dimension of ethics becomes even more immediate when we inquire into the responsibility of medicine for meeting the urgent sociomedical needs of large segments of our population. Can we absolve ourselves from responsibility for deficiencies in distribution, quality, and accessibility of even ordinary medical care for the poor, the uneducated, and the disenfranchised? Do we direct our health-care system to the young in ghettos and underdeveloped countries or to the affluent aged? Which course will make for a better world? These are vexing questions of the utmost social concern. Physicians have an ethical responsibility to raise these questions and, in answering them, to work with the community to set priorities that make optimal use of available medical skills.

It is not enough to hope that the good of the community will grow out of the summation of good acts of each physician for his own patients. Societies are necessary to insure enrichment of the life of each of their members. But they are more than the aggregate of persons within them. As T.S. Eliot puts it, "What life have you if you have not life together? There is no life that is not in community" (7).

Society supports the doctor in the expectation that he will direct himself to socially relevant health problems, not just those he finds interesting or remunerative. The commitment to social egalitarianism demands a greater sensitivity to social ethics than is to be found in traditional codes. Section Ten of the American Medical Association Principles of Medical Ethics (1946) explicitly recognizes the profession's responsibility to society. But a more explicit analysis of the relationships of individual and social ethics should be undertaken. Medicine, which touches on the most human problems of both the individual and society, cannot serve man without attending to both his personal and communal needs.

This is not to say that medical codes or physicians are to set social priorities. Clearly, the individual physician cannot quantitate the remote effects of each of his medical acts. Nor should he desert his patients to devote himself entirely to social issues. He cannot withhold specific treatment in hope of preventing some future perturbation of human ecology. Nor can society relegate solely to physicians such policy questions as how and for whom the major health effort will be expended.

In these matters, the physician serves best as an expert witness, providing the basis for informed public decisions. He must lead in pointing out deficiencies and raising the painful matter of choices. At the same time each doctor must honor his traditional contract to help his own patient. He cannot allow the larger social issues to undermine that solicitude. The ethically responsive doctor will thus find himself more and more involved in social and individual ethical values, impelled to act reponsibly in both spheres. The Hippocratic ethic and its later modifications were not required to confront such paradoxes. Today's conscientious physician is very much in need of an expanded ethic to cope with his double responsibility to the individual and to the community.

THE ETHICS OF INSTITUTIONALIZED MEDICINE

The institutionalization of all aspects of medical care is established fact. Within each institution, the health-care team is essential to the practice of comprehensive medicine. Physicians and non-physicians now cooperate in providing the spectrum of special services made possible by modern technology. Competence, confidentiality, integrity, and personal concern are far more difficult to assure when such diverse professionals have varying degrees of contact with the patient.

No current code of ethics fully defines how the traditional rights of the medical transaction are to be protected when responsibility is diffused throughout a team and an institution. Clearly, none of the health professions can elaborate such a code of team ethics by itself. We need a new medical ethic which permits the cooperative definition of normative guides to protect the patient served by a group, none of whose members has sole responsibility for care. Laymen, too, must participate because boards of trustees set the overall policies which affect patient care. Few trustees truly recognize that they are the ethical and legal surrogates of society for the patients who come to their institutions.

Thus, the most delicate of the physician's responsibilities, protecting the patient's welfare, must now be fulfilled in a new and complicated context. Instead of having the familiar, unique one-to-one relationship, the physician finds himself coordinator of a team, sharing with others some of the most sensitive areas of patient care. The physician is still bound to see that group assessment and management are rational, safe, and personalized. He must especially guard against the dehumanization so easily and inadvertently perpetrated by a group in the name of efficiency.

The doctor must acquire new attitudes. Since ancient times, he has been the sole dominant and authoritarian figure in the care of his patient. He has been supported in this position by traditional ethics. In the clinical emergency, his dominant role is still unchallenged, because he is well trained to make quick decisions in ambiguous situations. But he is not prepared for the negotiations, analysis, and ultimate compromise fundamental to group efforts and essential in nonemergency situations. A whole new set of clinical perspectives must be introduced, perspectives difficult for the classically trained physician to accept, but necessary if the patient is to benefit from contemporary technology and organization of health care.

THE ETHICS OF COMPETENCE

A central aim of the oath and other ethical treatises is to protect the patient and the profession from quackery and incompetence. In the main, competence is assumed as basic to fulfillment of the Hippocratic ideal of *primum non nocere*. In places, more specific admonitions are to be found. Thus, in *Law*, "Medicine is the most distinguished of all the arts, but through the ignorance of those who practice it, and those who casually judge such practitioners, it is now of all arts by far the least esteemed" (4, p. 263). The author of this treatise thus succinctly expressed the same concerns being voiced at greater length and with more hyperbole in our own times. In the treatise on fractures, specific advice is given to prevent curable cases from becoming incurable; to choose the simpler treatment; to attempt to help, even if the patient seems incurable; and to avoid unnecessary torment (8). Consultation is clearly advised in *Precepts* (3, pp. 323, 325). In *Decorum*, frequent visits and careful examination are enjoined (4, p. 295).

The Hippocratic works preach the wholly admirable commonsense ethos of the good artisan: careful work, maturation of skills, simplicity of approach, and knowledge of limitations. This was sound advice at a time when new discoveries were so often the product of speculation untinged with observation or experience. The speculative astringency of the Hippocratic ethic was a potent and necessary safeguard against the quackery of fanciful and dangerous "new" cures.

With the scientific era in medicine, the efficacy of new techniques and information in changing the natural history of disease was dramatically demonstrated. Today, the patient has a right to access to the vast stores of new medical knowledge. Failure of the physician to make this reservoir available and accessible is a moral failure. The ethos of the artisan, while still a necessary safeguard, is now far from being a sufficient one.

Maintaining competence today is a prime ethical challenge. Only the highest standard of initial and continuing professional proficiency is acceptable in a technological world. This imperative is so essential a feature of the patient-physician transaction that the ancient mandate, "Do no harm," must be supplemented: "Do all things essential to optimal solution of the patient's problem." Anything less makes the doctor's professional declaration a sham and a scandal.

Competence now has a far wider definition than in ancient times. Not only must the physician encompass expertly the knowledge pertinent to his own field, but he must be the instrument for bringing all other knowledge to bear on his patient's needs. He functions as one element in a vast matrix of consultants, technicians, apparatus, and institutions, all of which may contribute to his patient's well-being. He cannot provide all these things himself. To attempt to do so is to pursue the romantic and vanishing illusion of the physician as Renaissance man.

The enormous difficulties of its achievement notwithstanding, competence has become the first ethical precept for the modern physician, after integrity. It is also the prime humane precept and the one most peculiar to the physician's function in society. Even the current justifiable demands of patients and medical students for greater compassion must not obfuscate the centrality of competence in the physicians' existence. The simple intention to help others is commendable, but by itself not only insufficient but positively dangerous. What is more inhumane or more a violation of trust than incompetence? The consequence of a lack of compassion may be remediable, but a lack of competence may cost the patient his chance for recovery of life, function, and happiness. Clearly, medicine cannot attain the ethical eminence to which it is called without both compassion and competence.

Within this framework, a more rigorous ethic of competence must be elaborated. Continuing education, periodic recertification, and renewal of clinical privileges have become moral mandates, not just hopeful hortatory devices dependent upon individual physician responses. The Hippocratic ethic of the good artisan is now the point of departure for the wide options technology holds for individual and social health.

The one-to-one, patient-to-physician relationship so earnestly extolled for centuries makes the patient almost totally dependent upon his physician for entry into the vast complex of potentially useful services. We cannot leave to fortune or statistics the possibility that the patient's choice of a physician may impede his access to all he needs for optimal care. We must surround this one-to-one relationship with the safeguards of a corporate responsibility in which the whole profession dedicates itself to protecting the patient's right to competent care.

TOWARD A CORPORATE ETHIC AND AN ETHICAL SYNCYTIUM

The whole of the Hippocratic Corpus, including the ethical treatises, is the work of many authors in different historical periods. Thus the ethical precepts cannot be considered the formal position of a profession in today's sense. There is no evidence of recognition of true corporate responsibility for larger social issues or of sanctions to deter miscreant members. Indeed, in *Law*, there is a clear lament for the lack of penalties to restrain or punish the unethical physician: "medicine is the only art which our states have made subject to no penalty save that of dishonor. And dishonor does not wound those who are compacted of it" (4, p. 263). Again, in *Precepts*: "Now no harm would be done if bad practitioners received their due wages. But as it is, their innocent patients suffer, for whom the violence of their disorder did not appear sufficient without the addition of their physician's inexperience" (3, p. 315).

The Greek physician seems to have regarded himself as the member of an informal aristocratic brotherhood, in which each individual was expected to act ethically and to do so for love of the profession and respect of the patient. His reward was *doxa,* a good reputation, which in turn assured a successful practice. There is notably no sense of the larger responsibilities as a profession for the behavior of each member. Nowhere stated are the potentialities and responsibilities of a group of high-minded individuals to effect reforms and achieve purposes transcending the interests of individual members. In short, the Greek medical profession relied on the sum of individual ethical behaviors to assure the ethical behavior of the group.

This is still the dominant view of many physicians in the Western world who limit their ethical perspectives to their relationships with their own patients. Medical societies do censure unethical members with varying alacrity for the grosser forms of misconduct or breaches of professional etiquette. But there is as yet insufficient assumption of a corporate and shared responsibility for the actions of each member of the group. The power of physicians as a polity to effect reforms in quality of care, its organization, and its relevance to the needs of society is as yet unrealized.

Yet many of the dimensions of medical ethics touched upon in this essay can only be secured by the conscious assumption of a corporate responsibility on the part of all physicians for the final pertinence of their individual acts to promote better life for all. There is the need to develop, as it were, a functioning ethical syncytium in which the actions of each physician touch upon those of all physicians and in which it is clear that the ethical failings of each diminish the stature of all others to some degree.

This syncytial framework is at variance with the traditional notion that each physician acts as an individual and is primarily responsible only to himself and his patient. The shift of emphasis is dictated by the metamorphosis of all professions in our complex, highly organized, highly integrated, and egalitarian social order.

For most of its history, medicine has existed as a select and loosely organized brotherhood. For the past hundred years in our country, it has been more formally organized in the American Medical Association and countless other professional organizations dedicated to a high order of individual ethics. A new stage, however, in the evolution of medicine as a profession is about to begin as a consequence of three clear trends:

First, all professions are increasingly being regarded as services, even as public utilities, dedicated to fulfilling specific social needs not entirely defined by the profession. In the future professions themselves will acquire dignity and standing not so much from the tasks they perform, but from the intimacy of the connection between those tasks and the social life of which the profession is a part.

Second, the professions are being democratized, and it will be ever more difficult for any group to hold a privileged position. The automatic primacy of medicine is being challenged by the other health professions, whose functions are of increasing importance in patient care. This functionalization of the professions tends to emphasize what is done for a patient, and not who does it. Moreover, many tasks formerly performed only by physicians are now being done by other professionals and nonprofessionals.

Last, the socialization of all mankind affects the professions as well. Hence, the collectivity will increasingly be expected to take responsibility for how well or poorly each profession carries out the purposes for which it is supported by society.

Legal mechanisms will multiply to meet growing public demand for more regulation and accountability in the provision of health care. There will still remain a significant realm for the operation of professional ethics. To be effective, however, professional ethical codes will need to be expanded to include new realms of responsibility. Existing codes in medicine, except those that apply specifically to medical experimentation, are silent on these matters or leave them entirely to the judgment of the physician (9). The synergistic interplay of new legal means and an expanded professional ethic promises to avoid the impersonalization, standardization, and bureaucratic obfuscations that government interventions have inevitably brought.

Law can guarantee the validity of consent by providing that certain procedures be followed and recorded for later examination. It can penalize the professional who fails to meet statutory requirements for valid consent. It is a far more difficult thing to assure that the patient's decision and his consent to a given action are of high quality as a human action, that is, that the full dimensions of the medical encounter are taken into account. Here, we are more dependent on the ethical behavior of the physician. It becomes urgent for ethical codes to be more explicit about the physician's responsibility to make the patient's bill of rights a reality, not a mere adherence to formal procedures.

In a sense, the law is the coarse adjustment that guards against the grosser violations of human rights; ethics is the fine adjustment that sets a higher ideal than law can guarantee. Government must not become the sanction for a code of ethics, only a substitute that recognizes the human frailties of professionals. What is legal is not always ethical. Ethics is the realm in which professional conscience transcends law, strives for equity in its application, and anticipates the higher dimensions of assurance that human decisions shall be as truly human (i.e., as informed and free) as it is possible to make them.

Professional ethical codes have adapted too slowly to the new responsibilities the modern world demands from medicine. They need constant refurbishing. They should be ahead of the law in divining what duties should be required of professionals. Indeed, the separation of ethics and law in a free society is essential to prevent an unjust government from confusing what should be law with what is ethical. If government sanctions ethics in the form of statutes, then an infraction of the ethical code also is a crime against the state. The twentieth century has already seen too much of this abomination.

These changes will threaten medicine only if physicians hold to a simplistic ethic in which the agony of choices among individual and social values is dismissed as spurious or imaginary. The physician is the most highly educated of health professionals. He should be first to take on the burdens of a continuing self-reformation in terms of a new ethos, one in which the problematics of priorities and values are openly faced as common responsibilities of the entire profession. We must recognize the continuing validity of traditional ethics for the personal dimensions of patient care and their inadequacy for the newer social dimensions of health in contemporary life. It is the failure to appreciate this distinction that stimulates so much criticism of the profession at the same time that individual physicians are highly respected.

Accountability at the corporate level must match the degree of competence exercised at the individual level.

ASSURING COMPETENCE

In a technical society with knowledge increasing exponentially, all members of a profession cannot attain the same degree of competence. The whole body of physicians must assume responsibility for guaranteeing to society the highest possible competence in each member. A most effective way to assure this is for each professional group to require, as some already have, periodic demonstration of proficiency as a condition for continuing membership. Physicians should lead in requiring their own relicensure and recertification, setting standards of performance, and insisting on a remedial and not a punitive approach for those who need to refresh their knowledge for recertification. Implicit in this idea is the possibility that at some point each of us may fail to qualify for reasons such as age, illness, or loss of interest. A profession sensitive to its ethical responsibilities cannot tolerate fading competence, even for reasons beyond the physician's control. Instead, it must provide opportunities for remediation or for alternate, more suitable functions within medicine. Surely the wide range of uses for a medical education can provide a useful place for almost all physicians.

A most potent way to assure competence is to insist that all physicians practice within a context of competent colleague and peer surveillance. It is an ethical responsibility of the whole profession to see that every licensed physician is a member of a hospital staff. The privilege of using a hospital is primarily a privilege for the patient, not the doctor. To deprive any licensed physician of hospital privilege because of training, economics, race, or other reasons is to deprive his patient and to perpetrate a social injustice. We also thereby lose the best chance to help the physician improve himself by contact with his colleagues and with institutional standards, as well as with the informal network of teaching that links physicians together when they discuss their cases with one another. No rationalization based on economics or professional prerogatives can excuse our profession from its ethical responsibility to enable every practitioner to participate in the mainstream of medical care, both in the hospital and the medical school. This responsibility should extend to the osteopathic, as well as to the allopathic, physician.

Once every physician is on a hospital staff, the professions can do much to develop a context within which competence becomes a value of prime importance. Some institutional mechanisms for review of certain aspects of competence already exist in tissue and utilization committees, though these mechanisms are not universally applied with sufficient vigor. A well-functioning drug information

111

center in every hospital, a rigorous pharmacy and therapeutics committee, critical reviews of diagnostic accuracy and work-up, comparison of practices against national standards—these are examples of further institutional devices we should insist upon as ethical imperatives. Ultimately each physician should have available for his own edification a computerized record of his diagnostic acumen, therapeutic practices, complications, and autopsy correlations. The essential matter is not the specific mechanisms used, but acceptance of the dictum that the competence of each member of the group is, in some real sense, the responsibility of all.

These measures can easily be discounted as repressive, regimenting infringements on professional freedom. Or in a more enlightened ethical view, they can be the practical expression of corporate acceptance of the necessity for workable mechanisms to insure competence in a technological society. Is there a real ethical choice? The patient, after all, has no means whereby he can judge the competence of the services rendered. Individual physicians and the profession owe the patient every possible safeguard. If these measures are not forthcoming, they will be imposed by a public demanding more accountability in medicine and every other sphere of life.

One of the gravest and most easily visible social inequities today is the maldistribution of medical services among our population. This is another sphere in which the profession as a whole must assume responsibility for what individual physicians cannot do alone. The civil rights movement and the revolt of the black and minority populations have underscored the problem. Individual physicians have always tried to redress this evil, some in heroic ways. Now, however, the problem is a major ethical responsibility for the whole profession; we cannot dismiss the issue. We must engender a feeling that the entire profession suffers from ethical diminution whenever segments of the population lack adequate and accessible medical care. This extends to the provision of primary care for all, insistence on a system of coverage for all communities every hour of the day, proper distribution of the various medical specialties and facilities, and a system of fees no longer based on the usual imponderables but on more standardized norms.

Fulfilling such ethical imperatives is sure to cause discomfort for the doctor, as well as some loss of privileges and even of remuneration. But unless there is corporate concern translated into corporate action and self-imposed responsibilities, restrictive legislation to achieve these ends seems certain. To an ethically perceptive profession, such legislation not only should be unnecessary, but should be a scandal.

It is intrinsic to the very purposes of medicine that physicians exhibit the greatest sensitivity to any social injustice directly related to their mandate in society. The lack of this corporate sensitivity has been acutely perceived by some of today's students and has seriously disaffected them with medical education and practice (10). We hope, when they assume leadership of the profession, that they will feel these ethical discontinuities as clearly as they do now. If tomorrow's physicians practice what they now preach to their elders, they will indeed expand the ethical responsibilities of our profession into new and essential dimensions. To do so, they will need to supplement traditional medical ethics with a corporate ethical sense, as I have just described.

There are, perforce, reasonable limits to the social ills to which the individual physician and the profession can be expected to attend *qua* physician. Some have suggested that medicine concern itself with wars, the root causes of poverty, environmental pollution, drugs, housing, and racial injustice. It would be difficult to argue that all of these social ills are *primary* ethical responsibilities of individual physicians or even of the profession. To do so would hopelessly diffuse medical energies and manpower from their proper object—the promotion of health and the cure of illness. The profession can fight poverty, injustice, and war *through* medicine.

A distinction, therefore, must clearly be made between the physician's *primary* ethical responsibilities, which derive from the nature of his profession, and those which do not. Each physician must strike for himself an optimal balance between professional and civic responsibilities. This will depend upon his energy, capabilities, the nature of his specialty, his family responsibilities, and other factors. The extremes of this choice are dangerous: a narrowly technical life, or a free-floating social concern which at best is neurotic and ineffectual and at worst can seriously compromise competence. Ever present is the seductive hubris to which physicians are especially susceptible—the assumption of some special authority or capability to resolve all social issues.

113

THE ORDER OF ETHICAL RESPONSIBILITY

It becomes a matter of prime ethical concern for each physician consciously to establish some hierarchy of values and priorities which will define his individual and social ethical postures. The ethical responsibilities of the professional group should be broad; those of the individual may of necessity be narrow. Is there some reasonable order of values in the maze of conflicting duties thrust upon physicians today?

Surely the first order of responsibility for clinicians must remain with the patients they undertake to treat. Here, the moral imperatives are clear: competence of the highest order, integrity, compassion.

Although traditional, these priorities can be made more relevant to our times by extension in some of the directions indicated earlier in this essay. To fail in this realm is to violate the trust underlying the personal relationship which characterizes medical care. Nothing is more unconscionable or socially unacceptable.

Having satisfied his first order of ethical requirements, the physician is free to address himself to a second order of responsibilities. The alternatives generally fall into two categories: those which arise from medical progress and those which bear directly on the condition of life in the community.

The third order of responsibilities, which is more properly related to the physician as a citizen than as a physician, is among the most crucial for modern man. Yet, this set of issues is usually outside the physician's prerogatives and distant from his direct function in society. Important as they are, these issues—such as poverty, pollution, war, racism—require knowledge the doctor must acquire. If these are his major concerns, he should make no pretense at being also a clinician, or he will become one in the most limited sense. Medical education and experience make a legitimate base for service in new fields or for social and political action, but they do not legitimatize the neglect of clinical competence in individual medical acts. This distinction needs careful scrutiny by those who would have the physician cure the accumulated social ills of our times but who upbraid him for his failures to do this and to maintain professional competence as well. "If you try to act beyond your powers, you not only disgrace yourself in it, but you neglect the part which you could have filled with success" (11).

THE INTERPLAY OF INDIVIDUAL AND CORPORATE ETHICS

The individual physician can, and indeed should, limit the responsibilities he assumes in the second and third areas. The profession as a body can, but should not. Physicians as a group must assume ethical responsibility for all three orders of responsibility which may bind each physician. The profession, as we have shown, must attempt to do as a body what individuals cannot do by themselves—namely, span the full range of ethical imperatives. The profession is bound to assume responsibility for the ethical behavior of its members, for setting the context which best guarantees good behavior, and for taking sanctions against members who fall from their high estate, while at the same time effecting their rehabilitation. Physicians as individuals may eschew certain responsibilities as inappropriate, but the profession cannot.

Herein, then, lies the final guarantee for the patient and the community: the interplay of ethical responsibilities for each individual physician and of the whole body of physicians. Each physician must consciously define on several levels his personal moral responsibilities. The profession simultaneously must call for deep involvement of its members at all levels of ethical responsibility—the individual clinical medical transaction, the social consequences of medical acts, the quality and availability of medical services, and the duties of its educated group to engage in the larger social issues confronting contemporary man. This reinforcement of the ethical perspective of the individual physician by a heightened ethical perception of the community of physicians will refurbish traditional medical ethics, reflect the changes in moral climate, and effect greater sensitivity to the illnesses of society.

The axiologic approach always calls for an orderly analysis of the values underlying moral choices. The highest ethical call is still that of the conscience of an individual human person, a conscience which must be prepared at all times to take issue with social directives, corporate agreements, and political pressures. The dignity and the worth of the human being he treats must still remain the beacon that guides the physician's conscience through the ethical night. Marcel pinpoints this duty so peculiar to our times: "It is within the scope of each of us, within his own proper field, in his profession, to pursue an unrelaxing struggle for man, for the dignity of man against everything that today threatens to annihilate man and his dignity" (12, p. 241).

The individual physician needs more explicit guidelines than traditional codes afford to meet today's new problems. The needs lie largely in the realm of social and corporate ethics—realms of increasing significance in an egalitarian, highly structured, exquisitely interlocked social order. The Hippocratic ethic is one of the most admirable codes in the history of man. But even its ethical sensibilities and high moral tone are insufficient for the complexities of today's problems. There is ample opportunity for a critical reappraisal of the Hippocratic ethic and for the elaboration of a fuller and more comprehensive medical ethic suited to the profession as it nears the twenty-first century. This fuller ethic will build upon the noble precepts set forth so long ago in the Hippocratic Corpus. It will explicate, complement, and develop those precepts, but it must not be limited in its evolution by an unwarranted reluctance to question even so ancient and honorable a code as that of the Hippocratic writings.

Humanistic Basis of Professional Ethics

Too much is taken for granted about the way physicians conduct themselves. There is a need to reexamine the sources of the normative principles which should govern the behavior of physicians in the ordinary medical encounter—i.e., the situation in which one human in distress seeks out another who professes to have the knowledge and skill to help or heal.

The traditional view of professional ethics is derived from overemphasis on what physicians are and on what they ought to do for their patients as a consequence of their special position in society. The whole of these obligations is rooted in an image and a professional ethos which have served well but which require serious reappraisal in contemporary society. Beyond this, the more reliable source for a more humanistic professional ethics resides in the existential nature of illness and in the inequality between physician and patient intrinsic to that state. The ethical imperatives binding physicians are reducible to a meeting of the requirements of an impaired humanity which sickness implies. (Although I am speaking almost exclusively to and about physicians, what I say applies to other health professionals whose ethical conduct is similarly determined.)

What is at stake, I believe, is a fundamental recasting of the traditional image of physicians, one with profound implications for their social situation as well as their education and image of themselves. The need for this recasting is implicit in the disquietude expressed by many patients who call for a more "humanistic profession." Without such a redefinition of professional obligations, it will be impossible to close the widening gap between what physi-

Presented in part as the Jubilee Lecture, Memorial University of Newfoundland, St. John's, May 13, 1975, and at the 170th Annual Meeting of the Medical Society of the State of New York, New York City, General Sessions, November 8, 1976. Also published under the title "Humanistic Base for Professional Ethics in Medicine" in the *New York State Journal of Medicine*, Vol. 77, No. 9, August 1977, pp. 1456–62.

cians conceive themselves to be and what increasingly larger segments of the public expect them to be.

Anyone today who uses the noun *humanism* or the adjective *humanistic* is compelled at the outset to give at least an operational definition. The terms have become veritable shibboleths. They are used as a challenge, a claim, or an ideal, justifying all sorts of diverse and contradictory human activities. They are linked to every sort of political or social ideology, so that we hear of democratic, socialist, communist, and even totalitarian *humanisms*—all espousing the cause of man but on vastly differing suppositions. *Humanism* is piously affirmed by each professional or bureaucracy as precisely what *it* aims to be, but finds missing in others.

I will take the term in the loose sense, that applied by most people today to the health professions and other professions as well. *Humanism* encompasses a spirit of sincere concern for the centrality of human values in every aspect of professional activity. This concern focuses on respect for the freedom, dignity, worth, and belief systems of the individual person, and it implies a sensitive, non-humiliating, and empathetic way of helping with some problem or need.

I shall not use the term *humanism* in its more pristine meaning as a literary or educational ideal, or as dependent upon an in-depth education in the classics or the humanities. These older interpretations are admittedly more precise and, of course, still valid and important. But it is essential to distingush them from the more popular usage for two reasons: first, to be clear about the domain we are exploring and, second, to be sure that we do not link an intellectual, cognitive, and educational ideal too exclusively with what many people see lacking in the profession today.

With this operational definition of humanism serving as a bench mark, we can now consider what might be the most compelling derivation of a specifically humanistic professional ethics. Our inquiry will proceed from an examination of the more traditional source in the image and ethos of the physician to a source in the specifically human dimensions of being ill and in distress. I will argue that a more sensitive and compelling guide to the care of the sick is to be found in the fact of illness as a human experience than in the assigned role of the profession. Without supplanting traditional professional ethics, the intrinsic dehumanizing nature of illness imposes additional obligations of greater sensitivity—precisely those so often found wanting by the critics of medicine today.

THE TRADITIONAL SOURCE OF PROFESSIONAL ETHICS

For most of its history, the relationship of physician and patient has been dominated by the physician's point of view. Ethical codes have been established more on the basis of the obligation physicians feel than those patients may impose. The image of physicians that dominates the profession and society is still based in the Hippocratic ideal. Physicians are, in this tradition, represented as learned and noble men, members of a select brotherhood, which is largely self-regulating and autonomous. I have already noted some of the central precepts which formed and sustained the image of the Hippocratic physician in Chapter 6. They were Christianized in the Middle Ages, adapted to the spirit of eighteenth-century England by Thomas Percival, and have been modernized in the successive codes of ethics of the American Medical Association and similar codes in other countries. They remain the lineament of the ideal physician as interpreted by many in the profession. Indeed, this image has attained a quasi-scriptural stature. Only in the last several decades has there been any challenge to this traditional image. During that time the additional and often competing image of the physician as scientist has appeared. The benefactions of science and technology in medicine have given credence to an image of physicians quite at odds with older medical value systems. The public is genuinely ambivalent toward this new image. It recognizes the power of scientific medicine but simultaneously fears the loss of the virtue inherent in the older image. Physicians and patients have yet to amalgamate the older hieratic and the newer scientific conceptions of the physician.

This uncertain process of amalgamation is complicated by sharp changes in the social, political, and economic climate within which physicians now function. We no longer have consensus as a nation about what we expect from physicians and from medicine. Our attitudes about the authority, privileges, and superiority of professional groups have changed drastically. In a democratic society, we expect everyone to participate in decisions which will affect them.

Clearly, the easy congruence between the values of physician and patient commonplace in the past is rarely attainable in a democratic society which tolerates, and guarantees, plurality of values. Sharp differences of opinion now separate physician from physician, and patient from patient, in such matters as euthanasia, abortion, sterilization, prolongation of life, and the like. In an educated and liberalized society, the values of patients and physicians are as likely to be divergent as convergent.

Part of the problem also arises from the position of physicians as technical experts. We are all fearful of the potential tyranny of anyone with esoteric knowledge that can alter our lives in ways, and by means, we cannot fully understand. Physicians are constantly portrayed as the most powerful of modern thaumaturges. Their power is no longer related to their unique contact with the world of spirit, with which they might negotiate in behalf of their patients. Instead, their power is linked to mastery of impersonal instruments, tests, procedures, and medications which can too easily be used in injurious ways, or to advance professional rather than public interest.

Everywhere there are efforts to restrain not only this new magic, but also the old Aesculapian power and authority. The list of mechanisms being invoked is a long one: legislative control of quality, costs, and distribution of medical care, as well as the education of physicians and other health workers; demands for consumer participation in the management, accreditation, and licensing of medical institutions; the declaration of a patient's "bill of rights" to guarantee the elementary human rights of confidentiality and consent in medical transactions; and the growing tendency consciously to limit the growth of high technology and research. The most extreme reactions call for removing the larger part of medicine from the hands of physicians and returning it to the patient (1), or seeking redress in malpractice suits for every real, potential, or imagined injustice in the patient-physician encounter.

There is clearly an overt public disquietude with a large part of the spectrum of medical activity. Almost every serious ethical responsibility which had heretofore been delegated solely to the profession is today being at least partially withdrawn, or critically scrutinized. The traditional ideal of a self-regulating elite and of a trusted profession to whom society cedes moral and technical authority has been undergoing serious erosion. The ancient source of professional ethics, in the responsibilities assumed by physicians as members of a select group, has become insufficient in the eyes of many.

Before looking to an alternate source out of which we might develop more authentic and more lasting normative guidelines, it is useful to review briefly some of the social, cultural, and political forces which have irrevocably transformed the relationship of physicians with individual patients and with society. Such a survey is essential to understanding that the traditional view of the physician and of medicine is not likely to be resuscitated.

To begin with, the capabilities of modern medicine are now so expanded that physicians' decisions can have a profound effect on the quality of the individual's life. The right clinical decisions and their competent implementation can make the difference between life, health, and relief on the one hand and death, disability, or pain on the other. The quality of human existence is genuinely often in doctors' hands today, whereas it was only figuratively so in the past.

Moreover, the acts of modern physicians collectively can alter the quality of life for the whole of mankind. Already painfully obvious are the cumulative effects of such acts as prolonging life of the aged or the incapacitated, expansion of high technology to cover previously incurable disorders, and genetic manipulations and behavioral modification. Today separating the ethical impact of individual and social medical decisions is becoming more difficult. Medical progress and practice must of necessity answer questions of social purpose and value, questions which transcend the privileges any expert group might arrogate to itself.

In a democratic society we face, in addition, the crucial issues of how to enable people to participate as free individuals in the choices that affect them. These decisions cannot be delegated to the expert, whether a nuclear engineer, military expert, or physician. The community must generate the mandate under which experts can practice their technology as means toward ends society must define.

In a democracy too there must be some protection for pluralism of values about such fundamental matters as the value of life, the rights of the fetus, and the use or rejection of medical treatments. Values in these matters are no longer held in common, nor can they be established solely by the profession as they were of old. Many

121

things forbidden in the Hippocratic Oath have already been challenged in modern society—abortion, the proscription against euthanasia, and the use of dangerous medications, for example. These are instances where contemporary social values have taken precedence over professional ethical values previously held inviolate.

Complexities in the physician-patient relationship, introduced by the capabilities of medicine and the pluralism of values in a democratic society, are accentuated by the depersonalization inherent in the growing institutionalization and bureaucratization of the medical encounter. Authority is now diffused and partitioned among members of ever-larger teams of health workers, administrators, and other functionaries. The authority of the individual physician is increasingly transferred to institutional structures. This means standardization, reducing performance to an average uniformity and assuring outcomes by adherence to procedures and regulations, rather than depending on the initiatives of individual physicians.

Thus, at a time when medicine has begun seriously to threaten human values and therefore when the premium on humanizing medical care should be at its highest, the organization of medical practice is tending to the contrary. Patients not only have lost the person to whom they might make some assignment of moral values held in common, but they have also lost their personal advocate, who now recedes into the "system."

The final touch is added when, as in recent years, the profession subscribes to some of the economic values in its society. While legitimate for other professions or occupations, these are questionable in medicine. I refer to the growing tendency of physicians to adopt shorter work days and weeks, longer and more frequent vacations, and more regular hours. Many now take a unionist stance with respect to their "rights" and compensation. Whatever justification they might have, strikes or slow-downs by segments of the profession have seriously damaged the image of medicine as a profession dedicated to service above its own interests. One of the distinguishing features of the profession of medicine has thus been compromised by physicians themselves. Those who choose to pursue their self-interest, as union members may, cannot at the same time demand a superior moral position in society.

Factors like those just reviewed impart a vastly different quality to the relationship between physicians and patients. Its former hieratic quality has been challenged by the demands of a democratic society and diminished by contemporary patterns of medical organizations and practice. Physicians can no longer assume a moral stance for their patients or presume to derive moral authority from a unique position in society. In short, traditional professional ethics, as derived from the unique responsibilities the profession imposed on itself, have been damaged beyond rehabilitation. We must look elsewhere for a humanistic medical ethics.

THE HUMANISTIC SOURCE OF MEDICAL ETHICS

A more authentically humanistic basis for professional ethics is clearly needed, one more suited to contemporary society and less dependent on changing interpretations physicians or society may place on the role of medicine. This means we must derive physicians' obligations from the specific situation of the person seeking assistance in the state of illness. The most certain source of a humanistic ethics is the unique impact of illness (that is, the impact of *being* ill on the humanity of the person) because it is a source which gives meaning to the whole of the physician's activities. It is the need to repair specific damage done to patients' humanity by illness that imposes obligations on physicians.

To this state of "wounded" humanity we now turn—first to define its concrete features and then to delineate the ethical imperatives which stem from it. These imperatives cannot constitute anything but "humanistic" ethics because they are tied to a specifically human experience, not to a social or historical role for the profession.

The essence of humanistic ethics is this: particular features of illness diminish and obstruct a patient's capacity to live a specifically human existence to its fullest. These features create a relationship of inherent inequality between two human beings: one a physician, the other a patient. That inequality must be removed as fully as possible before the humanity of the patient can be restored. The obligation to restore the patient's humanity is intrinsic in the relationship physicians assume when they "profess" medicine. Specific obligations are derived from the "profession"—an active assumption by the physician as a free person entering a relationship with another person. These obligations transcend any responsibilities, rights, or privileges physicians may feel were conferred upon them by the degrees they possess.

I can now turn to a partial exemplification of this line of reasoning by first identifying the deficits in the patient's humanity imposed by illness, and then the obligation of physicians to repair them. It is the sum of the obligations which constitute an authentic, humanistic, professional medical ethics.

Those who are ill (that is, those who have experienced some event—a symptom, an injury, a disability—they regard as "ill-ness") suffer insult to their whole being. They experience a series of intimate insults to the aspects of their existence most integral to being human. Because of the event of illness, these patients lose their freedom to act; they lack the knowledge upon which to make rational choices or to regain their freedom to act; they must place themselves in the power of another human, as petitioners, to regain their humanity; their integrity (i.e., self-image) is shattered, or at least threatened.

In short, those patients who have just experienced illness as an acute event or who have lived with it as a chronic accompaniment of life are deprived in varying degrees of those things which distinguish humanity from other forms of existence. A closer inspection of these deficiencies will clarify the meaning of the state of "wounded" humanity and the resultant state of inequality that characterizes the relationship between physician and patient.

When we are ill, the body is no longer a ready instrument of the will; we lack the knowledge and the skill to make the choices which will restore it; we come necessarily under the power of others; and consequently the integrated image (our embodied selves) that gives meaning to our lives is shattered. The deficiencies in the humanity of those who are sick, therefore, can be examined under four headings: freedom of action, freedom to make rational choices, freedom from the power of others, and integrity of self-image, the latter of which gives meaning to the first three. A brief inquiry into each of these deficiencies and the obligations derived from them will illustrate what I mean by humanistically based professional ethics.

Freedom of Action.   Certainly, one essential attribute of being human is the ability to use the body as a ready instrument of our own purposes—to attain goals which transcend the needs of the body itself. The body is man's instrument for work, play, esthetic or physical pleasure, and creative activity of every kind. The bodies of plants, in contrast, are rooted and passive; those of animals are responsive largely to needs which do not transcend the body itself, though locomotion permits a more active pursuit of those bodily needs. In the human, the body is the agent for highly individualizing and personalizing activities, which serve purposes beyond the body's own needs.

Illness compromises the span of trans-bodily goals a person may set for himself, or attain. Pain, disability, or malaise make the body the center and end of existence rather than its means. Instead of being commanded, the body commands attention, and by that fact the patient moves closer to an animal or even a vegetative existence. Pursuit of the "good" life, however we define it, must stop until the body can be restored as the ready vehicle for that pursuit.

Freedom to Make Choices. The second deficiency in humanity caused by the fact of illness is the lack of the information and skill necessary to restore the body to its former state. The sick person lacks almost all the information needed to make rational choices and decisions of the utmost importance to his life. He does not know what is wrong; how he became ill or why; how serious his problem may be, whether he can recover; what treatments are available and whether they are effective; and what risk, cost, pain, or loss of dignity they may impose.

The freedom to make informed choices in matters affecting our well-being, one of the most fundamental of human prerogatives, is lost or seriously impaired in illness.

The freedom to make choices and take action in terms of one's own value system is impaired. In addition, the pain and discomfort of being ill make the patient susceptible to easier assent than would ordinarily be the case. Organic or functional disturbances of the brain add to this susceptibility or may even obviate completely free, informed consent or choice. In short, lacking knowledge to make decisions deprives the patient of his prime and intrinsic characteristics as a human agent.

Lack of information for rational decision making is common in a technological society. Even in ordinary daily affairs, it is manifestly impossible to comprehend all the alternatives. Dependence upon others is a practical necessity. In matters of health, however, the decisions penetrate too deeply into personal values and identities to be treated casually. Increasing numbers of patients perceive this difference and are expressing their dissatisfaction in a spate of patients' "bills of rights." The central thrust of these bills of rights is a plea for genuine participation in the process of medical decision making.

Freedom from the Power of Others. A consistent aim of a democratic and humanistic social order is to insure the widest individual self-determination consistent with the good of all. Each person wishes to be free of the power of others and to enter into personal associations on the basis of equality as much as possible. In illness this freedom, like the others, is seriously compromised. Even the most powerful, the most wealthy, and the best educated must become petitioners. Dependence on professionals, institutions, administrators, technicians—indeed the whole human apparatus of hospitals and clinics—is imposed of necessity upon the sick person. While the dependence is not as absolute as that of a passenger in an airliner landing in the fog, it is nonetheless of the same kind and lasts much longer.

The power of others to harm and to help is intermixed in every medical transaction. The patient is at the mercy of the integrity, competence, or motivation of others, most of whom are strangers. In today's complicated, technologic medicine a "team" is often necessary for vital aspects of a patient's care. The patient never sees many team members, others only fleetingly. The dangers of impersonalized use of power by team members are grave.

The fact of being ill, therefore, not only limits our freedom to act and to make free, rational choices, but places us in the most vulnerable position conceivable before those who have the power to make up these deficiencies.

Threats to Our Self-Image. Finally, these impediments to ordinary human freedoms occur within a context where the patient's image of himself is overtly or covertly threatened. Every illness is an assault on the integrity of the person. The assaults are of the most direct kind—the threat or actuality of death or disability, pain, discomfort, and limitations. The patient's idea of a satisfying life is threatened by the possibility of or need to adapt to chronic illness or repetition of acute episodes.

A lifelong construction of a personal image to balance abilities and limitations is eroded by the fact of illness. The challenge of rebuilding, the weakening of self-confidence, and the simple fact of vulnerability must be faced and a new image constructed. Some patients succeed completely or partially, and some fail. But, all in some measure or other must confront the test of an assault on the integrity of the person—and at the same time the other human freedoms enjoyed by the well have been lost or circumscribed.

MORAL OBLIGATIONS OF THE PROFESSIONAL

It is the undeniable fact of these specific disabilities in the humanity of the sick person that must be the infrangible base for the obligations of the physicians and all others who profess to heal. These obligations when codified and explicated constitute the substance of professional medical ethics. Professional ethics derived from the existential situation of the patient are more authentic and more human than the traditional ethics derived from the self-declared duties of the profession. If we accept this distinction, then we have the basis for a humanistic medical ethics—one rationally and humanely justifiable.

Obligations to the wounded humanity of the patient fall squarely upon the professional because inequalities in the relationship place all the power on his side. If the professional does not consciously remedy the four deficiencies which impair the patient's expression of humanity, his "profession" is inauthentic.

Clearly the body must be healed. This duty is the one most easily assumed by the health professional. The primary reason for the highest degree of competence then is a moral imperative, not professional satisfaction.

But in making his competence available, the physician must also attend to the other deficiencies created by illness. His technical decisions must be congruent with the patient's needs to participate in choices as freely and rationally as education, time, and circumstances permit. The facts of the illness; the degree of its gravity; the alternatives open; their relative effectiveness, costs, and dangers; the physician's own experience and skill in comparison with others; and the likelihood of success or failure must all be disclosed. Only when the information gap is closed can patients approach truly valid consent, one which permits participation as a human and enables the patient to incorporate the decision into his own value system.

127

Every clinical decision involves technical and value choices. These must to the most careful degree be dissected from each other to avoid imposing the physician's values. The professional can make a valid claim for technical authority, but no longer for moral authority. In a pluralistic society, the patient has the right to his own moral agency if he wishes to exercise it. The physician has the moral obligation to ascertain the degree to which the patient wishes to exercise his moral prerogatives and to provide the fullest exposition which will enable the privilege to be exercised.

Obviously, these obligations are conditioned by the acuteness of the clinical situation, the physiological state of the patient. But before excusing himself from them, the physician has the obligation to assure that he has exerted the care necessary to assure patient participation. A "humanistic basis" for professional ethics has to include the most careful management of the intersections of values that medical care so frequently entails.

This obligation extends beyond the patient to his surrogate in those circumstances when the patient cannot act for himself. Parents in the case of children, guardians in the case of the incompetent, and family or friends in the case of unconscious adults—all share with the physician the obligation to make decisions which will protect the patient's values to the extent they are known. The implications are obvious in such common clinical decisions as initiation and termination of life-support techniques, selection of treatment for incurable fatal disorders, or abortion whether for social, medical, or genetic reasons. An ever-present, subtle temptation for the physician and other health professionals is to impose their own values. The meaning of life, death, and quality of life; the exact content of a healthy existence; the relationship of spiritual to temporal concerns—each is a matter closely identified with our integrity as persons. Decisions affecting them cannot be humane unless they allow for individuals to express their values meaningfully.

The physician too has a set of values to which he owes allegiance. He has a double obligation: to protect those of the patient and to be faithful to his own. Conflicts will, of necessity, occur from time to time. To deal with them humanely, the physician must know enough about his own beliefs to decide when he can compromise, when he cannot, and when he must give the patient an opportunity to transfer his care to another physician whose values more closely coincide. A truly "humanistic" relationship allows the physician as well as the patient to express his humanity as fully as possible.

This is essential also in dealing with the threatened self-image of the person who is ill. He must consciously be assisted in integrating the experience of illness with his life. To do so requires his active participation in the decisions that affect him. Patient and physician must together reconstruct a meaning in the events of illness, even when it requires drastic alteration of the patient's conception of himself.

The moral obligations which arise from the fact of illness bear not only on the individual physician but on the institutions which "pro-fess" to provide medical care. Hospitals share the moral responsibility to repair the injuries to the patient's humanity. The responsibility is a corporate one, vested in the board of trustees, but it is not less binding. This responsibility cannot be delegated to the physician totally. When the physician uses a hospital, he is in a decision-making context that is no longer isolated. The degree to which he fulfills the moral requirements of a humanistic medical ethics must be a corporate concern as well. I am suggesting that the hospital too must be a moral agent. Ethical concerns involving this institution have yet to be adequately explored, and they lie in the realm of social ethics, one which I believe will increasingly require critical scrutiny in the years ahead (2).

Humanism in Medical Experimentation

Today, perhaps the first and only duty of the philosopher is to defend man against himself, to defend man against that extraordinary temptation to inhumanity to which— almost always without being aware of it—so many human beings today have yielded.

Gabriel Marcel (1)

The tension between human concerns and technologic possibility is exquisitely revealed in research with human subjects. Here the traditional mandate of the physician as helper comes increasingly into conflict with his new mandate as scientist and fact-gatherer. Can medicine remain faithful to both trusts—to be the most scientific of humanities and the most humanistic of the sciences (2)?

Francoeur even argues for a "technological imperative," which would impel man to use his new technology in medicine, even if it is dangerous. Man, Francoeur says, must join God in "creating future generations" and should apply his knowledge, always seeking the *via media* between the dangers and the benefits of technology (3). The perils of an overzealous pursuit of this view are obvious; the social consensus seems to favor some modified version of the technological imperative.

While recognizing the *de facto* necessity and reality of human experimentation, law does not explicitly sanction the practice. Medical practice acts do not assign experimentation explicitly to the physician. The prevailing social and legal opinion is that he does experiment only at his own risk. The pertinent citations in Professor Jay Katz's invaluable casebook on human experimentation refer only tangentially to experimentation (4). The courts use the term

Published in somewhat different form under the title "Humanism in Human Experimentation: Some Notes on the Investigator's Fiduciary Role" in *Texas Reports on Biology and Medicine*, 32:311–25 (Spring 1974).

loosely—and certainly not explicitly—to cover clinical investigation as it is practiced all over the world. Society clearly recognizes the value of human experimentation for all its members, but just as clearly avoids assigning the authority for its conduct. Paradoxically, regulatory mechanisms are being developed everywhere, often under governmental sponsorship. The investigator is always in the insecure state of being a hero at one moment and a villain the next.

Two important conclusions can be drawn from the inescapable conflict of values that society imposes on the investigator. Because society's mandate is a heavily conditioned one, the privilege to pursue investigations is absolutely contingent upon the investigator's willingness to accept the trust for preserving the integrity of the person of the subject. Society's mandate in this respect is far stronger than its mandate to do research—and far more important to its own health.

The second conclusion is that any experiment for therapeutic purposes or to further our understanding of disease mechanisms, by its nature, imperils the personal rights of the patient or the subject. Experimentation with humans cannot be conducted in a democratic society without some invasion of fundamental human rights. What must be sought is the degree to which society and the individual will permit these rights to be invaded, and under what conditions, in order that new knowledge may be obtained for the good of the subject or his neighbors (5).

The investigator does not enjoy, explicitly or implicitly, a social mandate to advance scientific knowledge as an end in itself. This is permissible in other scientific disciplines, but not where another person must yield up some of his inalienable rights, even if he volunteers to do so and consents freely. In short, contemporary social values sanction research involving humans if there is no alternative way, if there is reasonable expectation of good for the subject or for society, if the subject *genuinely* partakes in the decision to participate, if the study is worth doing, if it is carried out competently, and if the investigator assumes the fullness of his fiduciary role at every step. Only under these conditions will the social value system permit significant risks to well-being and to life—much as it does in space or underseas exploration, for example.

It is this highly qualified social mandate that the investigator must reflect upon and reexamine when his enthusiasm for the advance of science, his own career, or his intellectual delectation threaten to blur the sources of his privilege. The matter is uniquely important in the university setting where such high value is placed on research that its pursuit too frequently appears casual. No matter how minimal his contribution may be, each physician must realize that his fiduciary responsibility begins at the moment of his involvement. He has a fundamental obligation to adhere to the limitations of the social mandate, not only in his own behavior but also in his responses to the behavior of others. The investigator is party to a social contract between himself, the subject, and society. The fundamental obligation that arises, therefore, cannot be passed on to others, to group decision, or to "higher authority."

THE PERSONAL TRANSACTION
BETWEEN SUBJECT AND INVESTIGATOR

Granting he recognizes the heavily conditioned sanction under which he operates, the investigator must then fully appreciate the unequal nature of the transaction between himself and his patient or subject. The inequality will vary in magnitude, depending upon such factors as the subject's education and social level, emotional stability, and physical debility; or the subject's special circumstances (perhaps as prisoner, student, mentally retarded status, or his state of consciousness). Moreover, if the subject is a patient, his eagerness for a new cure or a new lease on life will alter his responses profoundly. The desire to be of service to others, in the cases of volunteers for nontherapeutic experiments, is an equally potent modulator of the delicate personal contract between investigator and subject.

Concealed forms of coercion are many: the overadulation of the unsophisticated for science and technology, the mystique that still surrounds the physician, the patient's desire to please, or the weight of group pressures to volunteer. Overriding these is the superior technical expertise of the physician-investigator. The patient or subject is totally dependent on him for information about the utility, probability of outcome, and risks involved in the proposed procedure. Both technical jargon and the subject's dependence upon the investigator's competence and goodwill at every stage of the procedure markedly accentuate the inequalities between them.

On the investigator's side, subtle but powerful forces may erode his fiduciary role. The investigator has chosen research using human beings as his life's work. His advancement and prestige depend upon publication of significant results. He must complete his work on a tight schedule. To compete successfully, he must be rigorous in his design, study a sufficient number of patients, and satisfy the canons of experimental elegance. The young investigator must break into the ranks of established investigators; the established investigator must maintain his hard-won prestigious position. Both are susceptible to that subtle shift of standards to which Professor S.E. Luria referred recently as "the ethics of competitive enterprise" (6).

These influences may be sublimated in apparently strenuous efforts to assist mankind. Self-deception is easy and readily rationalized. It is difficult to discern where legitimate dedication to high-quality humane research ends and the hubris peculiar to the physician-scientist begins. This intersection of personal human values with social and scientific goals is intense and crucial. No test of an investigator's humanism is more rigorous or revealing.

Yet it is within the context of these personal pressures and the inescapable inequality of his relationship with the patient or subject that the investigator must exercise his fiduciary responsibility. In the midst of this nexus, valid consent must be elicited, for this is the very first and the ineluctable requirement for ethical authenticity or humaneness in the transaction. In a free society and even with a social mandate permitting experimentation, only the subject is free to yield some of his rights over his body and run the risks of injury or discomfort inherent in any procedure—experimental, therapeutic, or diagnostic. Both physician and patient in this situation can never be wholly free or wholly informed in any absolute sense without meeting the minimum requirement, a valid consent; to fail to do so would mean indulging in the monumental arrogance of selecting "martyrs for society," to use Pappworth's phrase (7).

A valid consent is one in which the subject, the investigator, and subsequent reviewers agree that the subject is a full partner in the decision to participate and in understanding the conditions of participation.

Consent is neither free, informed, nor valid unless there is maximal opportunity for self-determination. This, in turn, requires full disclosure about the purposes of the experiment, the nature of the procedures, the dangers and discomforts they can produce, the benefits to be gained, the assurance that the subject may withdraw at any time, and information on whether the experiment is a substitute for standard treatment. When experimental design requires some concealment, the fact must be disclosed together with the general nature of what is to be concealed.

The phenomenology of human consent is extraordinarily complex, even in the ordinary affairs of mankind. It is essential to remember that, even in ordinary affairs, to consent is always to yield up one's will—at least in part—to another, and this act confers upon the elicitor of the consent the power to limit another person's freedom. When consent occurs in the medical and research relationship, its already complex dynamics are exponentially accentuated.

The necessity for valid consent is at the heart of any consideration of humanism in experimentation. It is the most crucial arena for the exercise of the physician's fiduciary role; it reveals most clearly the texture of his motivation, his veracity, and his humanism. The execution of a proper consent form, while necessary, is no substitute for the investigator's responsibility to assure *quality* of the consent. Like other regulatory measures, the form guards against gross abuses of privilege, but the authenticity of the consent rests with the investigator. It is the quality of human consent, therefore, that must be the central concern of the humane investigator, not the punctilious filling out of forms, however detailed or well intentioned. Indeed, the length and detail of a consent form may be inversely related to the quality of the subject's comprehension and consent (8).

There are other special features of the investigator's personal relationship with the patient-subject, such as the rights to privacy, to dignified treatment, to confidentiality, to redress—all of which bear on the genuineness of the investigator's fiduciary role. But if the original consent is invalid, there is no likelihood that these other human rights will be preserved with any assiduity. The spirit of the investigator's humane concerns, therefore, is best revealed in the quality of the consent he obtains.

AUTHENTICITY OF THE FIDUCIARY ROLE

Certain clear, personal, moral responsibilities are derived from the two unique features of human experimentation just discussed—

its limited social mandate and the inequality of the personal transactions it encompasses. There is no more stringent test of a physician's humanism than the way in which he exercises the fiduciary
responsibilities thrust upon him in every detail of a humanely conducted experiment with humans. Despite external regulations, the
fiduciary function must ultimately be self-monitored by the investigator. This means that each physician willing to undertake this
awesome duty must develop some set of values against which he
can judge the humaneness of his acts.

This is an especially onerous task in the face of the current trend
to moral relativism, in which every effort is expended to expunge
guilt from human affairs. Yet, without some conscious ordering of
values, accompanied by a sense of personal culpability for the injustices which erroneous values may impose, the fiduciary role can
never be authentic. No legal or institutional constraints can guard
against the cumulative evil that subtly evolves from small indiffer-
ences. The investigator is compelled, therefore, to scrutinize his
value choices and constantly examine and refurbish them. This demands a conscious reflection on some of the most fundamental issues of human existence—an exercise which to a culture infatuated
with means and unused to the contemplation of ends is inimical.

The investigator, therefore, is enjoined to deal with those questions that do not have a true or false answer, the "first order" questions, the stuff of philosophy (9). And it is precisely this mode of
thinking for which his scientific training does not prepare him. It is
these same questions that some philosophers, themselves overawed
by science and technology, call "meaningless." Yet our philosophical propositions govern behavior and justify actions. They demand
explicit cogitations, the lack of which depersonalizes the investigator and makes his actions automatic rather than human.

What are some of the dimensions of humane concern which the
investigator must ponder? Five areas of human concern will be
considered. The reader will, no doubt, have his own list and his
own ordering of it. The only indispensable activity is that there be
a list, a list which is consciously examined by the investigator whose
responsibility it is to assure its probity and humaneness.

The Realm of Metaethics. The first, and perhaps the most important and most difficult, level of inquiry deals with the conceptual
framework for ethical choices and values that lies in the realm of

metaethics. It conditions each concrete decision. It is the source of the ethical norms against which actions are measured and then labeled as right or wrong. Most of us quickly accept normative principles without any conscious reflection on their sources in our deepest convictions—those so identified with our conceptions of what we are that only the more intellectually and emotionally mature can probe to these depths without profound anxiety.

Our metaethical axioms have profound consequences for our patients. They transcend the mere fact of "acting according to conscience." On what, and how, is the conscience formed? There is a vast difference, for example, between the absolutist who makes his "principle" the final arbiter and the situational ethicist who uses the "situation" of the act and its consequences as his guide. In the first instance, right and wrong are antitheses, philosophical contradictories with little or no ground between them. This is the stance of much of classical ethics, and it can easily make "abstractions" of men. The situational ethicist, in contradistinction, may be the victim of an accommodating relativism that can be stretched to fit any subjective supposition he chooses. Lying, in the absolutist view, is always wrong; in the situational view, it may be the moral thing to do.

But in most of the circumstances the investigator encounters, the conflict is between two or more values, both having merit (10). Rather than choosing between good and evil, he is forced to choose between good and good, or better and worse: for example, telling the truth as against the mandate not to harm the patient or cause him anxiety; or the relief of suffering against the mandate to preserve life; or putting one person in the presence of risk to obtain good for many others.

Underscored here is the necessity of understanding how such decisions are made. To undertake this task in some reasonable fashion requires some understanding of the history of ethical theory—its origins in Aristotle and Plato, its infusion with Christian theology in Aquinas, its transformations and modulations in the thinking of Kant, Hegel, and the modern existentialists and pragmatists. The delineation of metaethical assumptions is a complex and lifelong task. It involves an understanding of the entire "attitude in the fact of the human condition," as Jacques Maritain has phrased it in his critical study of the presuppositions of ethical theory (11).

These presuppositions are themselves finally rooted in the idea of man. Explicitly or implicitly, every human subscribes to a metaphysics of man—the sum of the suppositions he makes about the meaning and the value of human existence and the existence or nonexistence of an order transcending man. Manifestly, it matters a great deal whether one subscribes to the views of a Marxian humanist like Adam Schaff, who believes that man's end is a happy life on earth (12); to those of a Christian humanist, who sees that life is fused by a spiritual element transcending man; or to those of a dozen other humanisms, each with its own spirit and values.

The physician must understand his own suppositions as well as he can and then make an attempt to understand those of the patient, an even more difficult task. Yet, without some intimation of the patient's values, he cannot guard against one of the more subtle forms of inhumane behavior: the imposition of his value sets on another person who is not free to resist or, worse still, is not afforded the opportunity to express his own values. Physicians are especially susceptible to the unthinking and condescending transfer of their authority in technical matters to the realm of human values.

Knowing, therefore, his own value choices and those of his patients is an essential for the humanist investigator. This is exquisitely the case at every stage of the process of consent, where the intersection, conflict, and harmonization of values proceed simultaneously. It is impossible to obtain a valid consent, much less one whose "quality" is that of a humane decision, without sensitivity to the issues that arise out of the metaethical geography of the beliefs held by subject and investigator.

The Ethics of Good Science. The second dimension of the fiduciary role is authenticity as scientist. Science has its own ethical base. To put a person at risk for ill-conceived scientific reasons or with bad experimental design is a serious violation of trust. Is the research question trivial? Is the experiment a duplication? Will the methods provide the answer sought? Is the investigator competent in the procedures involved, or will he be learning them in the study? Is the design rigorous, the control adequate, and the information worth having? Or, on the other side, is he being overly rigorous to satisfy the esthetic sense of what constitutes "elegant experimental design"?

Anyone reviewing experimental protocols or refereeing the papers that result from them must conclude that these questions are

137

not asked often enough. This is particularly true in drug evaluation, a form of clinical investigation too lightly entered into but the
most difficult of all investigations to conduct competently. Is the
drug worth pursuing for human use? How much preclinical testing
is enough? On whom shall it be tried first? Can such research be
justified when an effective treatment already exists?

These questions must be asked repeatedly before investigation.
Otherwise, the momentum generated by the research ambiance
will propel immoral exposure of humans to risk without sufficient
reason, or even uselessly if the design leads to erroneous or incon-
clusive results. The ethics of science may occasionally conflict with
the ethics of good patient care once an investigation is initiated,
but, if adverted to beforehand, the canons of good science are additional guarantees of the morality of the experiment.

The Quality of Consent.   The third dimension of the fiduciary
role is the quality of the consent obtained. Requirements for a valid
consent can be fulfilled to the letter, and still the consent can lack
those qualities that make it the consent of a free person.

As we are obtaining consent and after we have obtained it, we
must question ourselves closely. Did we gain consent more by sua-
vity, eloquence, or subtle duress than by frank disclosure of the information the patient needs to make a decision? Did our zeal for
the experiment override the patient's fear or reservation? Did we
tell the patient enough about the discomfort and the risks? Did we
excuse ourselves on the specious grounds that the patient would
not understand or might be made overly anxious? In a therapeutic
experiment, can we really offer the patient some probability of help
for his condition? Or is he merely another case we need to meet the
protocol? Having once obtained consent, do we regard it as immu-
table and also as a cover for new and unanticipated procedures the
experiments may later require? Are we sufficiently open to the patient's doubts after he has consented, and do we allow ample opportunity for a graceful withdrawal?

We cannot overstress the significance of the quality of human
consent. It is the pivotal point in the fiduciary process, the crucible
of our veracity, the place in which the psychological and intellectual integrity of the subject can be most subtly and unconsciously
invaded.

The Conduct of the Experiment.   The fourth dimension of humanism in the use of humans in experimentation is the actual conduct of the experiment. Have we taken the pains to make ourselves sufficiently skilled in the techniques involved? Do we insist on doing them out of motives of pride? Have we chosen the safer or the more spectacular and fashionable methodology? Do we know when to discontinue the experiment, whether because of patient discomfort, or because we have enough data even if the protocol has not been carried out to the letter, or because another investigator has already made our work redundant? Or are we thinking more of the eventual report, our survival on the academic scene, the approbation of our colleagues?

We might put the ultimate test to ourselves more often—perhaps routinely, as Lawrence Altman has suggested (13): are we prepared to submit to the experiment ourselves or even postpone seeking any subject's consent until we have performed the procedure on ourselves? The subject of auto-experimentation is a complex one, which I believe will be discussed more frequently as we look more critically at our humanist responsibilities. It is difficult to ignore the example of Nobelist Werner Forssman, who first performed two of the most important cardiological techniques, catheterization and angiocardiography, upon himself.

Corporate Responsibility.   The fifth dimension and the last, which illustrates the sort of self-examination the investigator must practice to keep the person of the patient or subject always in his consciousness, is his acceptance of corporate responsibility for the ethical behavior of the research group. The research team, commonplace today, is made up of a wide variety of people: physicians, basic scientists, nurses, students, fellows—each sharing some aspects of the protocol. Responsibility, under these conditions, is easy to diffuse even when there is a leader who takes prime responsibility. For a morally respectable experiment, the fiduciary responsibility must be shared by all who participate. Each member of the team must feel responsible for violations of trust in any of the dimensions iterated previously.

This may be an especially difficult duty for the student or the young physician, who is the junior member of the team. Yet, we cannot escape the conclusion that, if others fail in their trust, he must speak up, object, drop out of the team, or take action to end the injustice. If he does not, he easily becomes what Gabriel Marcel called the "auxiliary bureaucrat," the "small man" in a vast system who excuses himself for assenting to any order on the basis of his subordinate position.

SUMMARY

These are only a few of the questions each of us must answer as we enter the privileged and dangerous domain of human experimentation. They are derived from the personal responsibilities imposed by the social mandate that permits human experimentation and the unique characteristic of the physician's personal transaction with the patient as a subject. It is not too much to ask the investigator, at least periodically, to examine his conscience on points such as these. Each investigator conscientious about his fiduciary role will devise his own checklist.

The fiduciary role each investigator willingly assumes demands a conscious, critical, continual self-examination as the antidote for complacency and automatic behavior, which gradually lead to making an abstraction of our neighbors and which are the greatest dangers of technology. This self-examination need not impose either paralyzing scrupulosity or a neurotic and obsessive rumination on every past or future action. Rather, a mature, balanced self-examination, assisted by colleagues and patients, will enable the investigator to be both scientist and humanist.

Hospitals as Moral Agents

The subject of institutional ethics has significance beyond hospitals. Our country enters its third century in a state of moral disquietude about its own motives. There is widespread confusion about moral values. We suffer from an obsession with means and from a fear of ends and purpose. Institutions are particularly suspect. Most of them—whether we look at business, education, government, or the church—seem to have become disengaged from their human purpose. For economic, political, and fiscal considerations and self-interest are too often their dominant justifying principles. Rarely do our governmental or institutional leaders speak convincingly, as the founders of our country did, of the moral purposes of their enterprise. The inescapable challenge for all our institutions in the next century, the one upon which the revitalization of our national life depends, is to recapture the sense of a moral purpose transcending self-interest and self-preservation.

But it is not my purpose to moralize—this is very different from genuine moral discourse. I merely wish to set the question of the institutional obligations of hospitals against a backdrop of the general deficiency in the assumption of moral obligations that afflicts our nation. Because of the urgent and intensely human milieu within which it operates, the hospital must be among the first to attend to its institutional moral obligations. It can, in fact, be the paradigm for others.

In discussing these obligations, I shall reflect on three questions: *First,* what is the actual nature of the human relationship between a patient and a hospital in today's system of health care? *Second,* what obligations are derived from the nature of that relationship? And, *third,* what are some of the practical implications of these obligations?

Based on a speech entitled "Hospitals as Moral Agents: Some Notes on Institutional Ethics" which was published in *Proceedings* of the Third Annual Board of Trustees/Medical Staff Executive Committee Conference sponsored by Saint Joseph's Hospital in Saint Paul, Minnesota, on March 26, 1977, pp. 10-27.

INSTITUTIONAL ETHICS: WHAT IT IS; WHAT IT IS NOT

Before addressing these three questions, it is essential to clarify two propaedeutic issues—first, what I understand ethics to be, and, second, what I *do not* subsume under the rubric of institutional ethical obligation.

While there is a phenomenal resurgence of interest today in biomedical ethics, there is still much confusion and variability in interpretation of the term *ethics*. Many still believe ethics is an intuitive domain which consists entirely of personal beliefs that are not arguable and need no rational justification. Others believe that morals cannot be taught or that generally applicable principles cannot be derived. Both views, intuitionist and skeptical, are prominent among health professionals today. Discourse about ethics, they hold, is either impossible or meaningless.

I hold the traditional view of ethics as the systematic search for generalizable and rationally justifiable principles on how we ought to live and act in various relationships with our fellow men. Ethics is, therefore, a branch of practical philosophy. It includes the analysis of ethical statements but is not limited to that analysis. Ethics deals with what "ought" to be rather than with what "is." Institutional ethics, from this view, consists of the general normative principles which define the way institutions "ought" to act with respect to their obligations. It is a branch of social ethics in that it pertains to men when they act as members of a group rather than as individuals. The problems of institutional morality, those which emerge from the actions of organized groups, are more complex than those of individual ethics.

My second propaedeutic centers on what institutional ethics is not. It is not the sum of the ethical beliefs of the people who make up the institution—the individual physicians, nurses, administrators, and board members. Each has his own set of values and beliefs and in a pluralistic society must be permitted to express them as an individual. But institutional ethics consists of a definable set of obligations which transcends these individual beliefs. For example, individual physicians differ in their views on abortion and euthanasia, direct and indirect. What an institution must decide is whether it sanctions absolute or limited pluralism, and whether, on this or that issue, it will take some specific stance to which it feels morally obligated above others. Institutions, as we shall examine further, will be called upon increasingly to make their moral choices more explicit than has been customary.

Nor is institutional ethics to be equated with meeting only the legal requirements for accountability. Many obligations which derive from the nature of the hospital's mission in society are now being transferred to the realm of law. This is a forceful commentary on the tardiness of hospitals in sensing what should be ethical obligations. I refer to the sharpening of the definitions of legal and fiscal accountability of board and administrators for quality of care, protection of the rights of consent, managerial efficiency, equity in provision of services, and assuring rights of due process. Most of these obligations would have, and should have, been derived from a conscious reflection on the moral obligations implicit in what hospitals are all about. Their translation into legislation and patient pleas for a variety of bills of rights are signs of the ethical lassitude of our institutions.

But, if these rights and obligations are now being expressed in law, is this not sufficient? A brief look at the distinction between law and ethics will make the answer clearer. Law and ethics may often coincide, but they are not necessarily and always the same. In fact, as recent history shows, they may often be antipathetic. Law is in many ways the *coarse* adjustment of society to assure that certain obligations are fulfilled. It has been undeniably a positive force in enhancing human rights and freedom in our country. But as our lagging progress in civil rights and our Vietnam interlude illustrate, there is too often a disjunction between what is legal and what is moral.

Law, for example, can guarantee the validity of consent or minimum standards of quality by requiring hospitals to follow and record certain procedures and by imposing penalties for violations. But law, by its nature, seeks standardized and bureaucratized, often impersonalized solutions. What is transferred to law is by definition taken out of the realm of the voluntary recognition of moral responsibility. Something subtle and exquisite is lost. Law cannot guarantee the quality of human transactions even though it may protect the rights of the parties to the transactions.

Ethics, on the other hand, is the *fine* adjustment of men for the voluntary assumption of obligations because they are demanded by the very nature of certain relationships between humans. Ethics sets a higher ideal than law simply because it is not securable. An ethically sensitive institution takes the full dimension of the medical encounter into account—all those things which flow from the existential condition of humanity in the state of illness.

Law and ethics can reinforce each other, as do the coarse and fine adjustments of the microscope. Law assures that patients' rights will be protected from those who do not act from ethical motives; ethics guarantees that the institutional conscience will transcend law and attend to obligations whether covered by law or not. It also guarantees that law is applied humanely, always in the spirit of serving individual needs rather than justifying itself. Government, therefore, must never be the sanction for ethics but only a recourse when human frailty obfuscates moral sensibilities. Law seems indispensable to human life, but it cannot be totally sufficient for an institution consciously attending to its moral obligations.

Neither should ethics be confused with etiquette, the niceties of conduct between institutions and professionals which protect their mutual self-interests. Even in the so-called ethical treatises of the Hippocratic Corpus, these domains are confused. Intermingled with a few true ethical principles are many more precepts as to the physician's mien, conduct and comportment with patients and families, and courtesies he should afford his fellow physicians. In our times, the proscription against advertising or unseemly publicity and the rules for enlightened self-interest which govern the inevitable but subtle competition between institutions or professionals are in the "etiquette" category. There may be fragments of moral issues here, but they are not mandatory obligations whose violation undermines professional authenticity.

Finally, institutional ethics does not imply that a single rigid set of principles be uniformly practiced by all hospitals. This is manifestly impossible in a society with such a wide range of values as ours. Indeed, our moral pluralism may itself require some declaration by the institution of its values, if the patient's own values are to be fully protected.

Some commonly applicable principles will undoubtedly emerge, so that the final declaration of institutional morality will be an admixture of shared and unshared beliefs. What is important is that the points I have been emphasizing here be adverted to consciously by those in whom corporate responsibility is vested.

Ethics is a legitimate branch of practical philosophy, which systematically examines and rationally justifies claims about how we should live as individuals and members of society. Institutional ethics seeks out these principles as they apply to the moral obligations of institutions to the segment of mankind they profess to serve. There are several things institutional ethics is *not:* it is not the same as accountability to law, nor the simple addition of the ethical beliefs of those who work in the institution, nor professional etiquette or some unexamined universal set of norms which should be imposed upon all hospitals.

We can now examine briefly three further questions: the nature of the relationships of patients to hospitals that generate ethical obligations, the nature of these obligations, and their implications for everyday hospital practice.

THE HOSPITAL'S PROFESSION AND THE PATIENT'S NEED

We must look first at the genesis of the hospital's moral obligations as an institution to the patient. I find it useful to begin at what I call the hospital's "profession." By this, I mean that a hospital, by the very fact of its existence, makes a declaration—that is, it professes to concentrate and make available those resources which a person can call upon when he is ill. Implicit in that profession is the promise to assist the person in the condition of illness to regain what he has lost—his health—at least to the maximum degree possible.

If it is a community, voluntary, nonprofit hospital, the hospital makes a second declaration, namely, that it is available to all, that it will not profit from the patient's need, and that its self-interests are subservient to the community.

The hospital usually makes its resources available through the medium of the physician. But he too makes a public declaration that he possesses skills he will put at the services of those who are ill. In doing so, he incurs all the moral obligations traditionally delineated in professional codes of ethics: he must be competent, act in the patient's interest, never do deliberate harm, protect confidentiality, and treat the patient honestly, considerately, and personally. These obligations bind the physician within the hospital as they do in his office.

In using the hospital, however, the physician takes advantage of a community resource which he has not personally provided. The community places this resource in the trust of a board of directors, who act as surrogates for the community. The physician's moral obligations to the patient are no longer solely his concern. They now occur within an institutional framework, which modulates the relationship with his patient two ways. First, the physician's decisions directly or indirectly affect others. And, second, he shares his responsibilities with the institution through its board, which must carry out the obligations it incurs by virtue of its own declaration.

As a matter of fact, today an increasing number of patients now enter the same relationship with a hospital which formerly was obtained solely with physicians. The patient with no personal physician, or whose physician is unavailable, or who has an emergency expects the hospital to assume the same obligations for his care a physician would. When the hospital assigns a physician, technician, or nurse, it carries out its moral obligations through them, but it is not absolved of responsibility for how these obligations are fulfilled. When physicians are full-time employees of the hospital, the corporate obligation of the hospital is even more direct.

An even more fundamental and demanding source for the hospital's moral obligations is the special vulnerability of the person who is ill. The fact of illness is an insult to those aspects of existence most integral to being human. The patient is deprived in varying degrees of his humanity: his body is no longer the ready instrument of his will; he lacks the knowledge and skill to repair it or to make free and rational choices; he must place himself in the power of others. In short, illness deprives the patient of his distinctly human freedoms: to act, to make his own decisions, to be independent of the powers of others. The integrity of the patient's self-image as a human is shattered or, at the very least, threatened.

This state of vulnerability and injured humanity of the patient is one of grave inequality. All the power rests with those who have made the declaration that they will assist—the physician and the hospital. Even the most highly educated, powerful, or wealthy patient becomes a petitioner. Healing cannot be humane unless it does everything possible to restore these impaired freedoms, in a sense restoring the patient's humanity along with relieving him of pain, disability, or disease.

It is clear from the foregoing that hospitals as well as physicians incur serious moral obligations by the special nature of the fact of illness and the profession they voluntarily make to heal and assist. The central moral obligation is to make that profession fully authentic by fulfilling the expectations implicit in a relationship of such great inequality as exists between the helper and the one to be helped. A little closer look at the nature of the obligations themselves is now in order.

THE NATURE OF INSTITUTIONAL OBLIGATIONS

We have space to illustrate only a few of the specific obligations which flow from the special relationship between patients and those who profess to heal. Some have been touched upon already.

First, it seems clear that the institutionalization of so many aspects of medicine increasingly demands a moral relationship between the patient and the hospital which can be very similar to the patient/physician relationship. This means a great deal more than simply providing the setting in which medicine can be practiced safely and competently, as well as assuring its managerial efficiency and fiscal integrity, although the latter too are obligations. What is called for is a sharing of the same range of ethical responsibilities which have traditionally been implicit in the relationships between physician and patient. The board of trustees must feel moral as well as legal responsibility for the actions of the professional and nonprofessional workers within the hospital walls. This responsibility, even in presumably professional matters, cannot be delegated. Institutional morality, by necessity, must concern itself with every facet of the corporate life of that institution.

The result should be an overlapping and sharing of moral obligations in which the professional and the institution check and balance each other more intimately than is now customary. On this view, I take some exception to Professor Charles Fried's recent analysis of the partitioning of responsibilities between physicians and hospital authorities (1, 2). He assigns the hospital directors the bureaucratic decisions—those affecting efficiency, equity, and allocation of resources—and excuses them from responsibility for the personal dimensions of care given. These latter he assigns wholly to the physician, excusing him from concern with allocational decisions and suggesting that he must work within the framework of efficiency/equity decisions made by administrators or government.

Fried's division of responsibilities is reasonable so far as primary operational emphases are concerned. But these domains must not be compartmentalized; they must always be in dynamic equilibrium with each other. On the theses I am suggesting here, physicians and hospital directors are morally bound to see that their areas of primary responsibility do, in fact, interact. Each must fulfill the ethical obligation for the whole of what patients have a right to expect.

This mutuality of moral obligation becomes even more impelling in remediation of the injured humanity of the patient which illness entails. Both physician and hospital must reduce the inequalities in the relationship as well as the situation allows. The patient must be provided the knowledge necessary to participate rationally in the decisions which affect him. He must know what is wrong, what can be done, what the chances are for success, the dangers of treatment, the alternative procedures. The physician and the hospital share this obligation to enable the patient to make as free and rational a choice as possible. The obligation goes well beyond the mere legal requirement for valid consent. It demands consent of the highest quality and fullest sense of self-determination by the patient. The right to refuse specific treatment must be protected as well. The physician, the patient, and the hospital share obligations to each other, but because of the patient's vulnerability his needs are foremost.

This particular obligation assumes exquisite significance when a decision involves a moral question—a situation increasingly more pertinent as the capabilities of medicine expand the ways human life can be altered, shortened, or extended by technologic means. The questions in this realm are already matters of widespread public debate: abortion, continuing or discontinuing life-support measures, treatment or nontreatment of terminal or seemingly hopeless patients, participation in experimentation, and the like. The choices involve an intersection of the patient's values and those of the physician and the institution. Respect for the patient and humane treatment demand that these values be respected and that the patient be given the opportunity to act as his own moral agent if he wishes.

There are clear indications that more and more patients will wish to be their own moral agents and not delegate this agency to physicians as in the past. We live in a democratic society in which there is no uniformity of opinion on most medico-moral issues and no recognized authority to settle differences in ethical beliefs. There is also a growing tendency to distrust experts and institutions. The traditional moral authority of the physician has already been substantially eroded. Under these circumstances, the moral responsibility of hospitals, like that of the physician, must be to make its values clear so the patient can make his own choice among institutions. We can foresee a time, not too far distant, when hospitals will have to declare their positions on the major medico-moral questions for the patient's guidance. Catholic hospitals have customarily done so on certain specific procedures.

There is room for considerable variation in ethical practices among hospitals. A democratic society should offer each patient the possibility of care in institutions that declare the same moral values he holds. This right can be actualized only if boards of trustees are willing to state clearly, in more specific terms than is now the case the ethical principles to which they subscribe.

The immediacy of this issue is underscored by the excellent study by Diana Crane of the decisions physicians actually make in the care of the critically ill (3). She shows considerable disparity between the official medical position, that treatment be continued until the patient is physiologically dead, and actual practice, wherein treatment is discontinued in those patients for whom the possibility of meaningful social interactions is nonexistent. Patients and their families should know of this disparity. Hospitals have an obligation to see that clear guidelines for terminating support measures be developed and monitored. Here again we see the dynamics of interaction on a moral issue between the physician and the institution.

Katz and Capron, in their book, have carefully studied the decision-making process in catastrophic illness. They outline the professional and institutional interactions necessary to assure that decisions are made rationally, equitably, and responsively (4). Hospitals have the moral responsibility to provide these safeguards before they become matters of law.

What I am suggesting is that most decisions in a hospital are decisions in which technological and value choices are intermingled. Our society has developed a deep concern, not without foundation, that in deferring to the expert in technical matters it has lost control of the values and purposes of that technology. We need ways to control technology democratically, as Arthur Kantrowitz suggested recently (5). He called for the separation of the technical from the value components in the uses of technology, the delegation of decisions on mixed decisions to judges who are not advocates of science, and, finally, wider publication of the deliberations and decisions of judges and advocates.

Some parallel system is needed in hospitals and in society to distinguish between the professional medical advocacy for introduction and use of high technology and the social values of its employment. Institutional morality, if it is to be exercised fully, must grapple with such sensitive and even dangerous issues. Institutions are not immune to irrationality, the abuse of power, or the usurpation of morals.

An analysis of the obligations of professionals and hospitals indicates the need for a new balance between their roles as moral agents. Neither institutional nor individual professional ethics is sufficient for safeguarding the humanity of patients. Heretofore, professional ethics has been the dominant and even the sole influence. We are now entering a new era in which three-way interaction between the moral agencies of physicians, hospitals, and patients is necessary.

UNANSWERED QUESTIONS WITH PRACTICAL IMPLICATIONS

Many practical questions remain. How does the hospital balance its moral obligations to individuals who work for and with it and its obligations to those it serves, including the community as a whole? How are obligations defined and deployed among professionals, nonprofessionals, and administrators? What mechanisms can be designed to implement the hospital's moral agency? What is the best way to allocate moral responsibility in team care? The team is, after all, a transitory, mini-social system operating within the hospital. It illustrates in microcosm the difficulties of the ethics of group actions. How are conflicts of values and principles among individuals in the institution resolved? To what extent and to what degree of specificity should the institution declare the values it subscribes to? How are the legal and ethical values of everyday decisions reconciled with each other? Law may lag behind ethics in some instances. Can an institution take a stance which society has not yet sanctioned in law?

These and related questions constitute the domain of institutional ethics. They will, I feel sure, be subjected to deeper and more critical analysis in the years ahead. The field of ethics as it applies to humans acting in concert is in need of a sound theoretical base before practical steps can be rationally justified. But the issues are sufficiently urgent to require tentative actions even before a substantial body of theory can be elaborated. Hospital administrators and trustees are already engaging in some of these issues. Some collaboration between ethical theorists and health-care practitioners is essential if the principles developed in this special domain of social ethics are to be practicable as well as theoretically sound.

Even while these fundamental explorations are being conducted, there is immediate need for a more open discussion of the issues of institutional morality among physicians, other health workers, and trustees. These are delicate issues of the kind generally eschewed in our society. The adherents of the intuitionist or skeptical views of ethics will deny the utility of such discussions. Others will shy away from the personal and sometimes emotional tone of ethical discourse. Some authorities even feel that the "tragic decisions" we must make in hospitals should not be the subject of public debate.

In my view, there is no alternative to a more concrete development of the issues in institutional morality at this time in our history. Everywhere there is a rebirth of interest in questions of value and purpose. This is particularly exemplified in medical affairs where the issues of biomedical and professional ethics are receiving unprecedented attention. I have called elsewhere for an expansion of medical ethics beyond its traditional boundaries to incorporate obligations of a new kind (6). If this scrutiny is happening in professional medical ethics, can we realistically postpone consideration of the new relationships between institutional, professional, and personal ethics?

Moreover, as Professor Renee Fox has pointed out, the new interest in ethical issues in medicine is simply an expression of a deeper concern in America with the values, meanings, and purposes of life and institutions in general (7). I believe Dr. Fox is right. The assumption of a more explicit role of moral agency by hospitals is entirely consistent with this trend. I believe further that the hospital is a natural place to raise these questions because of the special sensitivity of its mission in society, one inextricably bound with the most human of needs.

Rather than shying away from the undeniable challenges of moral

151

agencies, hospitals can show the way toward a clearer conception of institutional morality. The main tasks of American medicine's third century are not managerial, fiscal, or technological, though such things pressure us daily. They are unequivocally moral and spiritual. The nation must rebuild that sense of moral purpose in the probity of human enterprises without which much of human activity becomes meaningless.

I do not mean to sermonize. But our nation will regain a sense of its worth only if its institutions exhibit the courage to pursue higher ideals than can be accomplished in a lifetime. People are less disappointed with high ideals sincerely enunciated and imperfectly attained than with their abnegation out of cynical or practical motives.

A simple, sincere, voluntary, and expeditious show of concern for moral issues untainted with self-interest must begin in some institutions. Are American hospitals ready for this challenge in their third century?

Part III
Humanistic Medical Education

CHAPTER TEN

Educating the Humanist Physician

We must understand what man is, for he is the subject mat-
ter of the science of medicine for whom it is promulgated.
To understand him is to understand the world, for he is
similar to the world in his construction. He is the micro-
cosm, the macrocosm in miniature.

The Caraka Samhita (1)

T he assertion that physicians are no longer humanists and that
medicine is no longer a learned profession is painful to hear
because there is some truth in it. Moreover, it comes from those
who experience our behavior—our students and our patients.
And, in truth, our art is indeed in danger of being engulfed by its
technological apparatus. But, most painful of all, the assertion
strikes at the reality which alone gives authenticity to our profession
—our unique charge to answer the appeal of a sick and anxious
person for help that is both competent and considerate.

The criticism is especially poignant for medical educators, at
whose door much of the responsibility is laid. We are told that we
neglect the teaching of human values and the *art* of medicine, that
in our zeal for science we ignore liberal studies, and, most telling of
all, that the patient care we provide in our teaching hospitals and
clinics is itself dehumanizing.

Even our friendlier critics are alarmed by the recent trend to
shorten medical education. They fear that our haste will further
erode the liberal education of future physicians and thus accentuate the dehumanization of the student and the depersonalization of
the patient. These anxieties reach crucial dimensions when viewed
against the context of the erosion of personal elements inherent in
medicine's increasing institutionalization and specialization.

Based on an article which appeared under the same title in *Journal of the Ameri-*
can Medical Association, 277:1288–94 (March 1974). Copyright 1974, American
Medical Association.

The terms *humanism, compassion,* and *liberal education* are all easily employed to advance one's own political, social, or educational ideologies. Without some clear display of the anatomy of these concepts, physicians will only respond with defensive denial, while their critics will yield to enraptured denunciations. As always, the patient will be victimized by this exchange of diatribes, rebuttals, and contumely. Worst of all, we will miss the opportunity to reexamine these terms and redefine them in their contemporary setting.

There is indeed a genuine and urgent dilemma. Society has the right to require that physicians be competent, that they practice with consideration for the integrity of the person, and that some of them also be educated men who can place medicine in its proper relationship to culture and society.

Medicine enjoys a unique position among disciplines as a humane science whose technology must ever be person-oriented. Its practitioners are therefore under an extraordinary mandate to live and work within a humanistic frame. What does it mean to educate a humanist physician in contemporary society?

The term *humanist* is too often appended to the term *physician* in an intuitive and altogether imprecise fashion. I shall suggest that the ideal encompasses two essential but distinct sets of components —one affective and one cognitive. These differ markedly in content; the one does not guarantee the other. In the best examples they are complementary, but they may also be in conflict. Each requires a different mode of learning and teaching.

The failure to make these distinctions leads to pretension, on the one hand, or unfilled expectations, on the other. In either case, the concept loses credibility and this must be prevented in our times, when medicine faces unprecedented demands upon all its humane components.

Two concepts of the idea of humanism were recognized by Aulus Gellius, the second century grammarian, when he spoke of the meaning of the word *humanitas,* from which *humanism* was later derived. He distinguished *humanitas*—education and training in the "good" arts—from a "good" feeling toward all men. *Humanitas* is more properly subsumed under the Greek term *paideia*—an educational and cognitive ideal; and the "good" feeling—what we would call compassion—is more akin to the Greek concept of *philanthropia* (2).

Following Aulus Gellius, we can discern the same two ideals when embodied in the term *humanism in medicine*. One, the cognitive, deals with the physician as a man, a cultural being possessing ideas, values, modes of expression in word and art. The other, the affective, concerns the feeling of the physician for the person-as-patient experiencing the existential trials of illness. Together, these ideals enable the physician to understand his science and also to identify with the humanity of those he serves.

These two ideals must further be built upon a firm basis of technical competence. Without clinical craftsmanship, the physician-humanist is without authenticity. Incompetence is inhumane because it betrays the trust the patient places in the physician's capacity to help and not to harm. Throughout this essay, we shall assume that education in clinical competence always proceeds, *pari passu*, with the affective and cognitive elements of humanism, which shall be our major concern.

The Compleat Physician is one who is capable in all three dimensions: he is a competent practitioner; he is compassionate; and he is an educated man. To use the classical terminology, he combines *techné* with *philanthropia* and *paideia*. Few men can perform with perfection, or even adequately, at all three levels. We must repress the tendency to apotheosize our profession by expecting all physicians to excel in all three. No educational formula, ancient or modern, can make of everyone who studies medicine the Renaissance man or polymath some vainly hope for (3). A more realistic educational goal is to open the possibility for all students and practitioners to live in some measure at each of these three levels. Competence and compassion are clearly requisites for each physician if he is to meet his social responsibilities adequately. The extent to which he must also be an educated man is more variable and less intimately related to his social utility.

THE AFFECTIVE COMPONENTS

Compassion: Its Meaning and Erosion.   Of the two components of humanism, the affective is more frequently mentioned by today's critics of medicine. They decry the lack of compassion they perceive in the case of patients. Compassion is most often equated with humaneness and even with *humanism*. What do we mean by compassion as an affective attribute of the humanist physician?

157

"Com-passion" means co-suffering, the capacity and the willing-ness of the physician somehow to share in the pain and anguish of those who seek help from him. It connotes some understanding of what sickness means to another person, together with a readiness to help and to see the situation as the patient does. Compassion de-mands that the physician be so disposed that his every action and word will be rooted in respect for the person he is serving. Compas-sion is reflected in a disposition to "feel" along with the patient. When genuine, compassion is unmistakably sensed by the patient; it can-not be feigned. It is not to be confused with pity, condescension, or paternalism. Clearly, compassion is an affective and behavioral characteristic that bears little relation to a cognitive appreciation of any of the humanities. Nor is compassion altogether synonymous with the political or activist bias of many students and young phy-sicians, however well motivated they may be, to help the socially and economically disenfranchised members of society.

Potent influences in modern medicine and society now conspire to erode and even extinguish compassion. Among the most influential are: the fascination with technology, gadgets, and instruments; the inherent depersonalizing influences of our highly institutionalized social structures; the replacement of care by individuals with care by the "team"; scientific medical education that focuses on man-the-object-of-study; and, finally, a medical education, fraught with rigidities, that does little to help the student develop his own humanity.

Can the affective components of humanism—the *philanthropia* of Gellius—be assured in the education of physicians? Formal edu-cation would appear to be of limited value because humaneness and compassion are not disciplines to be learned in classrooms. The study of man, even of his affective and behavioral compo-nents, must in some sense make him an object and distort him. This is true even of those disciplines, like the social sciences and the hu-manities, that look at the conscious and imaginative dimensions of man's existence. Study may help the student to understand human-ity abstractly, but it will not help him to behave compassionately. We must remember with Jung that "the patient is there to be treated and not to verify a theory" (4).

Compassion in the Student-Teacher Relationship.   Before the stu-dent can begin to feel the plight of his patient as a person seeking help, he must develop a fuller insight into his own developing humanity. The affective education of the student starts with the means most significant for him—the humanization of his medical experience. By dealing in a personalized and compassionate way with the special circumstances into which a medical education places young people, the teacher may forestall that subtle erosion of sensitivities which is a genuine danger of too much immersion in the study of man as an object of science.

The student-teacher relationship has many similarities to the patient-physician relationship. In both circumstances, one person is seeking help from another, who presumably is wiser and has power over the petitioner. Both student and patient must face personal challenges in emotionally trying situations. When the teacher helps the student in a compassionate and understanding way, he illustrates how the student can in turn give the same understanding to the patient, who is dependent upon his humaneness as the student is dependent upon the teacher's.

The rigidity of current curricula and testing methods, as well as the trial-by-ordeal proclivities of some faculty members, are perceived by many students as "dehumanizing." This experience erodes their own capacities for humane relationships with patients. Granting a certain inevitable hyperbole in such assertions, the only effective way to inculcate compassion is to practice it. In each of their contacts with students, patients, and even with experimental animals, the faculty must exhibit genuine care. The clinician-teacher has truly awesome responsibilities here. One careless action at the bedside will undo hours of lecturing about the dignity of patients. Conversely, one act of kindness and consideration will make compassion a reality and an authentic experience. Student disaffection is often a masked appeal for models they can sincerely imitate.

There are some obvious critical incidents in the life of a medical student that can have a profound effect on his emotional maturation. The way the faculty handles his responses to these experiences may determine whether or not the student later approaches his own patients humanely. Some of the nodal points at which a student may need help in dealing with his own feelings are: the first encounter with the cadaver or with the hopelessly ill or dying patient, the death of "his own" first patient, identifying with young patients who are seriously ill or disabled, trying to help patients seeking assistance in the vast, impersonalized, hurried, and often physically depressing surroundings prevalent in too many large teaching hospitals.

Opportunities must be provided for students to express their feelings of conflict and anxiety with many of these potentially shattering experiences. Some personal adaptation must be effected that avoids rejection of self or profession, or hasty acceptance of the inevitability of an impersonal attitude. A judicious and interested faculty can encourage students to persist in gaining competence while simultaneously working to make the care of patients more humane. Even the well-intentioned student may be tempted to subvert the effort required to attain competence by self-righteous attacks on the "system" and the human failings of the clinical faculty.

Compassion and the Patient.   Humaneness and compassion in dealing with patients is not easily measurable. Yet, there are some rather simple behavioral criteria that can be monitored specifically as a beginning effort to see whether the rudiments of humaneness and consideration are being exhibited. Clinical faculty and students might repeatedly ask themselves a series of very simple questions about every patient-physician encounter.

First, do we teach students to satisfy the fundamental questions every patient will want answered? The patient wants to know: What's wrong? How did he get that way? Is it serious? Can you cure it? What will it cost in money and loss of dignity? What are you going to do? Will it hurt? These are simple questions. But to an alarming degree, patients see many doctors, have many tests, pay many bills, but do not receive answers to these simple questions.

The issuance of a diagnosis and a standardized explanation may be convenient and time-saving for the physician, yet, this can be the first step in making the patient an object and not a person. Each patient wants answers to all these questions put into the context of *his* life. This is more than individual treatment, which merely means treatment as one unit. Personal treatment, instead, gets at the uniqueness of the person who is the unit. Or, as Thomas Merton said so sagely, "The person must be rescued from the individual" (5). Physicians who have neither time nor inclination for this degree of personalization are bound by the first rule of humaneness to see that other members of the health-care team are permitted to answer the personal questions that lie at the root of the patient's plea for help.

Second, can we accept the patient for what he is and not what we think he should be? The German novelist Hermann Hesse puts it well: "No man has ever been entirely and completely himself. Yet each one strives to become that—one in an awkward, the other in an intelligent way" (6). To be compassionate, we must accept the strivings of all persons—the ignorant and the intelligent, the successful, the failure, the poor, the wise, the weak, the strong, and even the evil. All must receive our expression of willingness to help. This is impossible unless we continue to grow as persons ourselves. "If the doctor wants to help a human being, he must be able to accept him as he is. And he can do this in reality only when he has already seen and accepted himself as he is" (7). We can never *feel* with another person when we pass judgment as a superior, only when we see our own frailties as well as his.

Third, do we handle our authority in a humane way that respects the life values of the patient? The health professional is always in danger of extending his authority in technical matters over the patient's system of beliefs and values. Dag Hammarskjöld articulated the unique responsibility of those in authority thus: "Your position never gives you the right to command. It only imposes on you the duty of so living your life that others can receive your orders without being humiliated" (8). This is sound advice to which we must attend whether we deal with patients, or students, or our professional colleagues. It has an important corollary: we must not "put down" the patient when he detects our uncertainties and even our errors. To be humane, we must ever be ready, as Galileo said, "to pronounce that wise, ingenious, and modest statement—'I do not know.'"

Compassion, practiced in these terms in each individual patient transaction, is the irreducible base for mitigating the inherent dehumanizing tendencies of today's highly institutionalized and technologically oriented patterns of patient care. The student's distress with deficiencies in our present system is meaningless unless he realizes he can remedy them by humanizing his own relationships with the patients he is privileged to examine and help.

Compassion and "Humanistic" Psychology.   Recently, a variety of means derived from "humanistic" psychology have been introduced to improve the experiential-affective elements of learning. Carl Rogers has called for the use of the encounter group involving faculty and students in an attempt to forge a better unity between cognitive and affective learning. He has urged a reappraisal of all education from this point of view and has already initiated a series of encounter sessions for medical educators for this purpose (9). Other measures, like psychodrama and psychosynthesis, are sure to be explored in an effort to remedy the defects in affective learning among medical faculty, students, and practitioners.

The success of such measures will be difficult to evaluate. For some, the measures will no doubt leave a lasting impression. Others will reject them. For many, a transient experience of limited value will probably occur. We must avoid the conclusion that the only way to learn the affective components of humane medicine lies in any particular psychological mode. There is as much danger in medical education of psychologic overkill as there is of scientific overkill. We cannot ignore the capacity of at least some students to become empathetic, humane, and sensitive practitioners without necessarily dissecting their emotional lives to this fine degree.

Little of a lasting nature will be achieved until the affective components in the student's learning become the conscious concern of the majority of clinical teachers. To limit this concern, and the teaching that goes with it, to those whose specialties are in psychology or the behavioral sciences is to create a pedagogic ghetto that many students and faculty will eschew.

Before they can be evaluated properly, the newer psychologic techniques must be continuing experiences for teachers and students in their own institutions. One possible achievement is a reduction in the emotional overtones that seriously impede discussions of even the cognitive elements in medical education. If encounter sessions encourage a more reasonable dialogue in the cognitive domain, they will be well worth the effort.

Affective experiences and behavioral enhancements of humane attitudes by newer psychological techniques are promising. But the affective elements in the patient-physician transaction must also be studied in an intellectually rigorous fashion. The Spanish medical philosopher Pedro Lain-Entralgo has undertaken a comprehensive analysis of this subject (10). His work is an excellent starting point for those who wish to approach the subject cognitively. Ideally, the affective training of both student and teacher should be united with the cognitive examination of the affective components in the personal relationships of patient and physician, student and teacher, and student and patient.

THE COGNITIVE COMPONENTS

The Domain of Liberal Studies.   Medical students today are, commendably, most concerned with the affective components. They exalt them perhaps too readily over the cognitive in their zeal to remedy some of the more obvious depersonalizing tendencies in medical education and practice. In the past, we have run the danger of suppressing the human values in medicine by an overadulation of its rational and scientific elements. We will not serve mankind any the better if we now yield to the dominance of romanticism, intuition, and introspection propounded by some under the heading of medical humanism.

As a cognitive entity, *humanism* has a complex history, which Kristeller and others have attempted to clarify. It originated in the nineteenth century with Niethammer as *humanismus* (11), an ideal of the classical and liberal forms of education to be set against the vocational and scientific then gaining ground in education. *Humanism* itself derives from the word *umanista* used in the Italian universities of the Renaissance to designate the teachers of the humanities—those studies included in the *studia humanitatis*, the language and literature of Rome and, to a lesser extent, of Greece.

In this older sense, humanism is a literary and educational ideal, one which has lost much ground in today's universities. But almost from the outset, the term became identified with certain values that set man as a central focus of concern—belief in the dignity and worth of the person, the democratic process, and human rationality. These values, as Edel has emphasized, are not a philosophical system *sui generis*, but rather what he terms a "philosophical strain" or "a corrective process, the guardian of a human balance against seeing man as more than a man or less than a man" (12). This "strain" is expressed in an extreme form in the religion of man proposed by Auguste Comte. More commonly, it is a bias found in many philosophical systems. Thus, we can speak of Christian, Marxist, atheistic, or scientific humanisms. The humanist strain deals with values, and it is thus quite different in cognitive content from the more classical form of literary humanism.

Classical and Literary Humanism.   Let us first examine the cognitive elements in traditional or literary humanism. This ideal was best exemplified in the lives of such physician-scholars as Linacre, Caius, and their modern counterpart, Sir William Osler. Gilbert Murray said of Osler, in nominating him for the presidency of the Classical Association, that ". . . he stands for a type of culture which the Classical Association does not wish to see die out of this world—the culture of a man who, while devoting himself to his special science, keeps nevertheless a broad basis of interest in letters of all kinds" (13).

Osler is essentially the physician as educated man, combining superb clinical talents, scientific perspective, and human concern with the capability to excell in those skills that traditionally have been identified with a liberal education—the ability to think, write, and speak with clarity, taste, persuasiveness, and moral sensitivity. As Else has pointed out, language was the principal means through which these goals were attained (14). These were the skills which freed man, liberated him, and made him human.

The cognitive skills thus subsumed in this sense of humanism were those most uniquely belonging to man—the capacity to speak, write, reason, invent, create the beautiful, and judge it. Traditionally, they were taught by formal study of the disciplines of languages, literature, history, and philosophy, and especially as exemplified in the writings of the Roman and Greek classics.

Education of this type is no longer a common denominator for professional people. Indeed, it is regarded by some as elitist and even antithetical to the major social responsibilities of physicians. It is, moreover, an education increasingly difficult to obtain by reason of today's "crisis" in the humanities. This crisis is the culmination of several factors: a decline in the teaching of the classical languages in which literary humanism is based, transformation of the humanities into technical specialties, and a decided shift in cultural ambience toward the nonliterary and more intuitive modes of communication and expression.

Genuine literary humanism has always been a rare accomplishment for physicians as for other men. Some medical educators and practitioners still persist in the hope that some formula can be found that will enable us to produce physicians who are educated men in this sense and that this is essential if medicine is to be "humanized." The cognitive elements of classical humanism are undeniably important for physicians as professionals, and even more so if physicians are to transcend the confines of even so broad a discipline as medicine. It is as Berenson said of the Italian painters of the Renaissance, "Painting therefore offers but a partial and not always the most adequate manifestation of their personality, and we feel the artist as greater than his work, and the man as soaring above the artist" (15). The cognitive elements in literary humanism can enable the physician to "soar above" his profession.

Humanities in Medicine—Approach for Today. We cannot permit the possibility of contact with traditional humanism to decay completely. Too much of man's capacity for a life of satisfaction is contained within it. We owe every student at least the opportunity for contact with liberal studies at some point in his education. But today we are required to offer this opportunity in a variety of ways not limited to the premedical years.

Some few students will continue to follow the pattern of a professional education built on a base in the liberal arts. For the majority, the most effective teaching of humanistic studies will occur within the context of medical education itself. Here, the student's motivation and goal directedness will help to focus the cognitive features of the humanities. The medical context is rich in possibilities for explicating the essential cognitive skills unique to humane and liberal studies. The pedagogic aim in the predegree years is to uncover the student's interest in these skills and, in the years of continuing education, to reinforce them in his own experiences as a person dealing with other persons in the medical transaction. This mode of teaching the cognitive components of humanism will require special adaptations of *what* is to be taught, *how* it is taught, and *who* teaches it.

First, what is to be learned? There is no one discipline or combination of disciplines that will assure acquisition of the requisite intellectual skills. Instead, what we must seek is to inculcate that knowledge an educated man must have to distinguish him from his colleagues who are merely competent. Professor Wayne Booth succinctly summarizes these skills as learning how to think critically for ourselves, how to experience beauty for ourselves, and to make our own choices among possible actions (16). These are the skills that make a man free—the "liberal arts." If he possesses them, he is no longer subservient to the thoughts, actions, or esthetics of those

165

who can examine these matters critically. Neither the sciences nor the humanities can encompass these skills entirely. Each can contribute to their development. The traditional emphasis on the literary content of the humanities must be expanded to include some of what the scientist now contributes to our cultural milieu.

Second, how shall these skills be taught? To be most effective with the goal-oriented medical student the cognitive skills should be taught within the framework of a medical education, indeed, as an integral part of that education. Medicine is admirably suited to this purpose. It abounds in experiential data about the human condition and illustrates easily the concrete importance of the cognitive skills of humanism in clinical decision making, the lack of which, in my opinion, is one of the major defects of clinical medicine today. Medicine is also the focal point for much of our most recent and important knowledge of man and his behavior.

Teaching in such a context necessarily proceeds from the concrete, personal, and immediate to the abstract, general, and more ultimate concerns of mankind. It requires use of the case method and seminar rather than the lecture and reading assignment. It centers on personal involvement by the student with the specific concerns of his patient and thus gains a relevance scarcely equaled in other types of teaching.

These teaching modes are quite unfamiliar to the usual teacher of the humanities, and this brings us to our last question: Who shall teach? Certain special characteristics are demanded of the teacher who essays to teach the cognitive skills of humanism in the medical setting. He must be an able and secure scholar in his own discipline; he must be committed to communicating that discipline to medical students and physicians; he must be willing to enter serious and continuing dialogue with the medical culture, while bringing his special viewpoint to bear on the phenomena of the medical experience.

Not many bona fide humanists are prepared for this sort of teaching. It is hoped that more of them will see challenges and benefits for their own studies in an intimate exchange with medicine. If current interest among medical educators grows, we will need to educate some humanists specifically for the engagement with medicine. There is some danger at present, as with any new field as yet unproven intellectually, that the field may fall to the willing and eager rather than to the most competent teachers.

Clearly, the cognitive components of traditional humanism embracing its literary elements and its intellectual attitudes are important in the education of the physician-humanist. To be effective and useful in today's university and with today's student requires a mode of teaching and a faculty with characteristics different from those that prevail in university departments of humanities at present (17, 18).

The Domain of Values.   Another domain of cognitive knowledge in the concept of the humanist-physician is the domain of values, as subjects for serious study in medical education. We cannot provide medical care within a humanist frame without knowledge of the intersections in values which occur at every stage of the medical transaction. The meanings of these intersections for the patient, the physician, and society bear directly on the outcome of medical management. Medical teaching now requires infusion of a perception of the value questions as a correlative device, much in the spirit of the humanistic strain alluded to by Edel (12).

At every step in the medical encounter, human values are set against each other: those of the patient with those of the physician; those of society with those of the individual; those of the physician as scientist and teacher with those of the physician as healer. Each person and each community is identified by commitment to a certain configuration of beliefs, choices, priorities about the things believed to be important. These values have meanings quite specific for each person and each community, and these meanings must be understood by anyone who presumes to treat either the person or the community.

Practitioners, students, and faculty members, therefore, need a formal knowledge of the meaning of values and the varieties of systems within which values are expressed. They need especially to understand the genesis of their own value systems and to recognize the gap that inevitably develops between the values of the professional and those of the society within which a profession may function.

Physicians do not reflect very often on the values peculiar to the process of professionalization through which they pass. Nor are they and their teachers sufficiently conscious of the imprint made by the prevailing mode of medical education and its traditional orientation on their own value systems. These values very soon become the prelogical foundations for the physician's behavior, for his normative ethics, and for his apodictic statements on what is good for the patient and society.

The significance of an orientation to values as subjects of more serious study and experience in medical education is very much heightened by the new problems of individual and social ethics derived from the enhanced capabilities of modern biomedical science (19). The physician's stance with reference to abortion, euthanasia, human experimentation, genetic manipulation, behavioral control, and a variety of other urgent and dramatic new issues in medical practice is based in a set of values whose foundations he rarely examines critically.

It is impossible to confront these and other new questions in the ethics of health care without a reconceptualization of the foundations of medical ethics. Such a restructuring of traditional normative and deontological ethics is dependent upon a reevaluation of the values upon which traditional contemporary ethics systems are based. Value questions underlie the legal, political, and social mechanisms for decision making in the public as well as the most private matters of medical and health care.

Medical axiology is an underdeveloped—indeed, almost non-existent—discipline at this time. It can be taught at several levels: at the fundamental level of value theory, then at the applied level of clinical decision making, and finally at the community level of public policy making. Integration of knowledge from a variety of disciplines is requisite if a true medical axiology is to emerge. Law, ethics, political science, philosophy, and social and cultural anthropology are intermingled in any critical inquiry into the value questions of health care.

"Medical" axiology, like "medical" philosophy, "medical" history, or "medical" sociology, demands an interdigitation of principles from the humanities and the social sciences with the concrete experiential data derived from specific clinical situations in which value questions influence the outcome for human beings seeking help. A whole new set of questions of very great human concern is emanating from the emerging dialogue between medicine and biology, on the one hand, and various of the humanities and social sciences, on the other.

These questions at the interzone between medicine and the other university disciplines have not been explored in depth. Yet, even at this early stage they must be taught and exemplified in medical education. The content and the methods requisite to teaching at the junctions of medicine, the humanities, and the social sciences are just beginning to receive explicit attention (20). No success-assured formula is available for wide application. The impatient student who hopes to humanize medicine overnight through some curricular thaumaturgy is sure to be disappointed.

In the immediate future, we face a tense period in our attempts to develop a more humanistic framework for medical education. Our knowledge of human values is rudimentary and needs deepening, but we also face the urgency and the high expectations of all who hope for elimination of deficiencies in our present modes of learning. Faculties in medicine and in the traditional disciplines must undergo significant attitudinal adjustments before these nascent studies can flourish. Concomitantly, they must also develop the intellectual rigor without which they cannot survive in the medical curriculum.

Nevertheless, the formal teaching of human values at all levels of medical education offers a sound mechanism for liberalizing and humanizing technical and professional learning. The study of values may well provide a more realistic and a more widely applicable avenue for liberal education for today's medical students than the cognitive elements of traditional or literary humanism. Without deprecating the latter, it seems more likely that the study of human values will open a more attractive road toward those attitudes of mind formerly associated with the best in traditional humanistic studies.

Learning the cognitive domain of human values will be totally ineffectual if not accompanied by affective learning and by explicit example in the behavior of the faculty, especially its clinical members. In the realm of values, the humanistic strain is attainable only where the patient is treated with full dignity as a person enabled to participate democratically in decisions that affect his being, and approached with tolerance for his fallibility and that of his physician.

THE IDEAL RESYNTHESIZED

To clarify the goals of his education, we have intentionally disassembled the ideal of the humanist-physician. This disassembly enables us to understand the spectrum of meanings within the ideal and to denote educational goals specifically designed to explicate each integral component of humanism. By so doing, we can avoid diffusing our educational goals over a vague territory more emotionally than rationally defined. More important, our dissection may perhaps permit a resynthesis of the ideal in terms more consistent with motivations of today's students and contemporary responsibilities of the profession.

The ideal humanist-physician would fuse all elements, the affective and the cognitive domains we have described, on a base of technical competence. Professional education, then, has as its goal the making of a competent clinical craftsman; affective learning has the goal of making a humane and compassionate practitioner; and the cognitive elements of humanism, modified in the two ways suggested, should make for an educated practitioner. These three levels in the life of the physician should reinforce each other. Very few persons will ever experience excellence in all dimensions, but recognition of the full expression of the ideal establishes a bench mark against which the degree of an individual's humanistic education can be assessed.

Medicine enjoys a special position among the disciplines. It centers on man in all his dimensions and shares some part of his reality with the humanities, the social sciences, and the experimental sciences. Pursued to its fullest expression, medicine can be truly humanizing, for its object of study and concern is Man.

John Ciardi's recent exposition of the concept of esthetic wisdom is apposite: "the sum total of all the great artist becomes in his life's exposure to his medium." "The artist's environment," he adds, "is not the world but the world as his medium reveals it" (21).

I would submit that medicine, like the arts, also provides a kind of human experience which makes it a special medium for revealing the world. It, too, can yield an esthetic wisdom of its own special object, man. Medicine taught within a humanistic framework prepares the student for its humane practice. Practice in a humanistic framework reveals even more about man the microcosm; and, as Caraka perceived, to understand man is to understand the world (1).

CHAPTER ELEVEN

The Ethics of Medical Education

Medical schools stand in a unique relationship to individuals and society, which imposes certain very special ethical obligations. They are the sole portals of entry into the profession and the sole instrumentality of society to assure an adequate supply of trained medical manpower. Simultaneously, medical schools are charged with the care, cultivation, and transmission of new and old medical knowledge. This essay in a preliminary way maps out the ethical issues derived from these special characteristics of medical schools in the contemporary world.

Despite the recent intense interest in bioethics and the ethics of medical practice, curiously little has been written about the ethics of medical education. To be sure, some probing and embarrassing questions were raised about the values and purposes of medical schools in the turbulence of the late sixties. Paticular attention was given to their responsibilities for minorities, for medical care to the poor, the quality of teaching, the presumed "dehumanizing" effects of the educational process, and even the relationships of medical schools to the drug industry or to the Vietnam War. But the climate of those days was openly and aggressively antirational, and the issues were submerged in polemicism, politics, and emotion. Analytic and formal assessments of the ethical dimensions of medical education were not possible.

In the seventies, medical educators have concentrated on reacting to the "revolutionary" thrust of the preceding years. The prevailing temper is one of quiet retreat to more traditional curricula and a more restrained definition of the scope of the medical school's responsibilities. Ethical questions about the educational process are only tangentially examined, although some form of teaching of med-

This chapter is based on an article that appeared under the title "Medical Education" in *Encyclopedia of Bioethics.* Copyright 1978 by Georgetown University, Washington, D.C. Used with permission of the Kennedy Institute, Georgetown University.

ical ethics has been adopted by the majority of medical schools (1).

Ethical questions once framed, however, have a disturbing tendency to recur. The audacious, though poorly articulated challenges of the last decade are still in need of critical examination. Indeed, the current social climate portends a renewed interest in questions of the value, purpose, and utility of all our social institutions. Medical schools cannot expect immunity from the emergent phenomenon of concern for accountability characterizing American society (2).

Clearly, the claims of medical schools for a special position in society must, in consequence, meet more explicit tests of ethical justification. What are the obligations of medical schools to the several communities they purport to serve: students, patients, and society at large? How do medical schools resolve the conflicts that arise in meeting the needs of each group? How do the obligations to students and society square with the obligation to preserve and advance medical knowledge? In whom are these obligations vested? To what extent are the actual values of medical educators congruent with the ethical obligations imposed by their special position in society?

Questions of this sort are only obliquely addressed in the vast literature on medical education. They are generally treated by exhortations to this or that practice, which is presumed to be "good" or "bad" for students, patients, or society. What is "good" is in turn grounded in suppositions more ideologically propounded than critically assessed. Only infrequently are there suggestions of a more ethical or philosophical foundation for the way medical schools function.

There are at present no rationally derived ethical norms against which existing values and practices can be examined. The ethics of medical education consists largely of homilies which parallel those in the Hippocratic Corpus defining the relationships between student and teacher. Inspiring and valuable as such homilies have been, they are inadequate in confronting all the complex problems of contemporary medical education. The ethics of medical education, like the ethics of medicine itself, requires extension beyond the rudimentary propositions scattered in the Hippocratic texts (3, 4).

Unexamined value systems are as customary in medical education as in other forms of human endeavor. One task of ethical discourse about medical education is to uncover these value systems and clarify their relationship to the obligations which inhere in the special position of medical schools in society. What are the potential or actual conflicts between ethical obligations to each of the constituencies served and the *de facto* beliefs of medical schools about what is "good" for these constituencies? Normative and descriptive considerations are inextricably intertwined here. They must, in part, be dissected free of each other, since *de facto* values may differ considerably from those derived through ethical analysis.

This inquiry must touch on a branch of social ethics only incompletely developed, namely, the ethics of corporate enterprises. When any organized group of humans assumes a common responsibility, in whom do the ethical obligations reside? Patently, faculty, students, and patients have certain responsibilities to each other as persons. But the obligations of institutions like medical schools are fulfilled through the corporate actions of boards, committees, faculties, administration, and the policies they create.

Institutions, therefore, act as moral agents, and hence certain normative principles must govern that agency. A fuller and deeper accounting of the ethics of medical education is impossible without a better understanding of those principles. Manifestly, it is inappropriate to develop the more general principles of the ethics of institutions here. Nevertheless, some reference to institutions as moral agents is unavoidable.

In this respect, it is important to note also that this discussion is being limited to medical schools. However, similar considerations pertain to education for the other health professions; they pertain also to a certain extent to all educational institutions, whether professionally oriented or not. And we must remember that the medical school is usually part of a multi-school, academic health center, which in turn is part of a university. These higher levels of organization share in the obligations of the medical school and, indeed, are responsible for some accounting of how it performs as moral agent.

THE MEDICAL SCHOOL: A MULTI-PURPOSE SOCIAL ORGANISM

The social and ethical obligations of institutions are derived ultimately from two sources: (a) the purposes for which men establish and support them, and (b) the extent to which they claim to serve these purposes. These are the bench marks against which we can assess their ethical authenticity. The ethical quality of an institutional or individual action depends upon the interaction between the expectations engendered by the nature of the institution and its expressions of willingness to meet those expectations.

In this regard, a commercial venture is a single-purpose institution whose ultimate, avowed, and expected goal is to make profits by providing services people are free to purchase or not. It pursues this goal according to the rules of a competitive and free economy. It is ethically constrained only by the ordinary obligations to persons accorded by law or common social consent. Although we speak of "ethical" manufacturers, the public still recognizes the primacy of profits as their goal.

When the services provided are as essential to human welfare as power, transportation, or communications, the profit goal is modulated by government regulation. Public utilities and quasi-public utilities operate under constraints because we are not entirely free to refuse their services.

A medical school, like a university or a church, is a very different kind of organization. It is a multi-purpose enterprise, whose several products are difficult to measure but are essential to human welfare. Profit is not an avowed or expected goal; the rules of the free-market economy do not apply. A monopoly exists because entrance to the profession is possible only under medical school aegis. The school is the only place where the esoteric knowledge needed to practice can be reliably transmitted, and it is a necessary gateway to licensure. Medical schools are also uniquely fitted to advance clinical knowledge.

This powerful position is tightly bound within a matrix of professional values that shapes goals and priorities. Through medical schools, the profession influences the numbers of those who may be trained, what they shall study, and the patterns of practice they learn. Freidson has pointed out that medicine is a "dominant" profession: it is virtually the sole determinant of what constitutes health and disease, it controls access to health-care services and the allocation of resources, and it directs the work of other health professionals (5).

Medical schools, and through them the profession, have *de facto* exclusive control over manpower production and the knowledge and skills that manpower needs to practice modern medicine. Simultaneously, medical schools affirm that they exist for the benefit of society. This combination of power and affirmation imposes certain very clear obligations, which society is justified in expecting.

At a minimum, the medical schools' ethical obligations which flow from the special confluence of powers that society vests in them would be: (a) to assure a continuous supply of medical manpower, adjusted in number and kind to the perceived and anticipated medical and health needs of the nation; (b) to provide equity of access to applicants from all segments of society for the available entering places; (c) to assure that medical manpower is competently and safely trained and that those who lack integrity will not be granted a medical degree; and (d) to preserve, validate, and transmit existing medical knowledge and generate a continuous supply of new knowledge.

Medical schools are supported by society because men are subject to ill health which can be cured or alleviated by the utilization of special knowledge not freely accessible to all men. Medical schools have sole trusteeship for both the manpower and the knowledge requisite for meeting this basic human need, and therefore they are morally bound to at least these four minimal requirements. Although I cannot discuss these in depth, my illustrative comments on each of these obligations are useful in adumbrating the sorts of issues which might be subsumed under this rubric.

The Supply of Medical Manpower.   The specific determination of how well manpower needs and supply are matched must, in my view, result from interaction between what the public deems to be in its interest and what educators define that interest to be. In the past, that interaction has been one-sided: medical schools determining what was "good" for society, and the public passively accepting that determination. The current disparity between the needs for generalists and their supply, as well as the paucity of manpower working in the neglected fields of primary, chronic, and preventive care, is an indicator of past dominance of medical over public value systems.

In recent years, federal and state legislation has been invoked to redress some of these imbalances. Should the public be forced to seek through law what appears to be an ethical responsibility growing out of the social functions of a medical school? A genuine sensitivity to its ethical obligations would require that a medical school undertake a continuous and responsive balancing between the kinds of physicians produced and the health needs of the society which supplies medical education. To be valid, the claim of the educational enterprise to serve public interest must be modulated by genuine dialogue with those outside the profession.

Does this mean that all medical schools should direct all their efforts to producing primary care physicians? Or, should schools vacillate with every change of public fashion in medical care at the expense of all other considerations—research or quality of education, for example? This sort of *reductio ad absurdum* is no more correct morally than is ignoring the issues completely. Medical schools have an equal obligation to contravene actions which might imperil the public health, directly or indirectly. The important point is: medical schools rarely have reflected on the ethical requirements of their special position as regulators of the flow of physician manpower. The laissez faire view of the past is no more justifiable that a complete capitulation to public pressures.

What is needed is a more effective, active interaction between medical educators and those who presume to speak in the "public" interest. Only in this way can the troublesome distinctions between needs, demands, wants, and whims be resolved. The dominance of either professional or public interests is open to serious question in a democratic society.

There are also limits to the obligations which can be reasonably imposed on medical schools in this regard. For example, there is no necessary connection between their special position in society and responsibility for distribution of medical manpower to underserved areas. This is a duty more properly assigned to licensing bodies, departments of health, or voluntary agencies. Medical schools have no prerogatives here, nor are any justifiable on the principle we have been explicating.

They have indirect responsibilities, to be sure. They must prepare a sufficient number of physicians of the kind needed by underserved populations; they should provide opportunities for students to experience those needs and the communities in which they arise; they should provide backup referral services, continuing education, and models to demonstrate how practice in such areas may be conducted efficiently and satisfyingly. These responsibilities are logical extrapolations of the principle of congruence between manpower production and manpower needs.

The optimum geographic distribution of physicians is, however, not a primary and direct ethical responsibility of medical schools. It is a duty which flows, rather, from the expectations society holds for other agencies charged with general regulatory functions. The unique position of a medical school does not extend this far. Physician distribution is a decision in the public realm to determine whether the right of professionals to choose where to practice takes precedence over the right of equity of access to medical and health services of the citizenry. Imposing this obligation on medical schools has no ethical foundation. It is an abnegation of responsibility by those public agencies charged with the establishment of priorities among the many good things a society wishes to have.

It is important that these obligations be distinguished from each other, for it is a fact that they can easily come into conflict. For example, legislative solutions have imposed on medical schools the teaching of family practice and the establishment of departments of family medicine. Under consideration in the legislatures are limitations on numbers and kinds of residents trained and a requirement that a certain percentage of entering students must be committed to practice in underserved areas. Educators protest that the principle of freedom of academic institutions to determine their curricula without outside interference must not be brooked. Legislators claim, to the contrary, the equity of access of all citizens to health and medical care has a higher priority than the principle of academic self-determination.

This conflict of obligations is among the more pressing problems awaiting a fuller analysis than is possible to note here of the sources and priorities of obligations of medical schools and of the regulatory agencies charged with the public welfare. The problem is an old one. There is ample warrant in the experience of other countries for the fears of political intrusion into the processes of education. But, there is also the undeniable fact that medical schools have been less than avid in their attention to the matter of congruence between manpower and social need.

Balancing the conflict between two good things like freedom of academic institutions and equity of access to health care for all is one of the most essential tasks of ethical discourse. It is hoped that a fuller analysis of the sources, content, and priority of obligations of medical schools will help to ground the discourse more rationally than heretofore possible. Where conflicts cannot be resolved

177

by ordering obligations in relationship to each other, political solutions inevitably supervene. In general, political answers to ethical dilemmas carry portents dangerous to a democratic society. Governments can too easily equate their own will with what is ethical, as history too abundantly demonstrates.

Equity of Access for Applicants.   As the sole channels to entry into the profession and its prerogatives, medical schools incur a second set of obligations. All who are qualified should have an equal access to entry; there can be little debate in principle on this point in our society. The grosser violations of this principle have been eliminated. The not-so-subtle ethnic "quotas" of years past have disappeared, though more subtle forms of discrimination persist sporadically.

One central ethical issue, however, is the admission of minorities, whose representation in the profession and in medical schools is drastically below their representation in our population. Although qualified minority candidates can readily gain admission, their percentage among medical students is still very low. Blacks, for example, made up 2.2 percent of the medical school population in 1968-69 and 6.3 percent in 1974-75. Latest figures indicate that inequitable distribution still exists. Because black physicians tend to practice among black people, it is clear that inequities in access to medical care will persist as long as the number of black students remains at the current low levels.

What should the criteria be for admission of minority students? Wellington studied the values used by the admission committee at one medical school which set out to admit one-fourth of its class from minority ranks. The criteria for selection appeared at first to be more personal than academic. But on closer analysis, Wellington concluded that "the committee continued to select from a limited pool of students with the highest academic records" (6). What are the ethical implications of goals or quotas? Should the values used in selection of one group be different from or the same as for others? How are conflicting claims of nonminority candidates balanced against the obvious social need for more minority physicians?

Two ethical principles seem to conflict: equity of access for all applicants and equity of access to medical care for all the people of this country. Which principle has priority? No answer is possible without first ordering our social and individual value systems in the light of current realities and past injustices.

As in the matter of the geographic distribution of physicians, we confront an intersection of several value systems requiring the most careful disentanglement. No matter how difficult the task has become, an ethical solution should be sought. Otherwise, more pragmatic solutions will be urged. Dr. Therman Evans, a black physician in Washington, proposes the establishment of eight predominantly black medical schools to redress the imbalance (7). Is this an optimal solution or simply a necessary effort to redress failure of the corporate ethical responsibility of all medical schools?

Assuring Competence and Integrity.   Society can rightfully expect that medical schools will not confer the medical degree on students who are incompetent or who have evidenced lack of integrity. This obligation is obvious when we contemplate the fact that only medical schools can provide the knowledge and experience needed to be a physician. Yet, the full ethical force of this obligation is infrequently invoked or implemented. The fact is that graduation from an American medical school is—as it should be—tantamount to licensure and therefore a guarantee of the right to practice. Medical schools owe society careful evaluation of the student's capacity to perform safely, competently, and with integrity.

Does the dominant pattern of clinical education allow for the close surveillance of students this ethical obligation implies? The closest and most continuous contact of students in the clinical years is with house staff rather than with the faculty. Although house staff may sometimes be harsher critics than faculty members, the possibility remains that they will more easily identify with students and will be more indulgent of their failings. Moreover, is it ethically sound to place the burden for such serious decisions on the youngest members of the teaching staff?

Few students are failed in the clinical years. Would not a little more reflection on the extent of this moral obligation to society result in a more conscious assessment of the clinical proficiency, judgment, and humaneness of medical students than is now the case? Some students, despite rigorous admission procedures, later reveal defects in character serious enough to disqualify them as practitioners. Do present methods of supervision detect these ade-

179

quately? What is the relation between questionable acts in medical school and later unethical behavior, or incompetent performance?

The ethical aspects of evaluation are more usually examined from the student's point of view—with particular attention to fairness, clarity of criteria, and a nonpunitive stance which emphasizes learning from one's errors. This is commendable and ethically sound when looked at in relationship to the school's duties to students (*vide infra*). But, can these values be reconciled with the equally weighty, perhaps greater, obligation to assure society that those upon whom the degree is conferred are indeed safe and honest practitioners? Again, the potential conflicts of opposing obligations require a more intensive inquiry into the ethical agency of medical schools than is currently available.

In this respect, another question must be posed: is it ethically sound to provide an education which exalts theoretical understanding at the expense of practical experiences? Only in the latter can the more subtle skills and attitudes be properly examined and lapses of integrity be properly uncovered. A medical school cannot excuse itself on the ground that these are matters for licensing agencies, professional societies, or specialty examining boards. These checkpoints may be too late: reluctance to take action about defects in competence, and especially in character, seems to increase each step along the way to final certification.

The want of fully reliable methodologies for evaluation and their subjective character make this a most exasperating and dangerous realm in which to make such serious judgments. The obligations of the medical school to provide competent as well as reasonably honest practitioners manifestly must be balanced against the rights of students to be evaluated fairly and with due respect to their rights as persons. The ethical obligations of the medical school to its students and to society may from time to time be incongruent. Which obligations shall take precedence, and under what circumstances?

Guardianship of Medical Knowledge. Although not the only place where the esoteric knowledge necessary for alleviation and prevention of human ills is pursued, the medical school is nevertheless society's most comprehensive reservoir of such knowledge. Its concentration of biomedical and clinical scientists, teachers of clinical practice, and research facilities represents society's largest and most expensive investment in medical knowledge. The medical school, therefore, incurs social obligations to act as guardian of that knowledge: to preserve what is known, continually culling it for error; to transmit it accurately and effectively to students, practitioners, and the public; and to generate new knowledge.

The medical school also is the preeminent locus for experimentation involving human beings because such experimentation requires both the apparatus of science and a setting in which patients are cared for. Moreover, future clinical investigators must be trained, and medical schools are the site for that training. Ideally, the medical school is the channel through which all the resources of the university disciplines as well as medical science can be applied to some of man's most pressing problems. The social sciences and the humanities as well as the biomedical sciences can be effectively and directly applied to questions of health and illness only under the aegis of the medical school and medical center.

The obligation to engage in research is therefore a moral one, grounded in the unique social situation of the school as the guardian of medical knowledge. The refurbishment, growth, and critical assessment of that knowledge is essential if the quality and rationality of medical care are to be advanced. Presumably, society expects medical schools (as a group, at least) to exercise their guardianship of knowledge in this way. This is the firmest social basis for the obligation to engage in research.

Difficulties arise when other justifications are advanced. For example, the prestige of a medical school, the quality of its faculty, the encouragement of critical attitudes among faculty and students are indirect and secondary justifications being questioned by policy makers. From the point of view of a social, ethical obligation, research by medical schools is not a luxury or refinement but a necessity.

The ethical dilemmas begin when this obligation is weighed against some of the other obligations outlined in this essay. Which activity has priority: care of patients, teaching, or advancement of knowledge? Again, the issue of reconciling and balancing conflicting responsibilities cannot be resolved by apodictic statements in favor of one or the other.

Only a more conscious selection of priorities by each school, based upon its strengths and resources, can possibly suffice. The facile promise of all medical schools to function equally in all three areas cannot be a responsible position. Moreover, in situations where the conflict is immediate and urgent, some ordering of priorities is requisite or decisions will be made by default.

We have adumbrated some of the ethical obligations which devolve upon medical schools because of their unique position in modern society. Thus, medical schools no less than individual professionals can be said to make a "profession." That is, they make a declaration that their whole enterprise is ultimately founded in the need society has for them and that, in consequence, their activities are in the public interest. If that "profession" is to be authentic, the medical school as a corporate entity—students, faculty, board of trustees—must assume explicit responsibility for the obligations reviewed here.

OBLIGATIONS TO STUDENTS AND PATIENTS

In addition to the ethical obligations of medical schools to society as a whole, there are important responsibilities to those who are taught, those who teach, and those to whom medical care is provided. A brief examination of obligations to two of these constituencies is in order.

The ethical obligations to faculty will not be specifically examined because these obligations are not particularly different from those in other types of educational institutions. Moreover, the matter of faculty rights has been widely propounded by such organizations as the American Association of University Professors and the faculty unions springing up in many universities.

Obligations to Medical Students.   The medical school has the same ethical obligations to its students as any other institution of higher learning. Students can rightfully expect to receive competent teaching, up-to-date information, introduction to the central theoretical and practical issues in their profession, and preparation for performing safely and competently as house officers and then as practitioners. Reasonable access to a faculty dedicated to teaching, fair modes of examination and evaluation, and participation in administrative decisions which affect them personally, are additional legitimate claims. The school also has the corollary obligation to detect inadequate and disinterested teachers and to rehabilitate or reassign them.

To these ordinary obligations must be added those peculiar to a clinical education. Practical experience must be provided in a sufficiently broad spectrum of clinical settings and clinical disorders. Careful, individualized, and graded responsibility in patient care is essential. The safety of the patient and the maturation of the student's clinical skills cannot be assured without active participation of mature clinical teachers. Delegating these tasks wholly to resident or junior house physicians compromises this obligation.

Attention should also be devoted to assisting students with the emotional challenges specific to a medical education: first encounters with a cadaver, dying or incurable patients, and the seemingly unredeemable victims of their own habits like alcoholics or drug addicts. The mechanisms students use to cope with these situations often condition their later behavior as independent practitioners. Faculty behavior should provide a model of humane and considerate attention to patient needs, so contradiction of the precept of humane medicine even by inadvertently humiliating a patient will not occur. If students turn to coping mechanisms that dehumanize and desensitize them, their approach to their own patients may lack those elements of humaneness so essential to healing (8).

In today's society, questions of value and purpose are entering every phase of medical decision making. Specific instruction in ethical and value issues is a new requirement of a medical education (9). The extent to which such a requirement is ethically founded is still problematic. Yet, it is at least arguable that such an obligation follows from society's expectations that a medical school will prepare its students adequately to confront the human as well as the technical aspects of illness. Such things as patients' bills of rights, the growing public concern about questions of bioethics, and the legal and social impetus to consumer participation all point to a new public view of obligations to patients. Education of future physicians without reference to these emergent concepts is at least ethically questionable.

What I am asserting is that obligations that customarily have been considered as merely academic or pedagogic are instead ethical. In any case, any serious inquiry into the ethics of medical education will need to address itself more explicitly to its obligations to students.

What is more, the same kinds of questions pertain to the education of residents and fellows, who also have moral claims on the school and its faculty. Their teaching shares the special characteristics of clinical education but at a more advanced level of responsibility. Their need for greater freedom in decision making can create conflicts with the simultaneous rights of patients to optimal care. Where does pedagogy end and independent responsibility by residents begin? How does the faculty meet simultaneously the differing learning needs of students and house staff? Which obligations take precedence: those to students, to house staff, or to patients? Can we avoid both extremes: the unsupervised, dominant house staff or the overprotective, overrestrictive attending physician who will not permit sufficient discretion to his residents?

Obligations to Patients.   Every medical school in the United States at least has responsibilities for care of some patients in its university and major affiliated teaching hospitals. These patients have moral claim to the same protection of their interests that every hospital must afford. They have a right to competent, personalized, and considerate care and to confidentiality, consent, and personal dignity. All of these obligations are complicated when they must be assured in a setting simultaneously dedicated to pedagogy and to generation of new knowledge. The most parlous conflicts of obligations can ensue. The judicious and ethical resolution of these conflicts can pose some of the most complex, sensitive questions of values and priorities.

The intricate nexus of human relationships, rights, duties, and expectations inherent in clinical instruction is rarely paralleled. The patient, first of all, is entitled to certain considerations for the special vulnerability he experiences in the fact of being ill. That fact curtails the patient's freedom—and thus his humanity is compromised. The sick man loses the free use of his body: he feels pain and disability; he lacks knowledge of what is awry and how to repair it; he is dependent upon the attention and knowledge of others.

In a teaching hospital, this special vulnerability must be removed or ameliorated in a context not exclusively therapeutic. Medical students, fellows, residents, students of other health professions, and clinical investigators all complicate the highly personal medical encounter. Each group has its own claims and expectations. There is no way for the medical school to fulfill all its obligations to society and individuals without constantly confronting the serious conflicts in this complicated skein of human relationships.

No matter how just may be the claim of students to a proper clinical education, their participation in the care of patients must always be a privilege and not an absolute right. When conflicts occur, there can be no question that the obligations to patient must take precedence. We still hear educators and academicians asserting that the prime purpose of a university hospital is teaching and the generation of new medical knowledge. This view cannot be justified morally when we consider the special vulnerability of the person who is ill. His needs must be primary even in a university hospital. It is the obligation of school and faculty to secure that primacy even when it may contravene the claims of students or house staff.

Admittedly, and necessarily, society permits some intrusion into the traditional privacy of the medical encounter because society must provide for a continuing supply of trained personnel. Every student must perform his first history and physical examination; every resident must perform his first operation; every new medication must be used for the first time in some human patient; every diagnostic or surgical procedure must be introduced in the care of some patient. There is no other way to teach or advance knowledge and assure its continuing availability to society.

Nonetheless, these permitted invasions must be sedulously guarded at every point so that the patient never becomes mere teaching "material" or a mere experimental "subject." Certain special obligations, therefore, bear upon a medical school and a university hospital in addition to those inherent in any medical transaction.

The patient must know who is taking care of him. Students must be introduced as such, and not as *doctor*; house staff must be clearly identified; the responsible attending physician must be known. The patient has a right to know who will perform a procedure and who will assist. These and all the sensitive rights of disclosure and consent in ordinary as well as experimental procedures must somehow be guaranteed while still providing the opportunity for graded clinical experiences for students and house officers.

In these relationships, the ordering of obligations and the whole social mandate that permits teaching and research deserve serious scrutiny for the ethical issues they expose. The added costs, loss of time, fragmentation of responsibility, and extra inconvenience consequent to the concomitant pursuit of teaching need more critical examination than has yet occurred. Medical schools argue, and with justification, that certain dimensions of medical care are superior in the teaching hospital. But how does that claim square with the primacy of patient needs the school must acknowledge when it staffs and operates a hospital?

It is inconceivable that society will force medical schools to abandon clinical education as it now exists. This would have even more deleterious social consequences than some of the abuses that admittedly occur in some instances. Physicians would be trained didactically only, required to perform their first independent procedures without supervision when they enter practice. The great strength of American medical education and the high quality of practice is in no small part related to our method of clinical instruction.

One of the most serious errors a clinical teacher can make is to fail to see the ethical implications of his behavior when obligations conflict. Today's medical schools are a major influence on the whole process of professionalization. The physician's image is sculpted by his teacher's ethical behavior. What is the ethical responsibility of the medical school for the unfavorable critique of the physician's image so many now render?

Setting the value rheostat to accomodate obligations to patients, students, and faculty and at the same time to meet the social needs for manpower and new knowledge is perhaps the most vexatious issue before medical schools today. Academic, fiscal, and managerial decisions cannot be isolated from the underlying value suppositions that predetermine alternatives chosen. Presuppositions about medical education need to be clearly identified and examined for their ethical content. The substance of the ensuing discourse and the normative principles evolved constitute the domain of the ethics of medical education.

The times demand a vigorous and frank examination of the ethical bases for the corporate behavior of medical schools and of the individuals who act in their behalf. The size, the cost, and the social significance of medical schools make the inquiry one of the most important on the agenda of any democratic society.

CHAPTER TWELVE

University Professions and Technical Expertise

SOCIETY, TECHNOLOGY, AND PROFESSIONAL EXPERTISE

No age has experienced as exquisitely as our own the problem of the expert—to be faithful to a narrow pursuit without universalizing and ideologizing it. In no other age has the expert been more necessary, more productive, or more suspect. Except in our own narrow spheres, we are all at the mercy of other experts, each protected by an arcane language and ritual closed to outsiders.

When expertise is raised to the status of a profession—especially as medicine, law, theology, or teaching—the tensions are accentuated. For a profession adds the dimensions of commitment and ethical imperatives. Expert knowledge must then be more than mere technicism. In addition, if we require educated professionals to see the relationship of their special knowledge to the whole of culture, we quintessentialize the dilemma. What society seeks is the technically competent person who not only is committed to the service of others, but does not succumb to the pretension of universalizing his technique.

It is precisely because of the rarity of such individuals that the professions are in a more ambiguous state today. The professions have never been more highly regarded (indeed, unrealistically exalted) or better rewarded, while at the same time more distrusted or suspect of self-serving. Everywhere demands grow for regulation and limitation of "discretionary space," that perimeter within which professions are permitted, nay trusted, to enjoy freedom of action and decision. Manifestly, the public has discerned a growing

---

Presented in part under the title "Society, Technology and Professional Expertise" and published in the *Proceedings* of the "Crossfire in Professional Education: Students, the Professions and Society" Conference sponsored by Northwestern University, October 16–17, 1975, Evanston, Illinois. Ed. Bruno A. Boley. New York, Pergamon Press, 1977, pp. 1–17.

disarticulation of technical prowess from commitment and integrity. The resultant confusion of values besets all professions.

Medicine is a paradigm of these dilemmas. It occupies a unique position at the juncture of the sciences and the humanities. Medicine demands a special balance of technical prowess and sensitivity to human values. Its spectacular successes render it particularly susceptible to technicism. Medicine's capabilities for fashioning a viable image of man suited to the times and enhancing human existence are unparalleled. Medicine, therefore, merits careful cogitation as an especially sensitive instance of the problem of the expert and the education he needs to balance his technical and human responsibilities.

That these two types of responsibilities are in genuine conflict has been apparent for almost a century. The physician is ever more dependent upon his technological apparatus, even being identified with it in some specialties. Medical students are selected and their education postulated on the thesis that medicine is largely a scientific enterprise. Medical insurance organizations wholly or in large part pay for procedures, but only partially or not at all for time spent with the patient.

Medicine is only part of a cultural mosaic increasingly dominated by the colors of the technological imperative. Until very recently the Western world had made an act of faith in salvation through technology based on the powerful evidence of miracles already manifest. In a country looking at the "bottom line," the practical and the palpable, technicism has had all the advantages.

Concomitantly the humanities, to which so many have looked for some competing salvation themes, have been in serious default. They have pursued specialization and methodologies, confusing both with scholarship and education. The liberal arts have become "relevant," homogenized to satisfy all tastes. Language, history, philosophy, and literature were too "elitist"; they have been transformed into communication skills, social studies, or "readings" in this or that to fit more easily the demands for college education for all.

Despite these pressures, there is a growing countercurrent of criticism of the inordinate trend to technicism. More frequently than ever we hear laments over the decline of humanistic or personal medicine. Educational and ethical reform is being demanded within and without medicine. The potential dangers of transforming the physician into solely a scientist or technician are matters of public debate.

Medicine, along with law and engineering, is now suspected of being among the innumerable "gods" that have failed to yield an earthly paradise while extracting a price man may not wish to pay. No one wishes to return to the unhealthy, unpleasant, rigorous, and repressive living conditions of our forebears. Society wants, and needs, what the professions of medicine, law, and engineering can confer—health, justice, and comfort. But society rightfully fears even these good things if they must be bought at the price of man used as a means, rather than *the end.*

The central question is: what can the university do to balance these opposing tensions between technology and human values in the professions? More specifically, what in the university can safeguard man against being overshadowed by his own creations and by the experts who have mastery over them?

I will consider this question as it applies to medicine—and, inferentially, all the other professions—by trying to define the responsibilities of the university to three constituencies: society, students, and the profession. From that base, I will attempt to define what the university can specifically contribute. A necessary propaedeutic, however, is to clarify first what I mean by medicine and by humanistic medicine.

WHAT IS MEDICINE AND WHAT IS HUMANISTIC MEDICINE?

It is curious and even distressing that there is confusion at this late date in our history about what we mean by medicine. Nonetheless, much of the conflict about what must be done to improve the social utility of medicine arises from this confusion. If universities are to contribute constructively to balancing technology and values in medical education, some distinctions are crucial.

Medicine has always been a peculiar intermingling of theory, praxis, and art. Too often one element has been exalted over the others, as past and recent history amply illustrate. Thus, in the earliest times and still in primitive societies, medicine is identified with religion and magic. In the Greek era, medicine first merged with philosophy as well as religion. Aristotle's treatise *On Ancient Medicine* sharply delineated it as a practical endeavor, separate from

philosophical speculation. Varro, the Roman encyclopedist, classified medicine with the humanities.

The debate continues, and its repercussions are felt to this day in
medical education, practice, and the expectations of the public.
The reductionists identify medicine with chemistry and physics;
others see it primarily as a social science. Those of a more practical
temperament regard it largely as a technical, empirical, or artistic
endeavor. Some extremists prefer to place it back with magic or, as
in the case of Ivan Illich, castigate it as an ideological instrument.

The views of medical academicians are not as simplistic, though
they are not free of the dilemma. Their attitudes are of crucial significance because they provide the models medical students emu-
late. Many practitioners fail to clarify that model later in life and
oscillate between the two major models they encounter in medical
school.

The dominant of the two is that of medicine as applied science,
presumably proceeding to solve clinical problems with the scientific methods of observation, hypothesis formulation, experimentation, and quantification. In this view, the aim of medical schools
is to produce scientific physicians or clinical scientists. The logical
extrapolations of this supposition include the overriding importance of scientific education and the capacity for quantitation in
the practice of modern medicine.

Those who hold this view do not deny the personal or practical
features of medicine. Rather, they relegate them to the realm of the
subjective and the nonquantifiable, to be taught by precept but not
as serious disciplines. Values and ethical issues are important, but
not enough so to displace time in the curriculum devoted to the sciences. Such issues are considered matters for premedical education
and not suitable in a professional school.

Although they are in the minority, a small number of faculty
members always have opposed this scientific model of medicine.
They emphasize instead a variety of elements in medicine which
are outside the ordinary realms of science. For example, they point
out that most human illness is psychosocial. Medical decisions are
more a matter of choosing the right course in ambiguous situations
than of scientific rigor. The genuine challenges, they say, are in the
personal relationship with the patient. In this view, values and ethical decisions are of paramount importance and should occupy
considerable segments of time in education and practice. Science,

for those who hold this view, is a useful language and method but not the primary ingredient of good medicine.

I have caricatured these positions to make my point as clearly as possible. To varying degrees, medical faculties champion one or the other, or unrealistically assert that physicians must be both scientist and humanist. The difficulties arise less out of the fact of these divergent interpretations than out of the failure to distinguish between medicine and science or biomedical science.

Medicine, however, cannot be simply science as science, even though some of its method and language is utilized. Science seeks to know as an end in itself, to find generalizable laws, to explain, and to predict. It is interested in particular cases as illustrations of universal principles. It studies the particular only to be able to prescind from it. Science must be objective; it must purge itself of the nonfactual and the unique. The basic and clinical biomedical sciences fit these criteria. They seek knowledge in man or other animals or in isolated parts of organisms; they seek generalizable laws about human biology.

But the biomedical sciences are not the same as medicine, even when applied in the clinical setting. Medicine simply does not exist until its knowledge and skills are particularized—that is, used to effect some good end in a particular human being. This act of particularization goes counter to the universalizing thrust of science. Medicine, as distinguished from biomedical science, does not seek generally applicable laws. It is not interested in knowledge alone. It deals with those very particulars of the life of a given human being that truly scientific methodology must eschew. Medical decisions have to be made with inadequate data most of the time. The right course of action is the end point—i.e., the action must optimize the benefits and minimize the dangers for the patient.

Medicine then comes into being not when it acts as basic or clinical science, but when it engages the existential condition of an individual person. This is a unique experiment every time, one in which all the pertinent particulars rarely can be ascertained. In science, verifiability hinges on repeated observations of the same phenomena under the same conditions. But in medicine, we cannot repeat the exact circumstances even with the same patient, let alone between patient and patient. Medicine in essence, then, is the science of the particular case—something quite different from science as developed in the last five hundred years.

191

Very often the most essential element of the medical transaction is precisely what science must ignore: the personal, nonquantifiable values and beliefs which identify the person of the patient. These are indivisible from his physiology and his anatomy. The Cartesianism of the biomedical scientist is inappropriate, and unequal to optimization of a course of action that involves physiology *and* values simultaneously.

If we take the view that medicine is not simply science and, parenthetically, not one of the humanities or social sciences either, then what do we mean when we speak of humanistic medicine? I use this term simply because it is very much current. It is used by many to sum up the whole of deficiencies critics find in modern medicine: the impersonal encounters, the overbureaucratization, institutionalization, lack of compassion, and a deterioration in ethical sensitivities.

Humanistic medicine exists when the science, technology, and craftsmanship of the physician are practiced with the deepest respect for the humanity of the patient. This means that everything is modulated by those values we call human: freedom to make informed decisions, preservation of dignity, absence of humiliation, and the responsible use of power. If medicine is indeed the science particularized in a unique way in the clinical situation, then it must, by definition, be humanistic. Otherwise, it is not medicine at all, but some conglomerate of techniques, craftsmanship, science, or psychology.

RESPONSIBILITIES OF THE UNIVERSITY: TO SOCIETY, THE PROFESSION, STUDENTS

The preceding lengthy propaedeutic was necessary to clarify terms and to delineate more precisely what the university can do to meet the modern dilemma of technology and value. We can now turn to a briefer inspection of the responsibilities of the university to its three major constituencies: society, the profession, and students.

The university, from society's point of view about the education of physicians and other health professionals, is an instrument for the preparation of people in the numbers, of the kinds, and with the attitudes that will not closely match the needs of society. In the case of an institution with a regional orientation, the health-care needs would be those of the region; and, in the case of an institution with a national perspective, the needs would be those of the nation.

Society expects institutions to prepare safe, competent practitioners who have the capacity to continue their education, adding to their knowledge and skills as their fields advance. If we place any credence in the definition of medicine to which I alluded earlier, and if we accept the proposition that medicine by nature must be humanistic, then the university has additional responsibilities. It must also prepare professionals not only to make technical decisions, but to disentangle from those decisions the intermingled human values. The university defaults, at least in part, in its responsibility to society if it educates only for technical competence.

With respect to the profession itself, the university has additional responsibilities. (I include under the term *profession* the intellectual disciplines which make up that profession.) The university is uniquely equipped to preserve, validate, teach, and advance human knowledge. Society would be ill-served if the university did not also engage in the pursuit of knowledge. Humans have an ineradicable desire to know; it is this desire which impels investigators into fields that have no apparent utility. Inevitably, such knowledge rebounds to mankind's benefit, either by expanding man's knowledge of himself and the universe or by direct application to his more immediate problems.

Lastly, the university has a responsibility to the student to provide him the opportunity to gain the skills necessary to be a competent practitioner. As I have already said, this obviously includes not only a knowledge of the technical fundaments, but also a sensitivity to the impact of technical decisions on individuals and on society. The university must insist that the student become technically competent; there is nothing more inhumane than the incompetent but affable physician or nurse.

The university has equal responsibility to assist the student to grow in his own education as a person. This responsibility is not fulfilled simply by providing a so-called liberal education in the premedical years. All experiences indicate that this premedical liberal education is not sufficient and that it must be reinforced through medical training. The student is short-changed if he has no opportunity to engage the issues of technology and values within his profession. He cannot mature as a person without a clear notion of his own values and of how to deal with value conflicts in his

193

attempts to help individuals or to improve the general condition of society. Looked at carefully, the responsibilities of the university to society, to the profession, and to students do not necessarily conflict but reinforce each other. Indeed, the failure to understand this has distorted medical education severely in many institutions.

No one these days can take lightly the pressures caused by allocation of resources, government agencies, and the requirements of accreditation, licensure, and such. Rather than taking the negative view of these, the university might well practice the kind of critical self-scrutiny it so strongly urges in others. The university cannot deal responsibly with these external forces unless it understands more clearly what society is trying to say to it.

In my opinion, most of the move to regulation by external agencies results from the failure of universities to realize their responsibilities for educating health professionals whose number, kinds, and attitudes meet the needs of society. This does not automatically mean applying the "trade school" approach. Rather, we must appreciate society's expectations that the majority of graduates will be practitioners and that the practitioner will serve the practical needs of society before serving the needs of his profession, as such. It is my contention that the responsibilities of the university to its three constituencies must be fulfilled. But the central issue is their order of priority.

For example, if it is true that most physicians and health professionals would be, or should be, practitioners, then schools should graduate a preponderance of practitioners who meet the major needs of society. This is why society supports the medical school and the university. In our country, the principal unmet needs are for primary health and medical care; a great majority of graduates should be prepared to meet these needs. A much smaller number is required to satisfy the specialty and subspecialty needs of society. An even smaller number is needed to advance the disciplines as such.

The error causing the lack of fulfillment of what appear to be conflicting responsibilities lies with the unfortunate academic assumption that everyone should be prepared for any possible career within medicine, whether as a primary-care practitioner, a specialist, or a research scientist.

This confusion is manifest in the densely packed medical curriculum, where every student is prepared by the same exposure in depth to the basic sciences and all the clinical specialties. The time required to impart this information is so great that it is almost impossible to teach how to make value decisions as well as technical decisions. Even more disturbing, this situation fosters the view that medicine *is* technology or science. Finally, there is little time as a student—and less as a house officer—to reflect upon one's values and one's conception of what it means to be a physician.

The question of resource allocation, really a secondary one, can be approached rationally only when a university defines its responsibilities and places them in some relationship to each other. This usually involves the first question of what kinds of practitioners to prepare. If the university seriously accepts its responsibility to society, it must conclude that today practitioners are required who will meet the needs of primary care, general and family medicine, chronic care, and preventive medicine in the broadest sense. The number of specialists and subspecialists required is much smaller, and the number of academicians and investigators smaller still.

There are some exceptions to this general distribution of the kinds of graduates—in those few medical schools heavily endowed with talent, facilities, and fiscal support to train research scientists and academicians. The unfortunate fact is that the majority of schools try to prepare every student for all careers and make little genuine effort to match output with needs. Even in those schools consciously attempting to alter the mix of graduates more favorably to meet social needs, there is tacit acceptance that the training of academicians is a superior undertaking.

Governmental or consumer interest in medical education is derived in a very significant degree from a confusion of ends and purposes. The university must be more explicit in its delineation of the way it intends to fulfill its responsibilities to each of its tripartite constituency.

These responsibilities will occasionally conflict. Should the number of students and the fields available to them be determined by social need or the students' desires? Some legislators believe every qualified student should have the chance to study medicine. Others say the determinant should be the number needed, though this figure may be arrived at in a most arbitrary way.

Decisions about the allocation of resources and the kinds of graduates a school should produce must be taken in a way that gives primacy to society's needs. When the student enters, he

195

knows what the aims of the institution are and, in fact, presumably accepts them by agreeing to attend. Once the student is enrolled, the university then must place the student's academic needs in the primary position—his intellectual and personal development within the larger framework becomes the prime consideration. When the social framework and the student's academic growth are assured, then the advancement of the profession or discipline becomes important. The best institutions are the ones that balance these sometimes conflicting responsibilities. Balance does not mean doing a little of everything. It means allocating resources realistically, so that the three responsibilities reinforce each other in a way unique to the institution in question.

THE UNIVERSITY AND THE CRISIS OF PROFESSIONAL EDUCATION

I have been speaking of the tripartite responsibilities of the university engaged in professional education. The responsibilities of the university in the undergraduate and graduate divisions in the arts and sciences are somewhat different. These divisions are the heart of the university, the *sine qua non* without which it cannot properly be a university. The prime responsibilities in these domains are to serve as society's mechanism for preserving, codifying, validating, reflecting upon, and transmitting the reservoir of human knowledge and adding to it by original research and thought. In addition, the university has the social obligation to bring the young into contact with this endowment so they may grow intellectually to the extent their potentialities allow, and to equip them with the tools of language, thought, and critical inquiry for whatever way of life they may choose.

A few students will devote themselves to furthering the proper work of the university as scholars and teachers. For these few, the liberal arts will become professional subjects. Most students will pursue other callings in the professions, business, or elsewhere. The professionals in medicine, law, engineering, and theology (those in the humanities not excluded) are increasingly subject to the crises of the professions: the divinization of small branches of knowledge and the susceptibility to being overwhelmed by their own and others' expertise.

It is precisely at this point that the university has its major intellectual responsibility to its professional schools, and particularly to medicine. That responsibility is to assure some degree of competence and sensitivity in language, reasoning, judging—the human arts. These are the "good arts" of Aulus Gellius, the liberal arts, those that free a man's mind from the tyranny of other minds. These competencies and sensitivities are derived now, as they have been for centuries, from the humanities and not from the professional disciplines.

Having said this, we immediately face specific questions which cast serious doubt about the effectiveness of such an easy prescription. Are not the humanities themselves in crisis? Does not the premedical exposure to liberal education suffice? What should be taught? Who will teach it?

The most vexing of these questions relates to the identity of the humanities in the universities today. The uncertain state of the traditional humanistic disciplines is well stated by humanists themselves (1). The history of this dilemma has been thoughtfully set forth by R.S. Crane (2). He underscores the dichotomy between those humanists who equate the humanities with value-free, textual scholarship and those who hold that their central function is the criticism of human values. He calls for a resuscitation of the humanities by encompassing four elements: the rigor of scholarship, the normative thrust of a criticism of values, preservation of the unique contribution of each discipline, and the addition of a theoretical strain which was lost in the dominant version of the humanities propagated by Cicero and Quintilian (3).

Whether the crisis in the humanities will be resolved this way or not is yet to be seen. For the needs of the professions, it would suffice if the humanities seriously extended their interest in the evaluation of human value and instilled some of the spirit of the critical intelligence into professional education. I refer here to the capacity to assess value questions and to introduce the elements of moral science to physicians so they can better understand the bases for their decisions. Physicians need a deeper perception of value conflicts in their decisions and how to deal with them. The techniques of medicine are becoming more potent, but at the same time more demanding of choices only the patient can make for himself. These choices involve his idea of the quality of life, its extent, and under what conditions he wishes to pursue it.

There are now signs that the urgency of value questions in medicine can serve to accelerate in some part recovery from the malaise of the humanities. For example, a substantial number of philosophers have become interested in teaching and research in the problems of biomedical ethics. Their interests have more recently spread to the broader issues medicine can offer: issues of a genuinely philosophical nature, such as the logic of clinical medicine, the epistemology of the medical knowledge, the meaning of medicine, disease and health, and the philosophical basis of medical ethics.

The engagement of medicine and the humanities is growing in other areas as well. Literature, history, and theology show signs of similar mutually rewarding exchanges in medical education. Medical ethics, previously offered exclusively to preprofessional students, is also becoming a popular subject in undergraduate programs. Medicine, in short, offers interesting, available, and rewarding matter for exercising the traditional skills and insights of the humanities.

This exchange between medicine and the humanities should be deepened. It must extend through the education of the physician from undergraduate through professional, graduate, and continuing education levels. If this movement continues to thrive, it should serve as a partial antidote to the hubris and the technicism which threaten the profession. In short, the physician may imbibe enough of the critical essence of the humanities to become critical about medicine and himself.

The precise content of courses in the humanities in medicine is variable, as a review of the extant programs indicates (4). Each program emphasizes some facet or another, but concentration on bioethics predominates in most programs. The experience with these programs thus far is insufficient to permit conclusions in favor of one approach over others. Some observations, however, are applicable even at this early stage (5, 6, 7). I will enumerate a few.

A premedical education in the liberal arts does not suffice for the majority of students. The humanities should be taught within the framework of medical education as well. For those who acquired the attitudes the liberal arts can foster, reinforcement in medical school will be welcome. The majority, who hurdled the humanities as obstacles to entry into medical school, will experience an awakening of interest if those disciplines are related to medical problems. For some, of course, no appreciable benefit or interest is to be expected.

All students should have some exposure to the analysis of ethical and value decisions involved in modern clinical medicine. The most effective approach for the majority will be through the case method, especially if the problem is one in which decisions are being made even as the case is discussed. Working from the particular case, the skilled humanist can proceed to the underlying principles, the methodology of his discipline, and the more theoretical considerations. Seminars are the next most useful teaching mode, and the lecture is last.

All students should have the opportunity for an introduction to the humanistic dimensions of medical practice. For those with a richer background or a deeper interest, more specialized courses and opportunities for independent work can be offered successfully.

Teaching of values and ethics in clinical medicine must be sustained throughout the physician's education. It must occupy some time in the clinical years. Such teaching is most effective if part of regular clinical teaching sessions, at least intermittently. The support and cooperation of academic clinicians is indispensable to student acceptance. Taught in the clinical setting, medical ethics or philosophy of medicine reaches students, house staff, and faculty simultaneously.

This type of teaching is not intended to displace the usual clinical modes of instruction or to be used to depreciate the scientific aspects of clinical medicine. The most effective attitude is one in which the teacher demonstrates how closely value and technological decisions are intertwined. They become legitimate subjects for inquiry in proportion to their importance to the actual clinical situation. It is a fatal error to force the discussion into ethical channels unless such matters are intrinsic to the case under consideration.

Teaching is best done by some combination of clinicians in respected positions together with humanists: philosophers, historians, specialists in literature, theology, and ethics. Careful planning of all sessions is an obvious requirement. It is disconcerting to see how often well-intentioned sessions fail for lack of preparation of the case, the reading materials, or the actual presentations. Good pedagogy is absolutely essential when new material is introduced in any curriculum.

A body of humanists is growing who share certain characteristics which equip them for the special problems of teaching in the medical setting. They are interested in communicating something of their discipline to health professionals because they are aware of the intermingling of technologic and value questions inherent in modern medicine. Then, they are bona fide humanists, well trained and confident in their own disciplines. This enables them to see medicine from a fresh point of view and to benefit their own research by an intimate look at the urgent human problems that surface in medicine today.

Intellectual rigor and sound scholarship are essential to success in the medical setting. Faculty and students may be skeptical or even resentful of the entry of humanists into their special precincts, but they will acknowledge academic competence. This is the first step in making an impact on medical education.

Even more important than the subject matter and who teaches it is stimulating or reinforcing in future physicians those skills and attitudes traditionally embodied in the liberal arts, the arts that "free." I refer to the capacity for critical and dialectical reasoning for evaluating evidence and raising significant questions. Having these capabilities can assure that the physician will reflect upon and understand his own values and those of his patients and society. These attitudes are ultimately the only assurance any of us can have that we will not be helpless in the face of our own values or those of someone else.

It is refurbishing the ancient aim of humanistic studies, their identification as liberating arts, which constitutes their central function in the university. The contemporary dilemma of the humanities rests primarily in confusing scholarship and specialization within this central function. The major responsibility of the university in resolving the central crisis of professional education is precisely its contribution to liberal education for students in general and for professionals in particular.

The educated man is distinguished not so much by his special knowledge as by his ability to think critically outside his special field. Aristotle stated it well in the first chapter of his *On the Parts of Animals:*

> For an educated man should be able to form a fair offhand judgment as to the goodness or badness of the method used by a professor in his exposition. To be educated is, in fact, to be able to do this, and even the man of universal education we deem to be such in virtue of having this ability. It will, however, of course, be understood that we only ascribe universal education to one

who is his own individual person, is thus critical in all or nearly all branches of knowledge, and not to one who has a like ability merely in some special subject. For it is possible for a man to have this competence in some one branch of knowledge without having it in all. (8)

This aim has become extraordinarily difficult to attain in contemporary education, where the number of specialties is unprecedented and exponentially expanding, as is the sheer volume of information. We must nevertheless sustain the hope that some of our citizens can be educated men in Aristotle's sense. They are society's protection against being victimized by whatever expert may be in the ascendant at any moment.

RECAPITULATION

The professional in contemporary society is under increasing scrutiny. The inevitable intercalation of values in all technical decisions makes the expert both a hope and a danger to society. The result is a gradual narrowing of the "discretionary space" being allowed to all experts. This space is being narrowed by external regulations, legislation, consumer participation, and surveillance of institutions. This is particularly noticeable in medicine, but also evident in the other professions.

The university faces a serious challenge today: preparing professionals who are competent and technically expert, yet sufficiently educated to understand the humane purposes of their special skills. The university has apparently conflicting responsibilities to students, society, and the professions. It must balance these responsibilities in society's and mankind's interest. The university must not only prepare competent professionals, but provide them and the whole of educated men with the critical faculties unique to the educated man. I refer to the capacity to question, criticize, and judge the value issues in fields outside our own. We must not confuse technological decisions with value decisions. The one is dependent upon the experts' knowledge, the other on the capabilities all educated men share as free men.

The university cannot meet all its responsibilities without refurbishing the traditional functions of the humanities as agencies for teaching the liberal arts, not only to the undergraduate, but also *pari passu* with professional and continuing education. This is a difficult assignment, but only in its ardent pursuit can the university remain authentic and regain the respect and support it seems to be losing in contemporary society.

Human Values in Medical Education

*What youth thinks of us is very important, for youth
is the beginning of our posterity.*
Juan Ramón Jiménez, *Aphorisms* (1)

THE STUDENT CHALLENGE

Students have cogently and feelingly presented a damaging case against contemporary medical education and practice. They have literally pleaded for their older colleagues to listen to this case. Their sincerity and their urgency demand not only that we listen, but that we *hear*, and that we *respond* responsibly and with a concern at least equal to theirs.

I write as one member of the educational establishment who shares their interest in change, relevance, and the primacy of human values in medicine. I must, however, underline the personal nature of this response. I disclaim any role as an official representative, but I hope some of my thoughts are representative of those entertained by other concerned educators and practitioners.

Students have detailed the deficiencies in human values which now characterize medical education. The crisis, they aver, is a crisis in human values. The present system induces a feeling of dehumanization, a blunting of sensitivities for people, and an obtundation of social awareness. They see their teachers emphasizing disease rather than the care of patients, and science at the expense of a concern for social ills. They describe the scene as a "wasteland." They fear, I presume, that they are being turned into "hollow men"—if I may use one of T.S. Eliot's more pungent phrases.

Finally, and most tellingly, they assert that we, their elders, who should be their models and their guides, have failed them. In our

Modified version of an article entitled "Human Values and the Medical Curriculum" which appeared in *Journal of the American Medical Association*, 209(9): 1349–53 (September 1969). Copyright 1969, American Medical Association.

practice we are characterized as inconsiderate, unresponsive to community and social needs, indifferent to the poor and the outcast, too concerned with money, prestige, and comfort. And this, they conclude, is the consequence of an education that has exalted all the wrong values—authoritarianism, rigidity, excessive respect for the intellectual, and under-recognition of the creative, the human, and the intuitive.

Despite these indictments, they turn to us for help. They plead that we awaken to our responsibility to help them humanize medicine and work toward a more just society.

How shall we respond? The temptation is to polarize our reactions into denial and righteous indignation or penitential acquiescence. Both positions are morally feeble. The former will terminate the dialogue but submerge the questions, only to have them reappear later in more violent form or action. The latter is irresponsible, for it does not confront the issue; it does not gain the student's respect and it admits too much. After all, a concern for human values is hardly new in medicine. Its actualization in terms of today's problems is that we must all seek.

Any morally sensitive person must first admit the many deficiencies of contemporary medical education as a humanizing experience. Such deficiencies cannot be tolerated in a profession so inextricably bound with the human condition and so necessary to improving it. The litany of errors recited by concerned educators almost parallels the one recited by today's students. This is so true that the response of medical educators to current student criticisms is frequently one of hurt surprise. How can this happen? Have we not been undergoing ferment, crisis, and even revolution in medical curricula and with the same aims in mind?

What is the "hang up"? It is worth analyzing the discontinuities separating the student viewpoint from that of the enlightened leaders of the establishment who also want to close the credibility gap between themselves, their patients, and their students.

SOME STUDENT-FACULTY DISCONTINUITIES

The first, and perhaps the most serious discontinuity is in behavior. This is more pertinent than the "credibility" or "generation" gaps.

Since the 1940s, educators have questioned the human and social values of medical education and have expounded reforms. They have effectively raised student and public expectations that changes would indeed occur. But sadly, little has actually happened in either medical education or patient care to make these reforms really operative. Our proclamations, which are essentially valid, have not had behavioral authenticity. Nothing is more demoralizing to the young, and nothing more quickly discerned, than the appearance of hypocrisy induced by failure to meet expectations.

Let us admit it—we still tolerate several standards of care in teaching hospitals. The very terms "private" and "teaching" service proclaim the differences. We have not yet learned how to meet a community on its own terms, to engage that community in the determination of its own needs. We have yet to learn how to meet those needs unselfishly.

We do preach and teach care of the person in a comprehensive and humane and respectful way. Yet, in our institutions there are still too many tolerated violations of the human dignity of the patients we serve.

The essential point is that we of the faculty and administration have not consciously undergone the necessary transformations of behavior in all our medical transactions. We have freely asserted that we are humane, and the student should also be, without providing consistent examples of this humaneness in all our own attitudes and actions. The big gap, then, is an existential and behavioral one which curricular design alone cannot possibly close.

A second source of frustration is uncertainty about the mechanisms through which the physician's concern for human values can be adequately taught. We hear a recurrent plea from the students—"please teach us to take care of people," "teach us how to be considerate and responsive," and "teach us to understand the roles of other health workers."

The classical roles of clinical clerk and house staff catapult the student immediately into positions of authority. They provide little opportunity for understanding the frightening experience of illness, the importance and the tediousness of meeting the needs of a sick person for comfort, feeding, and care of his bodily functions. These are things often done without comprehension and easily delegated to others. Even community medical experiences, while becoming common features of the new curricula, are usually designed as "teaching" sessions. They should also be "helping" and "serving" experiences, which derive their teaching value from their authenticity and concern for patient needs.

Students have shown imagination in devising experiences which they feel will teach them to care for people. Patient advocacy, family care in neighborhood clinics, and work as orderlies and as nursing and psychiatric aides bring them into literal touch with the odors, the pains, the anguish, and the helplessness of illness. Medical faculties should show more respect for student desire for nonauthoritarian, helping roles in clinical medicine.

What needs to be assessed is how far such experiences can be used to advance competency as well as compassion, how effective they really are in inculcating attitudes of concern for patients, and whether their benefits are lasting. Faculty members must realize that they cannot teach effectively in these service-oriented settings unless they are comfortable in them—i.e., they must believe in them and be sincerely interested in sharing the student experience. Faculty who cannot honestly see the "values" of such experiences ought not to undertake them.

One almost indispensable way to demonstrate concern for human values is to establish a model of patient care under faculty auspices. Here, teachers and students can openly state their own hypotheses on how best to deliver care which is technically competent and humanely delivered. Students and faculty can "lay it on the line," so to speak, as they cope with the vexing human problems of illness and try specifically to humanize the whole process. It is not perfection that the student wants to see, but rather a demonstration by his teacher of genuine commitment to confront the issues in a concrete situation outside the restricted setting of the university hospital. The student himself will learn from such a model that sheer good will and a romantic devotion to change are not enough. They must be coupled with patient and competent wrestling with frustrating and often petty obstacles; otherwise the result can only be greater confusion and more hypocrisy.

Perhaps the sharpest divergence occurs between the designers of new curricula and the student-critic on the matter of technical competence. This, too, is an issue of human values. The physician "professes" a certain knowledge and skill not possessed by his fellows in society. If he is not to be a fraud or a hypocrite, he must be competent in what he professes to know. There are few abnegations of the humane more blameworthy than incompetence under the guise of compassion. Not only is truth violated, but the patient is deceived in the contract he implicitly enters with the physician—the expectation that he will be helped. We all want to be treated courteously when we ride an airplane, but we expect the pilot to be competent; we do not want a pleasant trip to eternity. An incompetent pilot may in this way terminate his career, but an incompetent physician may spend a lifetime at his macabre enterprise.

The paucity of discussion about competence and proficiency in current student demands is disconcerting. This very important professional value is also an important human value without which the physician's whole being is compromised. We must guard as carefully against the romanticism of service without knowledge as against proficiency without compassion.

Compassion, too, is not enough, as we are learning in our ghetto experiences. We must *understand* our patient's responses, as well as *feel* for him, or else we cannot make our well-intentioned efforts effective for a culturally different group.

Another major area that may divide the educator interested in reform from students and public expectation is the need to recognize a certain "economy of pretensions," as the philosopher Ortega y Gasset put it in speaking of universities (2). The goals set for medical education are becoming global. Granting the profound influence of medicine, we can hardly expect medical schools to solve every social, political, and economic ill of the ghettos, the rural areas, suburbia, and the developing countries. Racism, poverty, environmental contamination, housing, welfare, the rights of workers, the wholeness of family life—any of these things obviously can affect health and induce disease.

We must be much clearer, however, about the extent to which these should become the primary concerns of medical schools. The physician sensitive to human beings as persons must, of course, concern himself with these matters. But, to the extent that they become his overwhelming concern, as student or practitioner, he becomes more a sociologist, economist, or political scientist—and an untrained one at that! Our curricula must discriminate between those things which enhance our primary functions and those which constitute the primary function itself. Much of the rhetoric generated about medical education and human values is an expression of deficits elsewhere in society or in individuals. Medicine, because of its involvement with the human condition, tends to become a light-ning rod attracting all of the students' dissatisfactions with the world.

Another point is the proper placement of the responsibility and control of medical education. I accept the view that medicine is an instrument of society, operating under a social mandate and ulti-mately responsible for the relevance of what it does. I accept, too, the concept of a community establishing the framework and even the ends to be served by medicine. Community participation in de-fining policies is justifiable and essential. But, to state that a com-munity should *control* the medical school is to assign a task which demands competence to those who lack that competence. The community should have a real and direct voice in the operation of the university hospital and clinics, for example. Likewise, students as the persons most seriously at risk in medical education must have a powerful influence on the goals and means of their educa-tion. But, here too, emotional charges notwithstanding, the faculty does possess the knowledge the students want and need. A balance of faculty and student power must be struck which drastically al-ters the present authoritarian academic structure without relieving the faculty of its responsibility to determine academic questions.

A final and particularly significant source of divergence between students and faculty members lies in their disparate expectations of the medical school. Each group sees the school as an instrument de-signed primarily to meet its own needs. The student expects it to concentrate on his learning and personal development. He assumes the faculty is also ordained almost exclusively for this purpose. The faculty member, for his part, sees the school as a source of his own satisfactions. Teaching is only one of these satisfactions. The op-portunity to engage in research, to care for a specific group of pa-tients, or to share intellectual experiences with colleagues of like interest is often of more importance to him. Protection by students or faculty of medical schools as the sources of their own satisfac-tions is at the root of many confrontations. It is essential to recog-nize and to admit the existence of these divergencies in expectations before they can be dealt with effectively. A rapprochement is im-possible without the early recognition that some accommodation of the needs of each group, not total capitulation, is the only rea-sonable goal.

This vexing question is further complicated if we also interject the expectations of the community, which are different from those of both students and faculty. For the community, the medical school is an instrument designed to provide services and personnel to meet public needs as defined by the public and not by the physician.

Much more conscious definition of these divergencies in expectations is needed if something positive is to come out of the current academic confrontation syndrome.

I have just reviewed some major points at which there should be more effective intersection of the hopes and desires of educators, students, and laymen for medical curricula with more sensitivity to human values. Much valuable time will certainly be lost in confrontations and maneuvers if the nature of the discontinuities separating students and faculties is not recognized. A more humane process of medical education is needed now. The teaching of human values should not be delayed while students and administrators indulge in the new academic gamesmanship of crisis and confrontation.

FEATURES OF A VALUE SENSITIVE CURRICULUM

With these considerations in mind, we can now present the essential configuration of a curriculum effectively attuned to human values.

First, the curriculum must have behavioral authenticity—the student must see the faculty in every medical transaction acting out its preaching about compassion and consideration. Every student experience, every teacher, and every patient-care activity should be scrutinized for behavioral credibility. Patient care is an invaluable model for demonstrating this credibility to students and faculty.

Second, a human-value oriented curriculum must provide a variety of experiences which introduce the student to the patient on a personal, nonprofessional level. In this way, he can see illness as a personal assault on the patient and understand the many nonprofessional levels of care which are often of prime importance to the patient.

Third, humane behavior and attention to humane values must be manifest in faculty behavior toward the student as well as the patient. Students must be admitted to medicine on a wider variety of criteria, not just the intellectual. Disparities in the educational, racial, ethnic, or social profile of a student body should be redressed. The course of study should be variable and individualized to meet the student's level of preparation and sophistication. Medicine can be entered at a variety of points—directly from high school in some cases or after one, two, three, or four years of college. A variety of pathways to the M.D. degree must be developed to recognize the differences in interests, personality, and preparation of students and the ultimate roles they will choose. Thus, no two students need have the same curriculum. For some roles in medicine, the current standard regimen of the basic sciences may be of cultural interest only. For others, it is vital. For many important new roles in medicine an entirely different set of basic sciences will be more relevant.

Professional competence, another human value, must be assured by evaluation of the student's ability to use knowledge in a skillful and considerate way. The evaluation must not be limited to the intellectual, but also should include functioning as a human being. The real test is not that all students pass the same kind of examination. Rather, each student should be evaluated in the pathway selected, i.e., the one he professes and intends to proclaim in society.

Students must share responsibility in curricular design and evaluation, and the community must participate in defining the purpose to which the curriculum is put. But neither group should usurp the faculty's responsibility to develop a curriculum relevant to those needs.

Finally, there must be concrete evidence of commitment on the part of faculty and administration to the importance of human values in the medical curriculum. Without this, much of our talk about "human values" will seem to be idle prating, which can only exacerbate tensions between students and faculties by adding the suggestion of hypocrisy to an ever-expanding catalog of errors.

THE NEED FOR A MEDICAL AXIOLOGY

The deep concern expressed by our students for a closer attention to human values in medical education is commendable, but it will suffer the attenuation characteristic of all intuitive movements if it is not given rational underpinnings. The activist student specializes in intuitive assertions about values and emphasizes the sampling of human experiences to teach them. Experience is assuredly an excellent teacher of what human beings feel. We need, in addition, a critical and cogitative analysis of those experiences. The study of human values on a more formal basis in all aspects of medicine—a medical axiology—should be established as a legitimate discipline. It would deal with the tensions in human values created by the progress of medicine itself; it would define how medicine might contribute to restructuring and resynthesizing a value systen for contemporary man. And, it would define those values which should determine the social and personal behavior of every physician.

The laboratory for medical axiology is at hand and waiting to be used. I refer to the clinical contacts and experiences of students at every level of their education. Conflicts in human values are experienced by students as they progress from nonprofessional helping and serving experiences to more professional roles as clerks and house staff members. Interdisciplinary analyses of these concrete experiences in a clinical context can introduce students to the study of values on a formal basis much more effectively than courses or lectures in sociology or the humanities. The cooperative involvement of clinicians, sociologists, philosophers, ministers, and others in these analyses will greatly enhance the medical student's liberal education. Moreover, questions of values must be examined rationally and critically if plans for future improvement of the health-care system and the behavior of health professionals within that system are to be developed.

MEDICINE AND THE SEARCH FOR VALUES

Every crisis in human affairs is indeed a crisis of values—those compass points by which a society orients itself and sets forth the things it cherishes. To challenge these values is to induce anxiety in those who proclaim them and expectations for relief in those excluded by them from full participation in life—the young, the disenfranchised, and the poor. The resultant mixture of anger and anxiety is an exceedingly unstable one easily detonated in demonstrations, confrontations, and rebellion.

Today's rebellion, as Camus so trenchantly put it, is a "metaphysical rebellion." Contemporary man, having actualized the Promethean myth, is forced to fabricate a new set of values—his own values—which will proclaim what human being means in a techno-logical society. Medicine cannot possibly detach itself from this search for values. Rather, it must seek direct and deep involvement.

Medicine is in convulsion today because society is in convulsion. Medicine offers hope for the amelioration of some of the vexations of our modern-day Prometheus, and it has a responsibility it can-not shun to reduce some of the explosive potentials which can bring our society to the edge of oblivion. Educators must respond creatively and work to rehumanize our curricula and our system of care. In this way, a medical education will become simultaneously an instrument for development of technical competence and the in-culcation of a sensitivity for human values.

Dimensions of the Medical Intellect

Men pursue knowledge and techniques for two reasons: the fulfillment of a role in society and the joy of understanding. The growth of the professional as a person depends on the concurrent development of both the societal and individual functions of the intellect. In the physician, their relationship is indissoluble.

The disquietude about medical education today centers much on the optimal fulfillment of a role in society and little on the other intellectual dimensions. This focus raises such questions as: How can we best educate for breadth and depth? How best provide a scientific education without a concomitant sacrifice of interest in social needs or the personal requirements of the patient? How best motivate the physician to ideals of service? These and like matters relate to the practical ends of medical education, the service of society. They are not to be depreciated in any sense.

But it is equally important to examine those dimensions of the intellectual life and those uses of the medical intellect to which medical education is not yet critically attuned—the individual functions. For the degree to which we achieve a life of satisfaction is contingent on how well we exploit the contemplative as well as the practical potentialities of our education.

Medical education has some blemishes, but there are ways this same education can be transmuted to serve the contemplative as well as the practical goals of human existence.

Alfred North Whitehead has defined the primary function of reason as "the promotion of the art of life" (1). He goes on to say that the intellect enables us to live, to live well, and to live with satisfaction. The chief business of education is the quickening of intellects not only to keep man alive by equipping him for a function in society, but equally to help him to satisfy that irresistible impulse to understand and to break free of the terrible ennui of a life too insis-

Modified version of an article which appeared under the same title in *The Pharos* (28:120, 1965) and which is being used with permission of the editor.

tently hemmed in by the practical. The medical life, like any other, can be lived in its fullest delectation only when the practical and the contemplative dimensions of reason are attained simultaneously.

How well does contemporary medical education prepare for each of the three levels of intellectual existence mentioned by Whitehead? Ordinarily, we measure the effectiveness of professional education in terms of competence and service. This is proper. However, the nonpractical goals of professional education may be the more permanent, and they are worthy of more direct attention than is now the case.

The utilitarian nature of medical education eminently fits its subjects to live and to live well—to survive and to obtain a degree of material comfort. Success, as the world reckons it, is virtually certain unless the physician falls victim to illness or moral desuetude. The need for his services and the determination of an affluent society that health shall be one of its preferred goals guarantee financial security and prestige. Except for the more catastrophic upheavals, his profession will be immune from social and political crises. He can look confidently, too, to the satisfactions of serving his fellows well in a work of unending interest, capable of engaging every type of mind and personality. Some will be wealthier, more famous, and more powerful than others. But these distinctions will be the result of forces largely external. Unless he falls into the sins of professional envy and the enthronement of prestige above quality of work, these distinctions can hardly threaten his security or contentment. It appears, then, that the person with a degree in medicine can count on protection from most of the palpable dangers of this world. In the popular phraseology, he has it made!

However, contemporary medical education geared to the encyclopedic accumulation of essential facts and techniques does not prepare in any specific way for the fullest development of physicians as people or for their participation in the life of the intellect for its own sake. Indeed, in the strenuous demands of a medical curriculum, the permanent and nonpractical goals are inevitably obscured. By the neglect of these intellectual dimensions, though, medicine can be reduced to a mere means of livelihood, or, what is even worse, medicine itself can become a bore. To a degree, failure to cultivate the intellectual life, in and out of the profession, robs persons of that delight in work and leisure so essential to a healthy emotional life, indeed to happiness.

In her novel, *Middlemarch*, George Eliot describes the moment when her hero Lydgate decides on his vocation as a physician. Reading for the first time of the wonders of the heart valves, he experiences the entrancements of medicine opening suddenly before him. As the author puts it, "The world was made new to him. From that hour Lydgate felt the growth of an intellectual passion" (2).

The moment of its onset may not be so clearly defined, but this same intellectual passion has probably stirred in most medical students at some time. In some, it may have been stillborn. In most, it suffers decline before the exigencies of the workaday world. But when this passion is sustained throughout life, it effects that harmony of the practical and the contemplative, of the interior and exterior self, which has distinguished the best physicians in every age.

In any hierarchy of values, responsibility to others is dominant in the lives of doctors; the first demand on the medical intellect is the moral imperative to maintain professional competence. Professional incompetence, the unfortunate collapse of the functions of accurate observation—correct logic and reasoned judgment—is a moral catastrophe. Wisely, medical education has traditionally concentrated on this responsibility.

But the intellectual passion of which Eliot speaks and the life of satisfaction to which Whitehead alludes imply intellectual dimensions beyond the moral requirements of competence. They imply nothing less than exercising the intellect to perceive the wonderful in the ordinary things of medical practice, to see their relation to the whole of being, and to delight in the understanding they can bring. Socrates in the *Theaetetus* said that "wonder is the beginning of philosophy" (3), and wonder is a necessary condition of the fullness of the intellectual life in medicine. The sense of wonder keeps minds plastic, enables them to marvel at the uniqueness of each patient, and sustains them in their unending confrontation with human suffering.

Is concern with the functions of the medical intellect just another bit of academic precocity, born of isolation from the exigencies of the real world? After all, to serve the sick compassionately and competently is a sufficiently difficult and worthy goal. Why complicate it by vague musings and strivings after intellectual aims which can only detract from the vigorous pursuit of competence?

The hard answer is that this very competence can no longer be defined just in terms of technical and professional efficiency. The

215

transformations in the nature of medicine now occurring, and sure to occur in the immediate future, will radically alter traditional definitions of competence. Most of these transformations will be in the intellectual order, and it is in this order that the physician must confront them.

There are problems to which the medical intellect will have to respond.

First is the speedy obsolescence of all knowledge and especially of the knowledge pertinent to medicine. Facts, and the techniques dependent upon them, are destined to double each decade. It is patent folly, therefore, to equilibrate competence with possessing any set of facts and skills. No mind can keep pace with even the essential data. All the emphasis must be on sharpening the medical intellect to learn better how to use facts, where to find them, how to discriminate between them, how to synthesize them creatively and how to generate new information. The challenge for those who wish to be competent will be to keep the intellect sharp yet resilient, so that it can cut through the information mass and select what is useful for patients.

Fortunately, there is at hand already a technologic advance which will help enormously in this task and further sharpen the intellectual dimensions of medical competence; this is the computer. No machine will have greater impact on lives. For the first time, man has a mechanism to extend the potentialities of his brain. If we can dispose of certain irrational fears, we can appreciate that the computer is superior to the human brain in precision and speed in all the mundane intellectual problems, like the storage and retrieval of vast amounts of information and the solution of predefined problems.

The physician can anticipate electronic aid in many phases of his daily practice. With it, he can improve his diagnostic precision, select and interpret laboratory tests, compare his case with all like recorded cases, select the most effective treatment, search the literature for related information, and even interpret electrocardiograms.

But the very skill of the computer in manipulative "thinking" highlights its inadequacy in what is called heuristic thinking: namely, formulating the problem, generating hypotheses, designing a mode of solution, selecting criteria for solution, and making ultimate value judgments on the wisdom of the solution. The human mind easily surpasses the computer in these higher intellectual functions. In the future, it is these latter functions that will comprise competence, not the personal possession of a large body of factual information or even experience in the ordinary sense. Only an intellect more specifically trained for these higher functions can be an effective partner in the man-computer relationship and, most important of all, undertake the delicate tasks of translating the result into action and making it understandable to the patient.

The increasing institutionalization of medical practice presents another set of demands on the medical intellect, which also will condition our concepts of competence. In response to the needs for specialization in an ever more complex society, there is a growing tendency to organize many aspects of medicine as a team effort. As we view patient needs more comprehensively, it is clear that the physician can no longer master all the requisite knowledge and techniques. Then too, there is little likelihood that the projected increases in the number of physicians can satisfy the needs of an expanding population or the variety of new ways in which physicians will function. As a consequence, teams of physicians, each with a special interest, working with an expanding number of allied health professionals, will become the dominant organizational pattern for many clinical problems. At the same time, many of the technical and manipulative procedures performed by the doctor today will of necessity be delegated to technically trained but less highly educated personnel.

The requirements of these organizational trends will be for physicians capable of leading and supervising groups of disparate individuals from different disciplines. The doctor will have to earn his role of leader by more than competence in the ordinarily accepted sense. His unique clinical knowledge will be less useful than his intellectual attainments in problem solving, and in grasping the essence of a large number of different fields and synthesizing them. In a sense, he will use the team as he does the computer—as a source of special information and skills and as a manipulative aid. But he will have the responsibility of posing the questions, evaluating the results, and making the value judgments.

A final example of how intellectual requirements in medicine are being transformed is the impact of the revolution in biology. In the last several decades, knowledge in human biology has undergone the same efflorescence that revolutionized the physical sciences over the last century. The exploitation of two unifying concepts, evolution and biochemical genetics, has illuminated every facet of

217

man's constitution and behavior. The potentialities for the metamorphosis of human existence when this knowledge is applied are just being appreciated. Some are already obvious: population control, organ transplantation, the chemical control of behavior and heredity, and the engineering of future generations.

Inevitably, society must ask the value questions of us: To what ends shall these forces be directed? What is good for mankind? Who will decide how to use the new tools and on what basis? Medicine as the emerging science of man is inextricably involved with such questions as they apply to the individual and society. There is every indication that the physician will be expected to apply these far-reaching advancements in biology. An urgent need already exists for serious discussion of these issues among physicians, philosophers, sociologists, and theologians.

These and the foregoing are surely questions of the contemplative and not the practical intellect. To answer them requires a taste for ideas, for generalization, speculation, and critical thinking about values. Our medical education does not of itself foster the attitudes requisite for consideration of such questions. Indeed, as Hofstadter has pointed out, the professional man lives *off* ideas and not *for* them. In his professional life, he uses ideas as instruments (4). Yet the transformations imminent in our profession must move it toward more intellectual and less pragmatic functions. As I see the choice, if we settle for competence in the present sense, we shall be replaced by technicians trained for specialized tasks and by the computer, which does manipulative thinking better than we do. Those impelled into medicine by something akin to Lydgate's "intellectual passion" and those who wish to live with satisfaction in Whitehead's sense cannot accept this eventuality.

With specific changes in emphases, a medical education can become a potent instrument for achieving both our societal and individual fulfillment. Properly integrated with other life experiences, the study of medicine equips the physician better than the education of most other professionals to advance in understanding the larger and smaller issues in life.

Having learned the scientific way of thinking and its power in exploring reality, we also know much about the psychosocial behavior of man and his growth as an individual and in society. We have had contact with a wide range of persons and have been privileged to examine the intricacies of human reaction in the full range of physical and emotional stress. No discipline offers so immediate a combination of scientific and humanistic values; no other discipline is capable of uniting these two cultures truly into one. There is likewise no better set of experiences with which the contemplative intellect can occupy itself and from which understanding can be generated.

What then are the obstacles to attainment of the intellectual dimensions in medicine? What changes are required in education and for the individual who desires to explore the spectrum of uses of the medical intellect?

First is a respect and appreciation of the intellect as a tool that must be trained for its own ends, regardless of the work it must do. Cardinal Newman put it well: "I say a cultivated intellect, because it is good in itself, brings with it a power and a grace to every work and occupation which it undertakes and enables us to be more useful to a greater number" (5). The intellect can be cultivated on all sorts of data, humanistic or scientific, provided we attend to its needs as well as the needs of the profession in which it is to be exercised. Educators concerned, as they should be, with the emotional lives of their students need an equal concern with the disorders of the intellect to which their students can fall prey as undergraduates and in their professional lives.

Second, we should recognize how anxious faculty and students have become about the enormity of medical knowledge. To avoid stuffing our students like Strasbourg geese, let us undertake the hard task of finding the common substratum of fact and principle which will be the base for enabling our students to undertake their chosen field after graduation. The courage must be found to state clearly that the goal of undergraduate education is the preparation of the intellect for its later work, not merely the hatching of the Compleat Physician.

Some will recognize this cultivation of the intellect as the essence of a liberal education, with which so few are equipped today. We in medical education cannot provide a liberal education for our students. This should primarily be the business of the colleges. But we can examine, more creatively than we have, the possibilities of imparting the "liberal attitude" or state of mind as we teach the data of medicine.

If we can resist the temptation to infuse our students with encyclopedic surveys of every last clinical subspecialty, time may be left

219

for more sophisticated approaches to a medical education based upon less classwork, more flexible curricula, more tutorial experiences, more problem solving, independent work, and elective experiences. Special attention to logic, the operation of computers, philosophic problems pertinent to medicine, and the philosophy of science might well advance intellectual training.

This would not cause a vast convulsion, but it would involve a change in emphasis and in goals and make for a more discriminating selection of intellectual as opposed to vocational experiences. Many of our university colleagues are sincerely concerned about our tendency to anti-intellectualism. Perhaps they would be willing to collaborate in some of these endeavors.

We all blame our education for not exposing us to everything we need to know in later life. The complaint should be rather that we were not taught how to use our intellects in an independent way, nor were we taught how to maintain our enthusiasm and joy in understanding the new and the unusual. The teacher's real task is to provide the setting in which the intellectual virtues can grow, to help define responsibilities to be met, and to educate intellects in the attitudes and methods needed for continuing self-education.

Our teachers can provide the seed of the intellectual passion and even nurture it by example, but each of us must give it life ourselves. The depth of the student's or the physician's participation in the intellectual life, inside and outside medicine, rests finally with him. The task in later life is only little helped by postgraduate courses, tapes, films, television, and all the highly vaunted media of mass communication and education. These will always be ancillary to the unglamorous hard work of self-study, critical and meditative appraisal of one's own experience, and imitation of the best models.

In order to resist the constriction of intellect a busy professional life forebodes, some preventive measures are useful. One must examine oneself daily for those attitudes that slowly, insidiously, and painlessly corrode the intellect: obscurity of expression, gratuitous assertion, exaltation of intuition over reason, the fear of ambiguity, the painful response to a new idea, and the mistrust of things academic. Early development of a serious interest in that which opens the mind to itself and to nature—like poetry, painting, art, or music—is essential. Goethe's admonition is as timely now as it was when he wrote it: "One ought, every day at least, to hear a little song, read a good poem, see a fine picture, and, if it were possible, to speak a few reasonable words" (*Man sollte . . . alle Tage wenig-stens ein kleines Lied hören, ein gutes Gedicht lesen, ein treffliches Gemälde sehen und, wenn es möglich zu machen wäre, einige ver-nünftigbe Worte sprechen*) (6).

We need to provide for some silence and some solitude, as well as time to be free to do nothing; we need, above all, to cultivate lei-sure, "the basis of all culture" (7), as a positive attribute—a time for letting the mind play freely on other than the pressing things. Aris-totle went so far as to say, "The goal of education is leisure."

Are these goals beyond our capacities? Each one must answer this question. There is no better spur than a slightly unattainable goal. "What I aspired to be and was not comforts me," said Rabbi Ben Ezra (8). Certain it is that some will come close to the ideal of a life lived well and with delectation. Those who do will join the company of the select man spoken of by Ortega y Gasset: "the man who demands more of himself than the rest" (9).

Each one must start now to be wary lest he become lost in the ap-propriate but insufficient utilitarian goals of his education; each must resist the temptations to put all his energy into the immediate and the practical; each must always leave some time for his devel-opment as a person. The great Chinese philosopher Lao-tzu had some advice we might heed:

> The race, the hunt, can drive men mad
> And their booty leave them no peace.
> Therefore a sensible man
> Prefers the inner to the outer eye:
> He has his yes, he has his no. (10).

Each must now look with his inner eye at his present and try to define his future, and each must begin to decide how he will say his *yes* and how his *no*. Perfection as both physician and man is mea-sured by the choices one makes; the spectrum of his acquiescences will reflect the quality of the life he lives.

The strengths in medical education today are offset by certain imperfections. Aware of the strengths and weaknesses in his educa-tion, the physician-student can transform his education in the years to come into the means for a life of satisfaction—a life in which service to mankind and personal growth as a man become one. This is the closest a human being can come to happiness in an imperfect world.

To Be a Physician

Wheresoever manners and fashions are corrupted,
language is. It imitates the public riot.
—Ben Jonson (1)

The world we perceive is the world we see through words
. . . hence the importance of teaching language
not so much as grammar as behaviour.
—Ashley Montagu (2)

These essays have dealt in one way or another with the many articulations between the idea of humanism and the idea of medicine. Ultimately, these seeming abstractions must be related to something concrete and immediate in the physician's daily experience. Is there some moral imperative in medical humanism which binds simply by the fact that we *are* physicians? Is there an irreducible and uncompromisable dimension by which we can measure the authenticity of a claim to humanism in medicine?

Authenticity is revealed ultimately in what we *are*, and this, in turn, by what we think it means to *be* a physician. Our being is revealed very often by what we take the words to mean which we use to justify our acts.

If we are to know something about what it is to *be* a physician, four words in common parlance are in need of rehabilitation: the words *profession*, *patient*, *compassion*, and *consent*. They are so ubiquitous in the speech of physician and patient that we all imagine we know what they mean. Yet language, as Jean Paul said, is "a cloud which everyone sees in a different shape" (3). It is essential,

---

This chapter is an amalgam of the following: "To *Be* A Physician," Convocation Address given at Texas A&M University in October 1977; and "Profession, Patient, Compassion, Consent: Meditations on Medical Philology" which was presented as the Commencement Address at the Hippocratic Oath Ceremony, University of California, Los Angeles, on June 3, 1977, and appeared in *Connecticut Medicine*, 42:3, March 1978, pp. 175–78.

therefore, for every physician to contemplate more closely the shape of the clouds these words make when he utters them.

The four key words I have chosen all have Latin derivations—that Latinity no longer respectable since it is easier to ignore what we do not comprehend. These four words entered the Anglo-Saxon language with the massive infusion of foreign words which followed the Norman Conquest. The entry of these words enriched the language because they expressed certain precise notions. As the *feeling* for words declined, these original meanings have been corrupted over the centuries.

But we must try to rescue those meanings because both Ben Jonson and Ashley Montagu are right: we do act in accordance with what we think words mean, and when our acts become morally dubious, we do distort their meanings to suit the aberrant act. What the enthusiasts for laxity of language see as enrichment may, in fact, be a mere excuse for submerging the stronger, and richer, earlier meaning.

PROFESSION

The first word is *profession* (4). With the receipt of the M.D. degree, the student officially becomes a member of a profession. In sociological terms, the student joins a body of individuals sharing certain specific knowledge, rules of conduct, ideals, and entry requirements. Some are impressed with their entry into a privileged social group which automatically entitles them to a certain respect, a wide discretionary space in decision making and considerable authority over others. The more crass may even rejoice in the license to charge fees for what only yesterday they did for nothing.

While each of these construals of the word has a certain truth, the original meaning is much more powerful, and specific, to being a physician. It comes from the Latin word *profiteri*, to declare aloud, to make a public avowal. It entered English in the thirteenth century, or thereabouts, to signify the act of public avowal and entry into a religious order. It was a public declaration of belief and an intent to practice certain ideals. In the sixteenth century, it included the public declaration of possession of certain skills to be placed in the service of others, as in the profession of medicine, law, or ministry. The word was visibly distorted in the nineteenth century when the language of an industrial society infected our parlance. A profession became simply a prestigious occupation. Instead of commitment, we began to talk of efficiency, productivity, utility—in Marxist as well as capitalist societies.

When a student consciously accepts his degree he makes a public avowal that he possesses competence to heal and that he will do so for the benefit of those who come to him. In that declaration, he binds himself publicly to competence as a moral obligation, not simply a legal one; he places the well-being of those he presumes to help above his own personal gain. If these two considerations do not shape every medical act and every encounter with the patient, the "pro-fession" becomes a lie: the physician is a fraud and his whole enterprise is undiluted hypocrisy.

These are strong words, but they derive ineluctably from the expectations engendered in others by the act of pro-fession—the personal and public voluntary acceptance of the obligations one is willing to assume in accepting a medical degree. This is the essence of the oaths—whether of Hippocrates, Maimonides, or any of the others—traditionally adminstered at graduations. These oaths are not meaningless condescensions to tradition but living witnesses to society of a personal commitment.

A few years ago, it was popular for medical graduates to refuse to take *any* oath. To their credit they took the oath seriously enough to resist when they could not agree with its content. I hope the more placid acquiescence of today is not evidence of moral lassitude or lack of the courage to dissent.

The physician remakes his pro-fession every time he dares to offer himself to a patient. The obligation is unavoidable. It leaves little room for incompetence, selfishness, or even legitimate personal concerns like fatigue, lack of time, or the demands of family. It is inconsistent with the prevalent bureaucratic ethos which buries individual acts in the faults of society, institutions, or, the "team." We must not be "auxiliary bureaucrats," the term Gabriel Marcel used for those in a mass society who excuse themselves as mere functionaries (5).

If our pro-fessions had, up to now, been authentic in the pristine sense, we would have less malpractice, governmental regulation, and consumerism to worry about. It is in the actual or perceived failure to act in accordance with the full meaning of the word *pro-*

fession which underlies much of the public disquietude with medicine today.

The next word to examine is *patient,* another badly tortured word whose original meaning has also been seriously attenuated. The Latin root is *patior-pati*—to suffer, to bear something. It was first used in its medical sense by Chaucer. A person becomes a patient when, in his perception of his own existence, he passes some point of tolerance for a symptom or a debility and seeks out another person who has professed to help. The patient bears and suffers something, and his expectation is that every act of the physician will be to relieve him of that burden and restore his lost wholeness—which is, incidentally, the meaning of the Anglo-Saxon word *heal.*

The patient therefore is a petitioner, a human in distress, and an especially vulnerable human. He enters a relationship of inequality. He is in pain, anxious, and lacking in the knowledge and skill necessary to heal himself or to make the decision about what is best for him. The person who has become a patient thus loses some of the most precious of human freedoms—freedom to move about as he wishes, to make his own decisions rationally, and freedom from the power of other persons. The patient bears, in a real sense, the burden of a wounded and afflicted humanity.

The patient is not a "client," a word appearing with distressing frequency in medical and medico-legal writing. *Client* is from the word *cliens* and has a lineage dating back to Roman times. The word referred to a plebeian and in the Middle Ages to a vassal under the protection of a patrician or lord. The client paid certain homage and performed services to the lord in return for this protection. Today, the client is a customer. It is alarming to see how the spirit of this word has come to pollute the relationship of physician and patient and how insensitive we have become to the original sense of what it means to be a patient.

Physicians all too frequently interpret the word "patient" to mean long-suffering or enduring trouble without discontent or complaint, a trait they ascribe to a "cooperative" patient. There are even a few physicians who see patients as their vassals, paternalistically protecting them in the distorted notion of their own moral authority, making decisions for rather than with the patient, and demanding compliant behavior from those they serve. We even talk, in a distorted way, of "educating" patients, meaning that they must conform to our notions of how to behave in illness.

COMPASSION

If we understand, and feel, the full meaning of the word *patient*, then we can also understand another word so often tortured on the rack of misuse—compassion. This word is simply a derivation of the same root, *patior* which gives us the word "patient." It means, literally, to suffer with, to bear together, to share in another's distress, and to be moved by desire to relieve distress.

Compassion is not some facile combination of talents in public relations under the rubric of bedside manner; nor is it some mystical quality or charisma which radiates only from the gifted; nor again is it synonymous with mawkish or demeaning pity for the sick, or a saccharine piety and self-righteousness. These construals are all offensive to true compassion and an insult to the wounded humanity of the patient.

Compassion means to feel genuinely the existential situation of the person who is bearing the burden and who has undergone the insult of sickness to his whole being. We can never enter wholly into the state of being of another human, but we must strive with all our might to *feel* it to the fullest extent our sensibilities will allow. It is our failure to feel along with the patient that leads to the complaint we hear so often today of humiliation and being demeaned.

CONSENT

If we understand the full flavor of meanings of *profession*, *patient*, and *compassion*, then we can easily understand the last word so prevalent in current legal and moral discourse, *consent*. Here, the Latin root is *sentire*, a word which has two senses: one in the emotional and physical sense and the other in an intellectual sense.

Therefore, *con-sent* is to *feel* together and to *know* something together.

Con-sent grows out of a human interaction between someone who seeks to know what to do and one who advises what should be done. It is not the mere satisfaction of some legal formality, a signature on a piece of paper duly witnessed. Con-sent demands, rather, that action be taken from the ground *between* patient and physician. Both must feel the action is the right one, and both must agree on the basis of knowledge that it is a rational choice as well.

It is not appropriate to undertake a detailed consideration of the moral and legal dimensions of consent which has become such a tendentious issue in medical relationships. It is necessary only to iterate that the word demands a joint and not a unilateral experience; it cannot be valid where one party, physician or patient, decides for another; it does demand that both parties feel the decision as their own.

Consent of this quality is morally indispensable if we only think of the vulnerable state of the patient and the inequality of the relationship with the physician. The obligation to obtain con-sent flows from the fact of being a pro-fessed healer, one who purports to repair wounded humanity. The physician must restore as much of the patient's lost freedom as possible. That means making available the knowledge—the alternatives and probabilities—necessary to a free and human decision to take one course as opposed to another, or to reject what the physician proposes.

It has been said that one picture can replace a thousand words. But we forget that one word can also paint a thousand different pictures in our minds. Pictures are static while words undergo constant change. If we destroy a painting, it no longer communicates; if we mutilate a word, it still has great power and can corrupt, where once it enhanced human existence.

But even these crucial four words express something which is still peripheral to the innermost center of humanistic medicine. Two more words must engage our reflections: *being* and *having*, and the difficult but crucial distinction between them.

Gabriel Marcel, the French philosopher, critic, and dramatist, said that "Everything really comes down to the distinction between what we *have*, and what we *are*" (6). This is not one of those meaningless messages so appealing to the minds of middle-aged moralists. Rather, it is a distillation of the dilemmas we face as persons

227

and institutions in forming an authentic image of ourselves, one in which we and others can believe.

Without indulging in all the complex subtleties of Marcel's thought, what he seems to be saying is this: to *have* something is to hold ownership and control over a thing acquired from without. Whether it is a profession, an idea, an education, or a fortune, what we *have* is always external to our being; it can never enter into or define the infinitely greater mystery of what we are. No matter how impressive the things we *have*, they must not be our identity. If they are, then we lose the chance to *be* something. We lose the freedom of a personal choice and testimony. It is we who put our possessions to use and not our possessions that use us.

Physicians have a medical education, an M.D. degree, a set of skills, knowledge, prestige, titles. They *possess* many things by which they may mistakenly identify themselves and their profession. Many of the health professions—medicine included—confuse the possession of packets of knowledge, a white coat, or a technique with *being* a physician or healer.

Far too many who possess these things fail to be authentic healers. It is a daring and transforming experience to attempt to heal another person. To do so is to penetrate in some way the mystery of the person's being, and that becomes disastrous unless we are clear about our own being. It is the disjunction between having and being that outrages patients with their physicians, and similarly sours students with their teachers and congregations with their preachers.

The matter is so difficult because there are so many conflicting conceptions about what medicine is. Is the only *true* medicine equated with radical cure, high technology, and specialization? Or should we believe the polemicists like Ivan Illich, who believes that "the medical establishment has become a major threat to health" (6)? They urge us to deprofessionalize medicine and return to self-care. Or, should we heed the romantics of the "back-to-nature" school who advise a return to yesterday's remedies, diet, exercise, and vitamins? Maybe truth is with those who want medicine to alleviate all the more unfortunate consequences of being human and want medicine to be the ultimate guarantor of human happiness. Is there something more fundamental than this cacophony of salvation themes to tell us what medicine *is*, and what it is *not*? What is medicine *for*?

Medicine is something of all of these things, yet none of them exclusively. Having these attributes does not make medicine what it *is*, anymore than *having* a medical education is *being* a physician. Whatever else it may be, medicine comes fully into existence as medicine only in the moment of clinical truth, in the act of making a clinical decision. In this act, the physician chooses a right healing action, one that will restore health or contain established disease or prevent new disease. Among the many things that can be done, the focal point on which all medical activity converges is a choice of those that should be done for this person, at this time, and in this life situation. The right decision is the one that is *good* for this patient—not patients in general, nor what is good for physicians, for science, or even for society as a whole.

As soon as we introduce the word *right* with respect to action and *good* with respect to an end, we introduce morality—some system of strongly held beliefs against which behavior is to be judged as good or bad. Medicine is, therefore, at the root a moral enterprise because values enter into every decision. The physician's art and science are necessarily shaped by the special human relationship between a vulnerable person seeking to be healed and another person professing to heal.

To be sure, medicine derives content and methodology from a wide range of primary studies as varied as biochemistry and ethics. But medicine itself cannot be equated with any one of them or even the sum of all of them.

All health professionals participate to some degree in this central function of medicine. But it is the physician who stands closest to the point of convergence of the whole process, and thus he has the broadest moral responsibility. The closer we are to this moral center, the more we are physicians; the further from it, or the narrower the range factors to be integrated, the less we are physicians, no matter how sophisticated our technical knowledge.

Whichever of the many conceptions of medicine one selects, one can be a physician only if one satisfies the essence of the medical act: to make a right choice that is "best" for this patient. Others may carry out the procedures required—and they need not be physicians at all—but what medicine uniquely *is*, is the capability morally to manage the clinical moment.

To *be* a physician is freely to commit oneself to the moral center of the relationship with the patient and to do so with one's whole person—that is the only condition for freedom, as Bergson so rightly observed. This is neither too harsh, nor too simplistic a judgment. The malaise of medicine—the moral desuetude so many see in us and the bewilderment of our students about what we *are*— is rooted in our failure to sense the dimension of *being* a physician.

Without this dimension, even the idea of service can become degraded into mere performance of a function. Many of us function, but few serve. To transform functions into service we need what Marcel called attachment: "dedication to the intrinsic quality of what is done, its adaptation to the needs of the person served and personal accountability for its quality. (7)"

We cannot distinguish *having* from *being* without the capacity for critical self-examination. This is what the humanities—philosophy, history, literature at their best—have always taught the educated man. These studies are, therefore, tools of that intellectual and moral honesty which gives the lie to self-assurance and forces a constant reexamination of motives and values. There is no more effective antidote to the overweening pride that can so easily beset the physician.

The most authentic humanist in that very great novel *The Plague*, by Camus, was Rieux the physician. He possessed the modesty to resist self-justification. He was a symbol against the moral indifference of the citizens of Oran who allow the plague to take possession of their fellows while they pursue their possessions and pleasures.

If we can educate humanists like Rieux, medicine may help to treat not only the personal plague of disease but the pestilence of moral indifference that seems, like a cultural plague, silently to have possessed our spirits.

REFERENCES

CHAPTER ONE

1. Lewis Mumford, *Technics and Civilization* (New York: Harcourt, Brace & World, 1973), p. 435.
2. Renee C. Fox, "The Sociology of Modern Medical Research," in *Asian Medical Systems,* ed. Charles Leslie (Berkeley: Univ. of California Press, 1976), pp. 102-13.
3. Abraham Edel, "Where is the Crisis in Humanism?" in *Rev. Int. Philosophie,* fasc, 3-4 (1968): 284-95.
4. Lewis Mumford, *The Myth of the Machine, the Pentagon of Power* (New York: Harcourt, Brace, Jovanovich, 1970), p. 420.

CHAPTER TWO

1. Marcus Fabius Quintilianus, *Institutio Oratoria,* II, v, 15; quoted in Norbert Guterman, *A Book of Latin Quotations, with English Translations* (New York: Anchor Books, 1966), p. 283.
2. Casey Truett, Arthur W. Couville, Bruce Fagel, and Merle Cunningham, "The Medical Curriculum and Human Values," panel discussion, 65th Annual Congress on Medical Education, *Journal of the American Medical Association,* 209 (Aug. 18, 1969) 7:1341.
3. Albert William Levi, *The Humanities Today* (Bloomington: Indiana Univ. Press, 1970).
4. Ibid., p. 92.
5. Northrop Frye, "The Instruments of Mental Production," in *The Knowledge Most Worth Having,* ed. Wayne C. Booth (Chicago: Univ. of Chicago Press, 1967), pp. 59-83.
6. Geoffrey Vickers, *Medicine's Contribution to Culture in Medicine and Culture,* ed. F.N.L. Poynter (London: Wellcome Institute of the History of Medicine, 1969), pp. 5-6.
7. *Aphorisms from Latham* (Peter Mere Latham), coll. and ed. William B. Bean (Iowa City: Prairie Press, 1962), p. 40.
8. Scott Buchanan, *The Doctrine of Signatures: A Defence of Theory in Medicine* (London: Kegan Paul, Trench, Trubner, 1938), p. 80.
9. Ibid., p. 94.

10. Charles P. Snow, *The Two Cultures and the Scientific Revolution* (New York: Cambridge Univ. Press, 1959).

11. Levi, *The Humanities Today*, p. 61.

12. Eric Ashby, *Technology and the Academics* (New York: Macmillan, 1969).

13. Werner Jaeger, *Paideia: The Ideals of Greek Culture*, trans. from the German by Gilbert Highet (New York: Oxford Univ. Press, 1944), 2:21.

CHAPTER THREE

1. Henry E. Sigerist, *A History of Medicine* (New York: Oxford Univ. Press, 1951), 1:31.

2. Ibid.

3. José Ortega y Gasset, *Mission of the University* (Princeton: Princeton Univ. Press, 1944).

4. Paul Radin, *Primitive Man as Philosopher* (New York: Dover, 1956).

5. R.D. Steuer and J.B.deC.M. Saunders, *Ancient Egyptian and Cnidian Medicine* (Berkeley: Univ. of California Press, 1959).

6. Sigerist, *A History of Medicine*, I, IV, p. 441.

7. *The Yellow Emperor's Classic of Internal Medicine*, trans. and intro. Ilza Veith (Berkeley: Univ. of California Press, 1966).

8. Manfred Porkert, "The Intellectual and Social Impulses Behind the Evolution of Traditional Chinese Medicine" in *Asian Medical Systems: A Comparative Study*, ed. Charles Leslie (Berkeley: Univ. of California Press, 1976) pp. 65–67.

9. Arturo Castiglioni, *A History of Medicine* (New York: Knopf, 1941), p. 135.

10. Pedro Lain-Entralgo, "The Health and Perfection of Man," *Diogenes*, Fall 1960, p. 6.

11. Jaeger, *Paideia: The Ideals of Greek Culture*, 3:19.

12. Virgil, *The Aeneid*, ed. W.F.J. Knight (Baltimore: Penguin, 1962), vi, ll. 847–58.

13. A.C. Pegis, "St. Thomas and the Unity of Man" in *Progress in Philosophy*, ed. J.A. McWilliams (Milwaukee: Bruce, 1955).

14. Maurice De Wulf, *Philosophy and Civilization in the Middle Ages* (New York: Dover, 1953).

15. René Descartes, cited in Étienne Gilson, *The Unity of Philosophical Experience* (New York: Scribner's, 1937), p. 132.

16. Gilson, ibid.

17. Immanuel Kant, *Critique of Pure Reason* (New York: Modern Library, 1958).

References

18. I. Galdston, "The Romantic Period in Medicine," *Bulletin of the New York Academy of Medicine*, 32:5 (1956), 349.

19. C.G. Jung, "The Spiritual Problem of Modern Man," in *Modern Man in Search of a Soul* (New York: Harcourt, Brace, 1933).

20. W. Weaver, "The Imperfections of Science," *American Scientist*, 49 (March 1961), 99.

21. R.G. Collingwood, *The Idea of History* (New York: Oxford Univ. Press, 1956), p. 205.

CHAPTER FOUR

1. Blaise Pascal, *Pensées*, trans. H.F. Stewart (New York: Pantheon, 1950), p. 161.

2. St. Augustine, *The Confessions*, trans. J.G. Pilkington (New York: Liveright, 1943), X, 6.

3. Ibid., X, 17.

4. Ibid., X, 33.

5. Martin Buber, *Between Man and Man*, trans. R.G. Smith (New York: Macmillan, 1972), ch. V.

6. Aristotle, *De Anima*, version of William of Moerbeke and the Commentary of St. Thomas Aquinas, trans. K. Foster and S. Humphries with intro. by I. Thomas (London: Routledge and Kegan Paul, 1951), II, 1, 220.

7. Ibid., II, 1, 234.

8. Ibid., I, 1, 23–24.

9. E. Gilson, *Elements of Christian Philosophy* (New York: Doubleday, 1960), p. 9.

10. E. Gilson, *The Spirit of Medieval Philosophy* (New York: Scribner's, 1963).

11. René Descartes, "Discourse on Method," in *Descartes' Selections*, ed. R.M. Eaton (New York: Scribner's, 1927), p. 30.

12. René Descartes, "Meditations on First Philosophy," in ibid., p. 99.

13. E. Gilson, *The Unity of Philosophical Experience*.

14. St. Thomas Aquinas, *In Aristotelis Libros De Sensu et Sensato, commentarium*, ed. III, 3 (Cura et studio, R.M. Spiazzi, Taurini, Marietti, 1949).

15. F. Molina, *Existentialism as Philosophy* (Englewood Cliffs, N.J.: Prentice-Hall, 1962).

16. R. Dubos, "Humanistic Biology," *American Scholar*, 35:179 (1965).

17. Ramon A. Di Nardo, "Depth Psychology and the Contribution of Existential Synthesis," *The New Scholasticism*, XXXII, 2 (April 1958), 195–99.

18. J. Edie, "Recent Work in Phenomenology," *Philosophy Quarterly*, 1 (1964).

19. Niedermeyer, quoted, *see* above, ref. 17, p. 195.

20. Aristotle, *De Sensu*, trans. J.I. Beare, in *The Works of Aristotle*, ed. W.D. Ross (New York: Oxford Univ. Press, 1931), Ch. 1, 436a, 16.

CHAPTER FIVE

1. Plato, *Phaedrus*, 270; *The Dialogues of Plato*, trans. B. Jowett (New York: Random House, 1937), 1:273.

2. L. Versenyi, *Socratic Humanism* (New Haven: Yale Univ. Press, 1963), pp. 33–35.

3. W. Jaeger, *see* Ch. 3, ref. 11, 3:3–45.

4. Plato, *Symposium*, *see* Ch. 5, ref. 1, 186, p. 313.

5. S. Rosen, *Plato's Symposium* (New Haven: Yale Univ. Press, 1969), pp. 90–119, 273–77.

6. Plato, *Symposium*, 186, *see* above, ref. 1, p. 313.

7. Plato, *Phaedo*, 67, *see* above ref. 1, p. 450.

8. C. Bernard, quoted in Walther Riese, "Philosophical Presuppositions of Present-Day Medicine," *Bulletin of the History of Medicine*, 30 (1956), 164.

9. S. Buchanan, *The Doctrine of Signatures: A Defence of Theory in Medicine* (London: Kegan Paul, Trench, Trubner, 1938), p. x.

10. M.W. Wartofsky, "Roundtable Discussion," in *Evaluation and Explanation in the Biomedical Sciences, Philosophy and Medicine*, ed. T. Engelhardt, Jr., and S. Spicker (Dordrecht: D. Reidel Publishing Co., 1975), 1:228.

11. E.D. Pellegrino, "Medicine and Philosophy: Some Notes on the Flirtations of Minerva and Aesculapius," Annual Oration of the Society for Health and Human Values, Washington, D.C., Nov. 8, 1973.

12. L. Edelstein, "Hippocrates of Cos," in *The Encyclopedia of Philosophy*, ed. Paul Edwards (New York: Macmillan, 1967), vol. 3.

13. W. Jaeger, *see* Ch. 3, ref. 11, 3–45.

14. Hippocrates, "De La Bien Séance," in *Hippocrates oevres completes*, ed. E. Littré (Paris: J.B. Balliere, 1839–61).

15. Aristotle, *see* Ch. 4, ref. 20, 435a.

16. C. Kuehn, ed., *Claudii Galeni* (Leipzig: Opera Omnia, 1820–33), 1:53–63, cited in John S. Kroffer, *Galen's Institutio Logica* (Baltimore: Johns Hopkins Univ. Press, 1964).

17. W. Jaeger, *see* Ch. 3, ref. 11.

18. G.B. Risse, "The Quest for Certainty in Medicine: John Brown's System of Medicine in France," *Bulletin of the History of Medicine*, 45:1–10 (Jan./Feb. 1971).

19. G.B. Risse, "Kant, Schelling and the Early Search for a Philosophical Science of Medicine in Germany," *Journal of the History of Medicine*, 27:145–58 (April 1972).

References

20. I. Galdston, "The Romantic Period in Medicine," *Bulletin of the New York Academy of Medicine*, 32:346–62 (May 1956).

21. E. McMullin, "Two Faces of Science," *Review of Metaphysics*, 27:655–76 (June 1974).

22. P. Edwards, ed.-in-chief, *The Encyclopedia of Philosophy* (New York: Macmillan and Free Press, 1972).

23. W. Szumowski, "La Philosophie de la Médecine, Son Histoire, Son Essence, Sa Dénomination et Sa Définition," *Archives Internationales d'Histoire des Sciences*, 9:1097–139 (Oct. 1949).

24. A. De Waelhens, "The Ontological Encounter of Human Science and Philosophy," in *Begegnung; Recontre, Encounter*, trans. F.B. Sullivan (Utrecht: Vitgerverij Het Spectrum, 1957), pp. 492–507, printed in *Philosophy Today*, 3 (Spring 1959).

25. G. Marcel, "Incarnate Being as the Central Datum of Metaphysical Reflection," in *Creative Fidelity*, trans. R. Rosthal (New York: Noonday Press, 1964), pp. 11–37.

26. M. Merleau-Ponty, "The Spatiality of the Lived Body and Motility," trans. C. Smith, in *The Philosophy of the Body*, ed. S. Spicker (Chicago: Quadrangle Books, 1970), pp. 241–71.

27. S. Spicker, "The Lived Body as Catalytic Agent: Reaction at the Interface of Medicine and Philosophy," in *Evaluation and Explanation in the Biomedical Sciences, Philosophy and Medicine*, ed. H.T. Engelhardt, Jr., and Stuart Spicker (Dordrecht: D. Reidel Publishing Co., 1975), 1: 181–204.

28. E. Straus, *Phenomenological Psychology, Selected Papers*, trans. in part by E. Eng (New York: Basic Books, 1966).

29. E. Straus, M. Natanson, and H. Ey, *Psychiatry and Philosophy*, ed. M. Natanson (New York: Springer-Verlag, 1969).

30. M. Grene, "People and Other Animals," *Philosophia Naturalis*, 14:25–38 (1973).

31. H.T. Engelhardt, Jr., "The Philosophy of Medicine: A New Endeavor," *Texas Reports on Biology and Medicine*, 31:443–52 (Fall 1973).

32. H.T. Engelhardt, Jr., "The Concepts of Health and Disease," *see* above, ref. 27, vol. 1.

33. F.J.J. Buytendijck, *Prolegomena to an Anthropological Physiology* (Pittsburgh: Duquesne Univ. Press, 1974).

34. P. Lain-Entralgo, *see* Ch. 3, ref. 10, pp. 1–19.

35. P. Lain-Entralgo, *The Therapy of the Word in Classical Antiquity*, trans. L.J. Rather and J.M. Sharp (New Haven: Yale Univ. Press, 1970).

36. P. Lain-Entralgo, *La Rélacion Médico-Enfermo Historia y Teoria* (Madrid: Revista de Occidente, 1964).

37. M.W. Wartofsky, "Roundtable Discussion," *see* above, ref. 27, p. 228.

38. R. Zaner, "The Radical Reality of the Human Body," *Humanitas* (1966) 2:73–87.

39. R. Zaner, "Context and Reflexivity: The Genealogy of Self," *see* above, ref. 27, pp. 154–74.

40. R. Zaner, "The Unanchored Leaf: Humanities and the Discipline of Care," *Texas Reports on Biology and Medicine*, 32:1–18 (Spring 1974).

41. *Evaluation and Explanation in the Biomedical Sciences, Philosophy and Medicine*, vol. 1.

42. J. Shaffer, "Roundtable Discussion," in ibid., pp. 215–22.

43. S. Toulmin, "Concepts of Function and Mechanism in Medicine and Medical Science" (Hommage à Claude Bernard), in ibid., p. 54.

44. W. Szumowski, "La Philosophie," p. 1138.

45. José Ortega y Gasset, *What Is Philosophy?*, trans. Mildred Adams (New York: Norton, 1960).

46. M. Heidegger, *An Introduction to Metaphysics*, trans. R. Manheim (New York: Doubleday, 1961).

47. E. Husserl, "Philosophy as Rigorous Science," in E. Husserl, *Phenomenology and the Crisis of Philosophy*, trans. Q. Lauer (New York: Harper & Row, 1965).

48. M. Merleau-Ponty, *In Praise of Philosophy* (Chicago: Northwestern Univ. Press, 1963).

49. S. Toulmin, *see* above, ref. 43.

50. Hans Jonas, "Technology and Responsibility," *Social Research*, 40:31–54 (1973).

51. O. Temkin, "On the Interrelationship of the History and the Philosophy of Medicine," *Bulletin of the History of Medicine*, 30:241–51 (May/June, 1956).

52. W. Osler, *A Way of Life and Selected Writings* (New York: Dover, 1951).

53. K.D. Clouser, "Medical Ethics: Some Uses, Abuses and Limitations," *New England Journal of Medicine*, 293:384–87 (Aug. 21, 1975).

54. R. Straus, "The Nature and Status of Medical Sociology," *American Sociological Review*, 22:203 (1957).

55. M. Heidegger, *What Is Called Thinking?* trans. F.D. Wieck and J.G. Gray (New York: Harper & Row, 1968), p. 33.

56. H. Dreyfus, "The Critique of Artificial Reason," in *Interpretations of Life and Mind: Essays Around the Problem of Reduction*, ed. M. Grene (London: Routledge and Kegan Paul, 1974), pp. 99–116.

57. M. Buber, *see* Ch. 4, ref. 5.

58. J. Scheler, *Man's Place in Nature* (New York: Noonday Press, 1961).

59. E. Cassirer, *An Essay on Man* (New York: Bantam Books, 1970).

60. G.S. Stent, "Limits to the Scientific Understanding of Man," *Science*, 187:1052–57 (March 21, 1975).

61. E.D. Pellegrino, "Physicians, Patients and Society: Some New Tensions in Medical Ethics," in *Human Aspects of Biomedical Innova-*

tion, ed. E. Mendelsohn, J. Swazey, and I. Taviss (Cambridge: Harvard Univ. Press, 1971), pp. 77–97, 210–20.

62. S. Gorovitz, "Bioethics and Social Responsibility," *Monist*, 60 (Jan. 1976).

63. J. Bronowski, *Science and Human Value* (Baltimore: Penguin, 1964), pp. 63–64.

64. G. Holton, "Modern Science and the Intellectual Tradition," *Science*, 131:1190 (Apr. 22, 1960).

65. H. Jonas, "Technology and Responsibility," *Social Research*, 40: 31–54 (1973).

66. D.K. Price, *The Scientific Estate* (Cambridge: Harvard Univ. Press, 1967), p. 105.

67. E.D. Pellegrino, "The Most Humane Science: Some Notes on Liberal Education in Medicine and the University," *Bulletin of the Medical College of Virginia*, 2:11–39 (Summer 1970).

68. M. Foucault, *The Birth of the Clinic: An Archaeology of Medical Perception* (New York: Random House, 1973).

69. E.D. Pellegrino, "Medicine, Philosophy and Man's Infirmity," in *Conditio Humana, Festschrift for Professor Erwin Straus on His 75th Birthday*, ed. W. von Beyer and R.H. Griffith (New York: Springer-Verlag, 1966).

70. A. MacIntyre, "Moral Philosophy and Medical Perplexity: Comments on 'How Virtues Become Vices,'" in *see* above, ref. 27, pp. 97–111.

71. M.W. Wartofsky, "Organs, Organisms and Disease: Human Ontology and Medical Practice," ibid., pp. 67–83.

72. *Human Values Teaching Programs for Health Professions*, Institute on Human Values in Medicine (Philadelphia: Society for Health and Human Values, April 1974).

73. Charles Fried, *Medical Experimentation: Personal Integrity and Social Policy* (Amsterdam: North-Holland Publishers, 1974, distributed by American Elsevier).

74. Scott Buchanan, *The Doctrine of Signatures: A Defence of Theory in Medicine* (London: Kegan Paul, Trench, Trubner, 1938). p. 194.

CHAPTER SIX

1. H.E. Sigerist, *The History of Medicine* (New York: Oxford Univ. Press, 1961), 11:260, 298.

2. W.A. Heidel, *Hippocratic Medicine: Its Spirit and Method* (New York: Columbia Univ. Press, 1941), p. 149.

3. W.H.S. Jones, trans. and ed., *Hippocrates* (New York: Putnam, 1923), I, 263–301.

4. Ibid., II, 263–65.

5. D. Leake, ed., *Percival's Medical Ethics* (Baltimore: William Wilkins, 1927), p. 291.

6. Albert R. Jonsen, "Do No Harm Axiom of Medical Ethics" in *Philosophy and Medicine*, ed. T. Engelhardt and S. Spicker, vol. 3, *Philosophical Medical Ethics: Its Nature and Significance*, pp. 26–41.

7. T.S. Eliot, "The Rock," in *The Complete Poems and Plays, 1909–1950* (New York: Harcourt, Brace, 1952), p. 101.

8. J. Michler, "Medical Ethics in Hippocratic Bone Surgery," *Bulletin of the History of Medicine*, 42:297–311 (1968).

9. E.F. Torrey, *Ethical Issues in Medicine* (Boston: Little, Brown, 1968).

10. C. Truett, A.W. Douville, B. Fagel, et al., "The Medical Curriculum and Human Values," *Journal of the American Medical Association*, 209:1341–45 (1969).

11. W. Oates, ed., *The Stoic and Epicurean Philosophers* (New York: Modern Library, 1957), p. 480.

12. G. Marcel, *Man Against Mass Society* (Chicago: Henry Regnery, 1962), p. 180.

CHAPTER SEVEN

1. Ivan D. Illich, *Medical Nemesis: The Expropriation of Health* (New York: Pantheon, 1975).

2. E.D. Pellegrino, "Hospitals as Moral Agents: Some Notes on Institutional Ethics," The Harvey M. Weiss Annual Lecture, 1976, in *Proceedings of the Third Annual Board of Trustees/Medical Staff Executive Committee Conference* (Saint Paul, Minn.: Sisters of Saint Joseph of Carondelet, March 26, 1977), pp. 10–27.

CHAPTER EIGHT

1. Gabriel Marcel, *see* Ch. 6, ref. 12, p. 257.

2. E.D. Pellegrino, *see* Ch. 5, ref. 67.

3. Paul Francoeur, "We Can—We Must: Reflections on the Technological Imperative," *Theological Studies*, 33 (1972).

4. Jay Katz, *Experimentation with Human Beings* (New York: Russell Sage Foundation, 1972), see esp. pp. 527–28.

5. E.D. Pellegrino, "The Necessity, Promise and Dangers of Human Experimentation," *Experiments With Man*, World Council Studies, no. 6 (New York: World Council of Churches and Friendship Press, 1969), pp. 31–56.

6. S.E. Luria, "On Research Styles and Allied Matters," *Daedalus*, 102:75–84 (Spring 1973).

References

7. M.H. Pappworth, *Human Guinea Pigs: Experimentation on Man* (London: Routledge and Kegan Paul, 1967).

8. L.D. Epstein and Louis Lasagna, "Obtaining Informed Consent," *Archives of Internal Medicine*, 123:682–88 (1969).

9. John Lange, "The Cognitivity Paradox," *An Inquiry Concerning the Claims of Philosophy* (Princeton: Princeton Univ. Press, 1970), p. 56.

10. Patrick Romanell, "Medical Ethics in Philosophical Perspective," *Humanistic Perspectives in Medical Ethics*, ed. Maurice B. Visscher (Buffalo: Prometheus Press, 1972), pp. 24–37.

11. Jacques Maritain, *Moral Philosophy* (New York: Scribner's, 1964), p. 452.

12. Adam Schaff, *A Philosophy of Man* (New York: Delta Books, 1963).

13. Lawrence K. Altman, "Auto-Experimentation: An Unappreciated Tradition in Medical Science," in *Hippocrates Revisited*, ed. R.J. Bulger (New York: MEDCOM Press, 1973), pp. 193–210.

CHAPTER NINE

1. Charles Fried, "Rights and Health Care—Beyond Equity and Efficiency," *New England Journal of Medicine*, 293:241–45 (July 31, 1975).

2. Charles Fried, *see* Ch. 5, ref. 73.

3. Diana Crane, *The Sanctity of Social Life: Physician's Treatment of Critically Ill Patients* (New York: Russell Sage Foundation, 1975).

4. Jay Katz and Alexander Morgan Capron, *Catastrophic Diseases: Who Decides What* (New York: Russell Sage Foundation, 1975).

5. Arthur Kantrowitz, "Controlling Technology Democratically," *American Scientist*, 63:505–9 (Sept.-Oct. 1975).

6. E.D. Pellegrino, "Toward an Expanded Medical Ethics: The Hippocratic Ethic Revisited," in *see* Ch. 8, ref. 13, pp. 133–48.

7. Renee C. Fox, "Ethical and Existential Developments in Contemporaneous American Medicine: Their Implications for Culture and Society," *Milbank Memorial Fund Quarterly* (Fall 1974), pp. 445–83.

CHAPTER TEN

1. *The Caraka Samhita*, vol. 1, trans. Shree Gulabkinverba (Jamnagar, India: Ayurvedic Society, 1949), p. 469.

2. Aulus Gellius, in R.S. Crane, *The Idea of the Humanities and Other Essays Critical and Historical* (Chicago: Univ. of Chicago Press, 1968) p. 23.

3. E.D. Pellegrino, "The Non-Renaissance Man," *The Pharos*, 32:16–17 (Jan. 1969).

4. Carl Jung, *Psychological Reflections*, ed. Jolande Jacobi (Princeton: Princeton Univ. Press, Bollingen Series 21, 1970), p. 84.

5. Thomas Merton, *New Seeds of Contemplation* (New York: New Directions, 1961), p. 38.

6. Hermann Hesse, *Demian* (New York: Bantam Books, 1970), prologue.

7. Jung, *see* above, ref. 4, p. 90.

8. Dag Hammarskjöld, *Markings* (New York: Knopf, 1965), p. 105.

9. Carl Rogers, "Bringing Together Ideas and Feeling in Learning," *Learning Today*, 5:32–43 (1972).

10. Pedro Lain-Entralgo, *see* Ch. 5, ref. 36.

11. Paul Oskar Kristeller, *Renaissance Thought: The Classic and Scholastic and Humanist Strains* (New York: Harper, 1961), pp. 8–23.

12. Abraham Edel, "Where is the Crisis in Humanism?" in *Revue Internationale de Philosophie*, fasc. 3–4 (1968), pp. 284–95.

13. Gilbert Murray, quoted by Harvey Cushing, *Introduction to Sir William Osler: The Old Humanities and the New Science* (Boston: Houghton Mifflin, 1920), p. x.

14. Gerald Else, "The Old and the New Humanities," *Daedalus*, 8:803–4 (Summer 1969).

15. Bernard Berenson, *Italian Painters of the Renaissance*, vol. 2, *Florentine and Central Italian Schools* (New York: Phaidon, 1968), p. 1.

16. Wayne Booth, ed., "Is There Any Knowledge That A Man Must Have?" in *see* Ch. 2, ref. 5, pp. 1–28.

17. E.D. Pellegrino, *see* Ch. 5, ref. 67.

18. E.D. Pellegrino, "Reflections, Refractions, and Prospectives," *Proceedings of the Institute on Human Values in Medicine*, vol. 1 (Philadelphia: Society for Health and Human Values, 1972), pp. 99–115.

19. E.D. Pellegrino, *see* Ch. 5, ref. 61.

20. Proceedings of the Institute on Human Values in Medicine, vol. 2, *see* above, ref. 18, pp. BP 1–83.

21. John Ciardi, "Esthetic Wisdom," *Saturday Review* (April 8, 1972), p. 22.

CHAPTER ELEVEN

1. Joel Alpert and Evan Charney, *The Education of Physicians for Primary Care*, U.S. Dept. of HEW Publication No. HRA 74-3133 (1973), 73 pp.

2. Samuel A. Banks and E.A. Vastyan, "Humanistic Studies in Medical Education," *Journal of Medical Education*, 48:283–57 (1973).

3. John Bryant, "America's Role in Medical Education," *Proceedings* of the Bicentennial Symposium, Univ. of Illinois, Sept. 14, 1976.

4. E.J. Moran Campbell, "Basic Science, Science, and Medical Education," *The Lancet* (Jan. 17, 1976), pp. 134–36.

5. *Evaluation in the Continuum of Medical Education,* Report of the Committee on Goals and Priorities of the National Board of Medical Examiners, Philadelphia, 1973, 94 pp.

6. Lester Evans, *The Crisis in Medical Education* (Ann Arbor: Univ. of Michigan, 1964), 101 pp.

7. Abraham Flexner, *Medical Education in the United States and Canada, A Report to the Carnegie Foundation for the Advancement of Teaching* (New York: Carnegie Foundation, 1910), esp. pp. 25, 106.

8. Renee C. Fox, *see* Ch. 9, ref. 7.

9. Renee C. Fox, "The Sociology of Modern Medical Research," in *Asian Medical Systems: A Comparative Study,* ed. Charles Leslie (Berkeley: Univ. of California Press, 1976), pp. 102–14.

CHAPTER TWELVE

1. J.H. Plumb, ed., *Crisis in the Humanities* (Baltimore: Penguin Books, 1964).

2. R.S. Crane, *The Idea of the Humanities,* part 1 (Chicago: Univ. of Chicago Press, 1967).

3. Ibid., p. 170.

4. *See* Ch. 5, ref. 72.

5. E.D. Pellegrino, *see* Ch. 5, ref. 67.

6. R.M. Veatch, W. Gaylin and C. Morgan, eds., *Reform and Innovation in Medical Education: The Role of Ethics in the Teaching of Medical Ethics* (Hastings-on-Hudson, N.Y.: Institute of Society, Ethics and the Life Sciences, 1973), pp. 150–65.

7. E.D. Pellegrino, "Viewpoints in the Teaching of Medical History: Medical History and Medical Education, Points of Engagement," *Clio Medica,* 10:295–303 (Dec. 1975).

8. Aristotle, *On the Parts of Animals,* trans. William Ogle, in *The Basic Works of Aristotle,* ed. and Intro. by Richard McKeon (New York: Random House, 1941), pp. 643, 5–14.

CHAPTER THIRTEEN

1. *The Selected Writings of Juan Ramón Jiménez,* trans. H.R. Hays, ed. with preface by Eugenio Florit Grove (New York: Aphorism, 1957), p. 258.

2. José Ortega y Gasset, *Mission of the University* (New York: Norton, 1966).

CHAPTER FOURTEEN

1. A.N. Whitehead, *The Functions of Reason* (Boston: Beacon, 1958), pp. 4, 8.
2. George Eliot, *Middlemarch* (New York: Washington Square Press, 1963), p. 140.
3. Plato, *Theaetetus* 155 D, in *see* Ch. 5, ref. 1, vol. II, p. 157.
4. R. Hofstadter, *Anti-Intellectualism in American Life* (New York: Knopf, 1963), p. 25.
5. J.H. Newman, *The Idea of a University* (New York: Doubleday, 1959), p. 183.
6. Goethe, *Wilhelm Meisters Lehrjahre,* bk. V, ch. 1, Hamburg edition, ed. Erich Trunz, VII, p. 284.
7. Josef Pieper, *Leisure, the Basis of Culture* (New York: Pantheon, 1952).
8. Robert Browning, "Rabbi Ben Ezra," in *Selected Poems of Robert Browning* (New York: W.J. Black, 1942), p. 242.
9. José Ortega y Gasset, *The Revolt of the Masses* (London: Unwin, 1961), p. 12.
10. *The Way of Life According to Lao-tzu* (New York: John Day, 1944), p. 31.

EPILOGUE

1. Ben Jonson, *Works,* ed. C.H. Hereford et al. (New York: Oxford Univ. Press, 1925–52), VIII (1940), p. 593.
2. Ashley Montagu, "The Language of Self-Deception," in *Language in America,* ed. Neil Postman, C. Weingartner, T. Moran (New York: Pegasus, 1969), pp. 82–95.
3. Max Picard, *Man and Language* (Chicago: Henry Regnery, 1963).
4. The derivations of each of the four words discussed are based on the *Oxford English Dictionary* accounts.
5. Gabriel Marcel, *see* Ch. 6, ref. 12, p. 257.
6. Ivan D. Illich, *see* Ch. 7, ref. 1.
7. Gabriel Marcel, *Being and Having: An Existential Dairy,* trans. Katherine Farrer (New York: Harper & Row, 1965).

Index

Medical school
    access to, 178–80, 209–10
    curriculum of, 23–25, 25–31, 159,
        194–95, 207, 209–10, 219–20
    ethics and values in, 83, 90
    functions and obligations of, 171–
        86, 203–12
    and models of medicine, 190–91
    and the university, 64, 173, 181
Medical transaction or encounter, 79, 126,
    167, 185
    compassion in, 160–61
    ethics in, 98–99, 104, 117
    in experimentation, 132–34
    as basis for medicine, 191–92
    teaching of, 165, 209
Medicine
    concepts of, 4–5, 33–35, 188, 190–
        91, 228–30
    ethos and telos of, 77, 78, 87
    humanistic, 10–15, 33–35, 189–92
    intellectual dimensions of, 213–21
    meanings of, 78–81, 189–92
    and philosophy, 54–65, 66–91
    power of, 121, 148
    as a profession, 22, 155, 188–89
    as science, 76–77, 188–89, 190–91
    and technology, 10–15. *See also*
        Profession
Mendel, Gregor, 49
Merleau-Ponty, Maurice, 72, 73, 76
Merton, Thomas, 160
Middle Ages, medicine in, 43–44, 44–46, 71
Montagu, Ashley, 223
Montaigne, Michel de, 58
More, Paul Elmer, 19
Mumford, Lewis, 11, 14
Murray, Gilbert, 164

Natanson, M., 74
Naturalism, 38, 45, 46
Neurology, 83, 85
Newman, John Henry, 21, 36, 219
Nicholas of Autrecourt, 58
Nicholas of Cusa, 58
Niedermeyer, Louis, 62, 63
Niethammer, Friedrich, 163
Nietzsche, Friedrich Wilhelm, 59
Nuremberg Code, 98

Ockham, William of, 58
Ortega y Gasset, José, 38, 76, 207, 221
Osler, Sir William, 81, 164

Paideia, 70, 156, 157
Pappworth, M.H., 133
Pascal, Blaise, 50, 54, 65
Patient
    "bills of rights" of, 109, 120, 127–28,
        183
    criticisms by, 117
    definition of, 222, 225–26
    education for care of, 23, 24, 160–
        61, 183, 205, 206
    in hospital, 141, 145–50, 184–86
    in medical ethics, 97–99
    in medical transaction, 78
    rights of, 98–99
    value system of, 3–4, 62, 100–102,
        128
    "wounded humanity" of, 123–27
Patient-physician relationship
    compassion in, 160–61
    competence, 107
    defined, 225–27
    in Hippocratic ethics, 97–99, 105–6
    inequalities in, 119, 123, 126, 127
    information gap in, 100, 106, 120,
        125–26
    modern problems of, 122–23
    study of, 162
    value differences in, 100–101, 120,
        128, 137
Paul, Jean, 222
Percival, Thomas, 97, 119
Pharmacology, 83
Phenomenology, 55, 61, 134
Philanthropia, 156, 157, 158
Philosophy
    Anglo-American v. European, 69,
        71, 72–73
    in history of medicine, 42–53, 56–
        62, 70–74
    and, in, and *of* medicine, 5, 14, 54–
        65, 66–91, 198
    of science, 84
Physician
    competence of, 106–7
    defined, 222–30
    ethical obligations of, 102, 103–4,
        105–10, 113–16, 123–29
    as expert, 101, 104, 120
    humanistic education of, 16–37,
        155–70, 213–21
    ideal images of, 119, 157, 169–70
    intellectual life of, 213–21
    and philosophy, 62–64, 89–90

246

Humanism and the Physician has been composed on the Compugraphic phototypesetter in eleven-point Palatino with one-point line spacing. Palatino was also used as display type. The book was designed by Jim Billingsley and set into type by Metricomp, Inc., Grundy Center, Iowa. It was printed offset by Thomson-Shore, Inc., Dexter, Michigan, and bound by John H. Dekker & Sons, Inc., Grand Rapids, Michigan. The paper on which the book is printed bears the watermark of S. D. Warren and is designed for an effective life of at least three hundred years.

THE UNIVERSITY OF TENNESSEE PRESS : KNOXVILLE